GETTING

INTO

ADVERTISING

GETTING
INTO
ADVERTISING

DAVID LASKIN

Ballantine Books · New York

The author is grateful for permission to quote from the following:
Ogilvy on Advertising by David Ogilvy; text © 1983 by David Ogilvy;
compilation © by Multimedia Publications Ltd. Used by permission
of Crown Publishers, Inc.

Library of Congress Catalog Card Number: 86-90721

ISBN: 0-345-32598-2

Cover photograph by Mort Engel
Text design by Michaelis/Carpelis Design Associates, Inc.
Manufactured in the United States of America
First Edition: September 1986

10 9 8 7 6 5 4 3 2 1

"I find this business to be the obvious—highly competitive and peopled by men and women of extraordinarily high energy and an enormous eclectic band of interests. The best people in this business could do almost anything in business. They are creative. They are interesting. They are almost to a person enormously active in the social fabric of their cities and their countries, contributors way beyond what most business people are.

"At heart this is a creative enterprise, where the exceptional people can make quite a mark and actualize their potential faster perhaps than in any other business, and deal with such a multitude of issues and problems on a worldwide basis.

"We have terrific jobs, dealing with the most changeable thing on earth—*human beings*, not human nature, but human beings and their interrelations."

—*ALEX KROLL*
President and Chief Executive Officer
Young & Rubicam

To my parents

Contents

P A R T   T H R E E

P A R T   F O U R

Acknowledgments

This book would not have been possible without the cooperation of people in all areas of the advertising industry. My first thanks go to all the people who gave so generously of their time in interviews and who granted me the permission to use their names, their pictures, and words in the book. Of these people, I'd like to single out Woody Walters, Denny O'Hearn, Nancy Schneider, Peter Cooper, and Dana Gioia for special thanks and appreciation.

I'm grateful to Alex Kroll, Amil Gargano, William Phillips, Tom Clark, Barry Loughrane, and Ed McCabe—chief executives and heads of major agencies who were extraordinarily generous with their time and knowledge.

Many other individuals who helped out did not receive mention by name in the book. I'd like to thank them here: Mark Lonnegren, Emily Arth, Lisa Wasser, Penny Westerbeck, Jack Sidebotham, George Berger, Myra Rothfeld, John Mittnacht, Tom Messner, Dave Berman, Simmy Sussman, Ed Keller, Adrian Lichter, Ann Magee, Barry Wagner, Walter Carlson, Frank DiSalvo, Angela Dailey, Joseph A. Berlinger, Fred Lamparter, Mark Kapsky, Kinder Essington, Karen Walter, Corrine Cofsky, Galene Cox, and Judy Kozuck. Much thanks also to my aunt Molly Bazel and friend Karen Pennar for providing contacts, articles, advice, and information, and to Priscilla Flood for introductions to advertising people.

Gratitude to my editors Joëlle Delbourgo and Ginny Faber for continuing support and guidance, and for signing me up in the first place.

And a huge thank you to my wife, Kathleen O'Neill, for finding 1,001 ways to make this book easier to research and write.

Preface

Advertising is a people business. That's the first thing you'll hear about it. People—talented, committed, vibrant people—are the most important resource of every advertising agency and department. People imagining, planning, and creating are the essence of this $96 billion business. And so, correspondingly, this is a book full of people. People talking about their jobs. People recounting the stories—some funny, some quite odd—of how they got those jobs. People talking about what they love, and what drives them a little crazy, about the advertising business. Agency presidents and art directors, media planners and product managers, famous creative directors and obscure-but-hopeful junior copywriters, veterans of the creative revolution and tough business-minded researchers and account managers who quelled that revolution: this book belongs to them. If you want to hear what they have to say about *Getting Into Advertising*, stay tuned.

The second thing you'll hear about advertising is: great business, but *really* tough to break into. And you'll hear it and hear it until you're ready to scream. Don't scream. Listen, but don't give up. Advertising is tough to get into, there's no getting around it. There aren't that many jobs, and lots and lots of people want them. These jobs will go to the people who want them most. The people who try hardest to get them. The people who know how to try hardest. So this is also a book of advice on how to try hardest. And the advice, fittingly, comes from people who have succeeded and are now in a position to help you succeed. They'll tell you how they did it then, how they'd do it differently now, what impresses them in a job applicant, and what turns them off. It's good to get to know these people. They're your future colleagues.

I just said there aren't that many advertising jobs, which is certainly true compared with the professions of law, medicine, or business in general. But within the relatively small scope of advertising, there are many, many types of jobs, probably many more than you're even aware of—and many more than can be described in this book. As you make your rounds, you'll hear about openings in unlikely sounding areas—bullpen, traffic, media buying. Don't necessarily rule them out. Keep an open mind. The more you get into advertising, the more you may discover that it's not at all what you expected. Infinite variety—that's what lots of admen and adwomen find most wonderful about their jobs.

PART ONE

THE BIG PICTURE

WHO ARE ALL THOSE TERRIFIC PEOPLE AND HOW DID THEY GET THOSE TERRIFIC JOBS?

"I came to New York with about $75 in my pocket, and, after a week of interviews I was running out of money. But, of course, I couldn't go back home, because how could one admit failure at such an early age? I hung on through the following Monday, when the head of a small agency took pity upon my sad and sullen countenance and offered me a job—in the mailroom at $45 a week."

"In the back of my mind, advertising was something I had always thought about and, after taking some time off after college, I decided I had to go to New York. My initial goal was to get into account management. I had probably written or contacted the top twenty-five or thirty agencies in New York and didn't get any interviews. The few interviews I did get were through connections, but it all seemed to lead nowhere because I didn't have an MBA. I was beginning to think I'd be banging my head against the wall for a year when someone suggested I try getting into the media department. One of the first interviews I had in media was at BBDO and I got the job. At which I point I said EUREKA! Now I have something to go on."

"I came to this country twenty years ago, and I absolutely fell in love with New York. I didn't want to leave. My English was very bad, and I had to figure out how to make a living here. I worked for eight months as a glorified au pair girl in Scarsdale. Then I moved to the city and got a job as a girl Friday for a photographer. He did a lot of work for advertising agencies and so I learned what they were all about. After a year I was ready for a more serious job and I chose Cunningham & Walsh because I knew where it was on Madison Avenue. I walked into the agency and said, 'I need a job.' And Cunningham & Walsh said, 'You have six weeks in research to prove yourself.' I stayed there four years."

These are all true stories. The guy with $75 in his pocket is Tom Clark, president and chief operating officer of BBDO. The guy who considered banging his head against the wall is now an account supervisor at Grey Advertising and rising fast. The au pair turned researcher is Edith Gilson, senior vice president in charge of the Consumer Behavior Group at J. Walter Thompson/New York (and the only woman on the Thompson management committee). They are some of the people who have the "terrific jobs" Alex Kroll was talking about in the quotation that prefaces this section (he's got a pretty terrific job himself).

Advertising agencies and departments are full of people like them—people who stumbled or fell into advertising; people who lucked or chanced into their first job; people who were desperate for a break and got one, though maybe not the break they were hoping for. Advertising is that kind of field. There are all sorts of ways of getting into it and all sorts of ways of succeeding. People change jobs all the time. They hop from agency to agency or leap from the agency side to the client side and back. One executive I interviewed started as an apprentice in a small agency, became a copywriter, moved into account management, then joined the advertising department of a large chain of retail stores, moved back to the agency side, and ended up doing promotion and public relations for a large corporation. This kind of zigzagging career path may be less common now than it used to be, but it still happens. Advertising does not demand or reward uniformity or conventionality: it rewards creativity above all else. Create a new image for a tired old product, find a way to really *move* people about chickens, cars, or delivering parcels overnight, and you're well on your way.

AD PEOPLE: WHAT THEY DO

Creating something new may be the heart of advertising, but it takes a lot more than a heart to make an industry. An enormous number of people are needed to support, plan, guide, realize, execute, produce, schedule, and distribute this creation. And each one of these functions involves a number of different jobs. Let's take the thirty-second

DAVIS: Do you know me?

GARFIELD: Who cares?

DAVIS: That of course, is Garfield. He's fat.
GARFIELD: Full figured.

DAVIS: Ill mannered . . . and to think I created him.
But sometimes when I travel without . . .

GARFIELD: Mmmmm.
DAVIS: . . . the tubby tabby . . .

people don't know my name.

So, I carry the American Express card and
wherever I go, folks treat me like a fat cat.

GARFIELD: Fat chance.

(SFX: Print Out)

ANNCR: (VO) To apply for the card, look for an
application and take one.

DAVIS: The American Express Card. Don't leave
. . . ummm, home . . . ummm . . .

without it.®

Thirty second commercial spot for American Express featuring Jim Davis and Garfield: "Do You Know Me?" (GARFIELD: ©1978 United Features Syndicate, Inc.)

4

American Express spot featuring Jim Davis (creator of Garfield, the bestselling cat). Part of the American Express "Do You Know Me?" campaign, it opens with this question and closes with the unforgettable slogan: "The American Express card. Don't leave home without it." Start with the obvious jobs: somebody wrote Davis's and Garfield's lines and designed (or found) the restaurant setting in which they appear—this would be the copywriter and art director at Ogilvy & Mather, the agency that devised this campaign. Then there was the production of the actual commercial film, involving a director and an independent production company, cameramen and crew (almost always hired, like the director, on a job-by-job basis), producers—one from the agency and one from the production company, usually, plus their assistants—to coordinate the myriad details of making a commercial including set design and construction, props, wardrobe, scheduling, casting. The director shoots raw footage which is delivered to a commercial editor to refine, and he in turn farms out the job to outside suppliers for sound mixing, special effects, titles, etc. An animator working out of an animation house would handle the insertion of the Garfield cartoons into the spot.

So now you have a commercial—but how do you know what TV shows to run it on? Should it be spot television (airtime purchased from individual local stations) or network (airtime purchased from one of the three networks to be broadcast nationally)? Or maybe cable? All airtime is negotiable, so you need someone with experience in bartering for and approving packages of commercial times bought from the networks and the media reps who work for the local stations. Enter the media department with media planners, buyers, and researchers. But wait a minute: who's going to make sure the commercial actually gets to the right stations or networks on time, that it's going to make the necessary rounds of completion and approval? This work is handled by the agency broadcast traffic department. And there's also the matter of bills to be paid to director, editor, etc., and commissions and fees to be collected from client and media. Finance and accounting take their place in the agency structure.

This is just the beginning, the tip of the iceberg of advertising jobs. Any commercial, any advertisement for that matter, is a joint enterprise—the collaboration between client (the advertiser) and advertising agency (creator and placer of the ads). There's got to be somebody in the middle to communicate the wishes of agency to client and client to agency, to guide and coordinate the input of all the agency functions, to iron out problems and oversee decision making. These are the responsibilities—*some* of the responsibilities—of account managers. These people also take care of a lot of business that may not be quite so visible: there's a marketing side of the job in which they work with the client on building business, a strategy side of the job in which they size up the consumer and figure out ways to reach him/her, a report-writing side of the job, and a lot more.

We're leaving out research—the people who devise endless studies aimed at understanding the person who is going to apply for and use that American Express card, or whatever. Is Jim Davis really a good choice of "personality" for a "Do you know me?" commercial—or would Judith Krantz, David Hockney, or Julia Child bring in more business? How effective was this spot compared with the Mastercard personality spot featuring James Coburn? Who remembered what about the commercial? What are the psychographics (key psychological characteristics) of the typical American Express card user? The agency research staff concerns itself with these and related issues, working closely with creative, account management, and media people.

There are still more players of the ad game. Agency management—the presidents, chairmen, and chief operating officers who run these "shops" (familiar term for agency)—travel to the offices around the world, bring in new business, and keep old business happy. There's a legal staff to make sure that commercials abide by regulations. There's print production to oversee the translation of the art director's layout into a finished ad to be run in a magazine or newspaper. There are type directors, proofreaders, casting directors, secretaries, receptionists, and assistants of all sorts in almost all agency departments.

We're still not nearly done. We're forgetting all those advertising and advertising-related jobs on the other side, the side of the advertiser with the products to be advertised. At American Express there's an advertising department with managers and directors who oversee the work of the agency, collaborate with agency people on every phase of the ad campaign; they have budgets to adhere to and top management to report to, and they must see that the advertising is carried out effectively within the limits of these budgets. Large packaged goods corporations, such as Procter & Gamble and General Foods, have product (or brand) managers with responsibility for all aspects of the production and marketing of a particular product, and among these responsibilities is advertising. Large retailers—department and chain stores—often have fully staffed advertising departments including copywriters, art directors, production personnel, media people; this staff often takes care of all the advertising needs without relying on an agency. In fact, just about any company of any size advertises itself and its products, and though the actual creation and placement of the ads may be handled by an advertising agency, there are people in-house in charge of the company's advertising— whether this means approving the work of the agency, hiring and firing the agency, or actually sharing the work with agency departments.

So now we've got our commercial created, produced, researched, scheduled by the agency; we've got the client side guiding and approving the agency's work and determining how many more commercials are needed and how much they can spend on them. We still need a medium on which to run the commercial, and this means more jobs—jobs on the networks selling airtime to agencies, jobs for companies that represent local stations, jobs on those local stations selling airtime to local advertisers, and the same setup for newspapers and magazines. The whole area of media sales opens up an entirely different sphere of advertising jobs.

Even this list does not tell the whole story. The more you look into advertising, the more jobs you'll discover. Computer jobs. Public relations jobs. Meeting planners. Account planners. Though this book can't claim to cover them all, it does cover all the *major* ones. There are chapters devoted to all the functions and areas mentioned above. So take your pick—creative, account management, media, research, traffic and production, client side, retail, media selling—and immerse yourself. Or, if you're not sure where you want to be, flip through these chapters, read the interviews, and try to imagine yourself in various jobs. Remember, it helps to keep an open mind, both to the jobs described here and to the jobs not described that you may hear about or even be offered. As one agency chairman said: "My first advice if you think you want to go into the agency business is to get a job. Once you're inside the agency, you can usually wiggle your way up. Because agencies tend to be unstructured, people who can solve problems and do a good job get ahead very quickly." It's true. Get your foot in the door and see for yourself.

AD PEOPLE: WHAT THEY'RE LIKE

Are they all neurotic? Do they all have ulcers? Do they wear gray flannel suits—or black leather and motorcycle chains? Do they usually work all day and all night? Are they parasites on society? Do they all make fabulous amounts of money? Are they slick, shallow, sleazy, and superficial?

There are some pretty strange rumors going around about advertising people. Their reputations are not exactly sterling. And such popular novels as *The Man in the Gray Flannel Suit* (1955) and *The Hucksters* (1946) have done nothing to improve the image. It's time to inject a little up-to-date reality into the fantasy of old novels, movies, and gossip.

First of all, the answers to the questions in the paragraph above: No, they're no more neurotic than most people in high-pressure, demanding, and creative careers. No, most of them don't have ulcers. They dress for the most part in normal business attire, maybe a shade less formal than people in large corporations, except for some creatives, who run the gamut from urban cowboy to urban guerrilla. They do work long hours, and a lot of them have put in all-nighters on occasion, but certainly not *usually*. Yes, they are very well paid (see below). As for parasitic, slick, and sleazy—if you thought that, you wouldn't be trying to join their ranks.

What else? Let's pry a little bit beneath the surface and consider some of the intellectual, moral, and, to use a favorite advertising term, demographic qualities typical of ad people (keeping in mind that no one is really *typical* in this business):

Smart. This is practically the sine qua non of advertising people. This is not to say that they're all Einsteins or Shakespeares, but they are all brainy, and brainy in a peculiar, hard-to-put-your-finger-on way. Some executives have described it as *street smarts*. Others talked about a broad range of interests, a basic curiosity about people and culture. An openness to new experiences. A willingness to experiment and take risks. It's all of these things. Ad people have their fingers on the pulse; they can sniff out cultural, psychological, behavioral, financial, or lifestyle trends and changes on the merest puff of wind. They're plugged in—to movies, books, plays, restaurants, and above all, to the tastes and desires of the man on the street, whether that street be 42nd Street or Main Street, USA. They're honest with themselves and they have senses of humor. They're with it. You don't get this kind of smarts from self-help books or fancy colleges or knowing the right people. You get it most of all from being alive to and in your time. Advertising people are, with a vengeance.

Creative. The most overused and abused word in advertising, but still as useful as it is unavoidable. Being creative in the advertising sense means knowing how to translate all of the qualities listed under *smart* into communication. Being creative is not something that agency creatives (copywriters, art directors, producers, creative directors) have cornered the market on. All key advertising people—account managers, researchers, media people, production staff, top management—are creative. The whole business is based on creating—making up new messages and images, figuring out new ways to reach consumers, asking questions no one has ever thought to ask before. Tom Clark, president and chief operating officer of BBDO, summed this up when he told me what has kept him in the agency business for over thirty years: "It's the creative process. It's the application of marketing strategy to the creative process. I absolutely love being involved in the creative process and by that I mean contributing thoughts, watching a campaign evolve, being involved in its development, its strategic direction, selling it to the client, watching it come to fruition as it's produced, and then watching the results when it works."

Committed. "This job is *always* with you" is a comment you'll hear frequently from advertising people. You think about it on evenings and weekends. You frequently work at it on evenings and weekends. A working day that lasts from nine to five is practically unheard of in advertising. But it's not just the amount of time, it's the quality of the time spent on the job. Advertising people—successful advertising people—really are committed to what they do. They believe in it. They enjoy it. They're fulfilled by it. Sometimes they're consumed by it.

Of course, there's a downside to this. Advertising can be so demanding and intense it will grind you up if you're not careful. "This business really sucks you dry," one management supervisor who has risen fairly high fairly fast told me. "Because it's a service business, you have to answer to people all the time and try to please people all the time and try to meet people's needs and demands. There are times when I think I'm not going to be able to do this for years longer." Commitments get brittle and snap; people burn out; and lots of people who were once fulfilled by advertising are now desperate to get out. You need to exercise a bit of caution before you sign your life away. Advertising is not the kind of field you can dabble in.

Young. Thirty-one-year-old executive creative directors of international agencies. Twenty-six-year-old art directors handling hundreds of thousands of dollars on commercial extravaganzas. Twenty-nine-year-old account managers earning $65,000 a year. Forty-year-old presidents of major agencies.

These are by no means rarities in advertising today. Advertising is a young industry with fabulous opportunities for people in their twenties and thirties to rise quickly, make a mark (and quite a bit of money), travel, take charge of major responsibilities. Boy and girl wonders really do exist. If you've got the talent and the drive, no one's going to care that you're still sort of wet behind the ears. Youth may even be an advantage, especially for creatives. After all, youth is practically worshipped by America's consumer culture, and young people constitute a crucial, trendsetting segment of any market. Who better to communicate with this segment than their peers?

Again, there's a downside: a lot of bright young talent burns itself out or simply can't sustain the pace. "Sometimes we wonder: where do all these people go when they reach forty?" one youngish executive confided nervously. It's something worth thinking about. It can be great to rise fast and wow the world before you hit thirty. But the higher you climb in advertising, the fewer jobs there are and the more intense the competition becomes. You start seeing a whole new crop of twenty-five-year-olds coming in and rewriting the rules, as you did five or seven years ago. You may feel a bit like a baseball player or a ballet dancer—out to pasture when your friends in other careers are just hitting their stride.

If you're looking for long-term job security and an industry that rewards loyalty, steadiness, and consistent performance, keep looking. Advertising heaven is full of shooting stars.

Varied. They come in all shapes and colors, and with all sorts of racial, ethnic, and educational backgrounds. More and more of them are women. There are priests and taxi drivers who became copywriters; Asian language scholars and students of advanced aeronautics who went into research; stand-up comics and, yes, even bankers who were welcomed into exclusive creative agencies. Alex Kroll played a season of professional football before deciding that Young & Rubicam was where he belonged *[see page 15 for the full story of how he got into advertising]*, and before too many years Y&R decided to make him president and chief executive officer. Ed McCabe, a high school dropout, got a job in an agency mailroom because no one else would hire him; now he's worldwide creative director of super-hot creative agency Scali, McCabe, Sloves *[see Chapter Four for an interview with and profile of McCabe]*. There's no telling where they come from or what they've done. I've sat talking with an incredibly smooth, urbane creative director who gave the impression of growing up in the Museum of Modern Art with summer vacations divided between East Hampton and Provence—only to learn that he hailed from blue-collar Detroit, from which he catapulted himself to the top of New York by sheer force of talent and will. Then again, I've met an exuberant, earthy account manager, the type you just *know* had spent five years making sculpture in Tangiers before joining the business world—and it turns out she went right from University of Pennsylvania to the Wharton School to account work on Procter & Gamble.

It takes all kinds. Lots of them have come out of business schools and art schools—and lots haven't. Lots of copywriters majored in English and lots majored in odd jobs or television-watching or hanging out at rock clubs. This diversity in advertising people across all major departments is no coincidence. Many creative directors and agency presidents actually seek it out. As one president of a major agency explained, "While the MBAs from eastern schools may fit certain kinds of clients or situations, they will actually not fit others. If we have an army of these people, then we really do have a gray-suit kind of mentality. I look for a mixture of people." And as a young art director whose career was just opening up before her said, "What's great about advertising is you can be yourself. You can be crazy if you want to. So long as you're creative and you sell, you can be anything."

Team Players. Yes, some of them have egos the size of the Goodyear blimp. And some are a touch temperamental. There is the occasional tantrum thrown or vendetta sworn because the client or the account supervisor wants one itsy-bitsy more revision. Emotions do run high and passions may flare. But generally, ad people are an extremely cooperative bunch. They have to be. Advertising, as we'll see in the following chapters, is a collaborative enterprise from start to finish. The art director and copywriter don't just lock themselves up in a studio and whip up a brilliant campaign and toss it at the client with an arrogant glare that signals, Here is a work of true genius with which only a FOOL would tamper. No way. There are endless meetings, rehashings, strategy sessions, revision sessions; the researchers and media people have their increasingly important input; the account managers prod, the creative directors coax, the client insists, and the campaign *evolves* from all of these people working together. You watch your brilliant ideas turned upside down and inside out and you do the same to the brilliant (or not so brilliant) ideas of your colleagues. It's not like writing a novel all alone in your apartment or running a start-up technology company with a staff of three computer whizzes. It's a lot more like making a movie—one of those seemingly simple, artless films that has credits that run for seven minutes at the end with the names of the hundreds of people who contributed to the work. In one way or other, you're going to be collaborating and cooperating with all the people in the agency or in the advertising department or with the client and his/her advertising department or all of the above. So park your ego at the curb before you get down to business.

MYTHOLOGY, REALITY, AND EXPECTATION

Myth: Advertising is a cutthroat, back-stabbing, hypercompetitive business in which you can't even trust your best friend, let alone your boss.

Reality: I'm not going to tell you that it's a breeze or that everyone you meet in advertising is going to bend over backwards to help you rise to the top. There *is* a lot of competition and pressure to produce, to succeed, to make deadlines. Some offices do get tangled up in complicated and destructive internal politics. Others might be best described as hot houses full of exotic, delicate flowers. The occasional Machiavelli may be seen lurking in the shadows with dagger in hand. This sort of thing might happen a little more in advertising than in other businesses because advertising does attract some fairly intense, creative, and bright people. But for every time you hear "cutthroat," you hear "cultured," "civilized," "gentle," "humane," applied to ad people five or six

WOMEN IN ADVERTISING

The good news is: advertising, a field traditionally open to women, has terrific opportunities for women who want to break in today. Creative, media, account management, research are all hiring women at the entry and middle levels, and talented, ambitious women are rising fast. Even large corporations, usually more conservative, are hiring more and more women for their advertising and marketing departments and training programs.

The bad news is: women are still for the most part poorly represented at the very top ranks of agency management. You'll find lots of female vice presidents, a handful of senior vice presidents, a scattering of executive vice presidents, but women presidents, chief executive officers, and chairmen are a scarce commodity indeed. As one of the few women who has made it to the executive committee of a major agency summed up: "Since I am the senior woman in the agency in terms of budget and influence and the only woman on the executive committee, I am under a certain burden to be a role model for the younger women. There is some conflict, however, because I don't know how much hope I can hold out for them. In advertising, a woman can get up higher than in most places, but there are still very, very few women at the highest levels of power. It's a great field for women to start in, but most women can only rise so high."

This, however, is true not only in advertising but in most fields, even those traditionally open to women. Things *are* changing, but it's going to be a good many years before fifty percent of the presidents of America's corporations—or advertising agencies—are women.

times. The leaders, the people who set the tone and the pace of the business, are some of the most intelligent, articulate, witty, and informed people you'll ever meet. And they clearly got where they are now by hard work, honesty, and ability, though no one's going to deny that charm, luck, business savvy, and aggressiveness helped too. The odds are, if you've never stabbed anyone else in the back, you won't have to worry much about your own.

Myth: Forget about job security. Every time an agency loses an account, you and everyone else on that account lose your jobs in what's familiarly known as a "bloodbath."

Reality: Maybe once true but not any more. Blood no longer flows down Madison Avenue when a company pulls its business out of one agency and hands it over to another. Greater job security is one benefit of scientific management and the predominance of larger agencies. Now that the agency business has matured and become very big business, the agencies are run with the same careful planning that other large American corporations feature. For the most part, they can absorb account losses without mass firings.

This is not to say, however, that advertising is the world's cushiest business and that no one ever gets fired. The pressure to produce and sell is always there. The pressure of being a service business is always there—and this means the pressure to get along with people. And there's also a pressure to keep moving. There's no such thing as a cozy berth or a free ride. Find yourself stagnating or resting too long on past laurels, and you might find yourself tossed out. So no, it's not the most secure profession around—but then again, it's never boring.

Myth: It's a glamour field. You rub shoulders with movie stars. You eat in fancy restaurants. You're always jetting off to the Coast. You do a lot of kissing and calling people "babe."

Reality: Well, yes and no. I asked a lot of people this glamour question, and everyone had the exact same response: Absolutely not. It's hard work and more hard work, they say, and there's no glamour in it whatsoever. Then they tell you about the time they met J. Paul Getty. Or what it was like to shoot a commercial with Christie Brinkley or to travel with James Coburn to the south of France. Or how Michael Jackson is a "really beautiful kid" and was terrific to work with on those Pepsi spots. Or how they can't wait to work with the Rolling Stones. Again, this is really a matter of degree and comparison.

If you think it's glamorous to be on the same set with Michael Jackson or Christie Brinkley, then you're in for a lot of fun. But first of all, keep in mind that this is only a minute part of your job, even if you're in the creative end. And secondly, for every hour you spend in a limo with a star (or more likely in a taxi trying to catch up to the limo), you'll be spending ten or twelve or twenty hours sweating over the lines that the star is supposed to say or sing, or the fee that star's agent is demanding, or the numbers of people who are likely to buy the product because the star tells them to. And those winter "jaunts" to Hollywood can get pretty grueling when you're separated from your family once again and when you realize that you'll be putting in sixteen-hour days and probably won't even have a tan to show for it.

While we're on the subject of glamour, we might as well clear up a few more misperceptions: The wining and dining aspect of the job is vastly overstated. Account people don't while away their time in four-star restaurants (or golf courses) trying to impress/soothe/con clients. More likely they're grabbing a sandwich at their desk or talking business with a client in the company cafeteria. None of the account people say that entertainment is a major factor in their jobs, and few of the agency presidents say that either. Yes, there is a certain amount of partying and carrying on—agency people celebrate when they win a new account or when it's "a wrap" on a big-budget commercial. It's a lot of fun, but it's more in the way of a *reward* for hard and successful work than a normal part of the job. More and more, advertising is run like and feels like a business. The excesses of yesteryear—both lavish expense accounts and the "bloodbaths"—are more and more a part of advertising history.

Myth: People change jobs constantly because it's the only way to get ahead.

Reality: This myth happens to coincide to a large extent with the truth. Changing jobs has become a way of life in advertising. You'll meet thirty-three-year-old creatives who have worked at four agencies and researchers who have moved on to a new agency on the average of every two years. Agency-hopping is actually encouraged in advertising because it's frequently the only way to get a raise or a promotion. If you don't move around you don't move forward. There are, of course, exceptions. Young & Rubicam and Ogilvy & Mather both have reputations for rewarding loyalty and promoting from within, and as a result people stay on and make a career of working at these agencies. As proof of this policy, Ogilvy's chairman William Phillips and Y&R's president Alex Kroll have been with their respective companies their entire careers in the agency business *[see Chapter Ten on agency chief executives for more on these two]*. But these are exceptional men and exceptional career paths. Generally speaking, if you're a nest builder who prefers to settle in at one company, you may get your feathers ruffled in the agency business.

Myth: You make an awful lot of money.

Reality: You certainly *can* but you won't when you start out. It's pretty safe to say that advertising salaries begin on the low side ($12,000 to $18,000 a year is a ballpark range) and shoot up fairly high fairly quickly. After two years, if you're doing well, you may be making $30,000 and after five your pay could easily be $60,000, bearing in mind that you may very well have switched agencies a couple of times and put the screws on your various bosses. At a certain point of success, the sky's the limit. One copy chief at a very hot, prestigious agency was almost *embarrassed* to reveal that he made $300,000 a year with bonus and this guy is a few years shy of forty. Agency presidents not uncommonly make off with more than a half a million dollars a year. The same goes for successful commercial directors. There's a lot of money floating around those office towers in New York, Chicago, Los Angeles, Dallas, and Boston. So don't get upset when someone who's earning $150,000 offers you a job at $15,000. You'll get there soon enough. Advertising, whatever else it may be, is not stingy.

Though pay levels fluctuate a good deal from agency to agency and from city to city, for the most part creatives can expect to earn the highest advertising salaries; account people come next, then media and then research. See the individual chapters for more detailed discussion of advertising salaries.

ALEXANDER KROLL
President and Chief Executive Officer
Young & Rubicam

If you want to feel inspired about advertising, there's probably no better source of inspiration than Alex Kroll. Kroll is inspiring not only because of *who* he is—the leader of the world's largest ad agency—but because of *how* he is. There's something a little old-fashioned, a little larger-than-life (there's no doubt he's large at 6′2″, 220 lbs.), something very *basic* about Alex Kroll. The man's a believer—in advertising, in the people who make advertising, in himself, in the people advertising is made for. He not only likes what he does, he relishes it.

His energy can be a bit daunting. His dedication, while powerful, has nothing of the self-righteous fervor of the proselytizer. Kroll is an enormously gifted, creative businessman who just happened to land in the right business. At forty-seven years old, he heads an agency that has 8,400 employees around the world, some thirty-five U.S. offices, and world billings of $3.2 billion in 1984. Its clients include AT&T, Lincoln-Mercury, General Foods, Campbell Soup, U.S. Postal Service, Metropolitan Life, Dr Pepper *[see illustrations of some outstanding recent ads]*. Kroll is the sixty-two-year-old agency's seventh chief executive and the first to come from the creative ranks in twenty years.

In Kroll there survives some of the romance of advertising that one associates with advertising greats from years gone by—Albert Lasker (Chicago advertising giant of the first half of this century and head of Lord & Thomas), Stanley Resor (who turned J. Walter Thompson into the world's largest agency in the 1950s), Raymond Rubicam (founder of Y&R), Bill Bernbach (legendary creative leader of Doyle Dane Bernbach), Leo Burnett (founder of the agency, dean of the so-called Chicago school of advertising), David Ogilvy (who remains involved in the affairs of Ogilvy & Mather from the comfort and splendor of Touffou, his chateau in France). The romance that Kroll represents is not the plutocratic luxury and tyranny of Lasker, who told his agency staff that "Lord & Thomas is the trade name for Albert D. Lasker practicing advertising," and kept an estate outside Chicago staffed by fifty servants. Nor is it Bernbach's razzle-dazzle iconoclasm, nor Burnett's homespun, sod-busting innocence. No. Kroll is brains and brawn and determination. Kroll, an enthusiast himself, is an exciter of enthusiasm—and creativity—in others. Kroll is the ultimate team player. He gets his colleagues and staff to hustle, to keep running forward. He gets them worked up about winning and helps them shake off upsets. He expects the best and gets it. The sports images are chosen deliberately, for of course Alex Kroll is famous as the football player adman. The Alex Kroll story is becoming part of advertising lore. Here it is in his own words:

"My first job—I was about twelve at the time—was delivering the *Valley Daily News* in [the small mill and mining town of] Leechburg, Pennsylvania, from door to door, rain or shine, wind or snow.

"When I graduated from college, because I was an All-American football player [in 1961 on the Rutgers eleven], I was the subject of a small essay in *Newsweek*. I really didn't have a very secure idea of what I wanted to do when I got out of college beyond playing football, which I'd been doing for a long time. When I was in the Army I'd

YOUNG & RUBICAM NEW YORK

CLIENT: DR PEPPER
PRODUCT: DR PEPPER
TITLE: "GODZILLA"

LENGTH: 60 SECONDS
COMM. NO.: DPYT-4696
DATE: 3/18/85

(SFX: ANIMAL ROARS)

(SFX: SOUNDS OF DESTRUCTION)

(SFX: FRIGHTENED CRIES AND SCREAMS CONTINUE UNDER)

JAPANESE MAN: The Monster! Godzilla!

The monster!

AMERICAN REPORTER: We must stop Godzilla

before he destroys the city . . .

I'm saying a prayer . . . a prayer for the whole world.

What could he want? Unless we find something to appease him . . .

we're doomed!

CHORUS: HOLD OUT . . .

HOLD OUT . . .

FOR THE OUT OF THE ORDINARY . . .

HOLD OUT FOR DR PEPPER.

DON'T BE SOLD OUT . . .

HOLD OUT . . .

IT'S A TASTE THAT'S EXTRAORDINARY . . .

NO DOUBT IT'S DR PEPPER . . .

DR PEPPER.

(SFX: BURP!!)

Saved by Dr Pepper: Frames from a recent television spot created by Kroll's Young & Rubicam creative team.

Snoopy gets Met:
A highly visible
print campaign from
Young & Rubicam.

been drafted by the Los Angeles Rams and I just sort of assumed that I'd go out to the Rams and play center until my knees turned to Jell-O at the age of thirty. That was sort of my long-range plan, and I didn't quite see beyond the end of the last quarter of football. That's not totally unusual for guys in their twenties who think that they're immortal.

"However, the reporter who did the story for *Newsweek* followed me around the campus—at the time I was writing a senior thesis on Lawrence Durrell who had just written the Alexandria Quartet. At the end of the article, he asked what I intended to do other than play football and, being stumped for an answer, I said, 'Well, I might go to law school, and I might go into the advertising business.' This was in the late fall, and lo and behold, I got a phone call a few days later from a man named Harry Carpenter who was a vice president at Young & Rubicam and a Rutgers graduate. Harry said to me, 'You know, Alex, I read this article in *Newsweek* and I want you to know that we have lawyers in the advertising business at Young & Rubicam, so you could do both things. Why don't you come up and pay me a visit when you're in town?'

"I did come to Young & Rubicam, in fact I came to this floor, and Harry Carpenter introduced me to a few men, including Ed Bond and George Gribbin who were running the agency then. They were impressive in an unusual way. They were direct, candid men. In the end, after a couple of conversations, Bond said, 'Look, we have a training program here and it starts in the research department and it goes into merchandising and media and ends up in account management. You could do that and then take six months off and play football for a couple of years. After two years you decide what you want to be—an advertising person or a football player.' It was so simple and these guys were so terrific that I said, 'Yes, absolutely. I'd love to try it.'

"So I went into the research department, the first part of the training program, and I was *terrible* at it. I found myself falling asleep at meetings or doodling or drawing ads—that should have been some indication about what my real bent was. I spent about four and a half months at it and then I took off six or seven months to play a season with the New York Titans. When I returned to Y&R I went to the personnel guy and admitted that research was not my forte. He asked if I could write. Y&R had a modest copy test that they gave people who didn't have a portfolio. I took the test and they hired me as a cub copywriter.

"It was a thrilling job. It was *so different* and so different every day. I remember one time we were playing the Buffalo Bills here in New York, and we were ahead about 14 to 0. It was a Friday night game and it was raining and about 33°. They were wearing white covered with mud and our blood. We had the ball on about the two yard line and we came up to the line of scrimmage and I just absolutely froze in my tracks. I stopped, and the guy behind me ran into me and the back ran into him. They said, 'What's the matter with you?' I had had this vision. A small one. Not an epiphany, not exactly like Saul on the road to Damascus. But here we were on the two or three yard line and we were going to run an off tackle play to the left and I was going to take a little jab step with my left foot and then duck my head and move my right shoulder and I thought, 'I've been doing this motion, exactly the same dance step for about fourteen years. *Exactly the same*. The people are bigger and faster, and I'm bigger and faster. The place is different but we're the same automatons dancing through the night.' The one thing that was true about writing copy was that *it was never the same on any day or night*. It was never automatic. There were no set steps. It was always fresh and interesting and a stretch.

"I started out on the usual kinds of accounts, writing trade ads and those sorts of things. It was wonderful. By July, when Weeb Ewbank called to say it was time to come back and throw myself at those other guys, I said no, I'd really found something that was really exciting. I was an odd cub copywriter as you may guess. I weighed 240 pounds then and had a bullet-shaved head. I didn't look like the other thin, ascetic boys and girls who were struggling to become writers and art directors. But that's not the most important thing. The advertising business seems to accept you regardless of race, color, creed, or size.

"So that is how I got into the advertising business."

[For the rest of Alex Kroll's story, as well as his thoughts on leadership, creativity, and breaking into the business, see Chapter Ten on agency chief executives.]

THE INDUSTRY IN FOCUS

Imagine the world without advertising. Skimpy little magazines with only articles. Cityscapes bare of billboards and posters. Subways and buses with nothing to look at but graffiti. Radio just music and news. TV just shows without a break. No Marlboro cowboy. No Pepsi generation. No Jolly Green Giant. No "We try harder . . ." No legendary women wrapped in Blackglama minks.

The fact is, advertising has become not only a part of our economy, but part of our culture. It shapes not only the way we buy, but the way we think, feel, speak, and imagine. Some say it's too powerful, too pervasive, and too insidious. Others contend that it's only begun to realize its potential commercially and artistically. There's no doubt that advertising is bound up with the very core of modern existence. No wonder so many people are trying to get into it.

Advertising is not only important business, it's *big* business—very big and growing fast. During the last three years, domestic advertising expenditures grew at a faster rate than the economy as a whole. In 1984, while the GNP expanded 11%, domestic advertising spending rose by more than 15% to about $87 billion. Now the Commerce Department is predicting that an average growth rate of 10% in advertising will continue for the next five years. According to the 1982 Census of Service Industries, advertising agencies experienced a "period of unparalleled growth" from 1977 to 1982, with employment up 28% to 175,000 people, annual payroll up an impressive 79%, and the number of agencies climbing 18%. Not bad. Other good news about the advertising industry is that when the economy as a whole stumbles, advertising expenditures don't usually fall—in fact, they often *rise* as companies try harder to boost their sales. How's that for built-in security?

Although there are lots of young people working in it, advertising itself has become a "mature" industry. It has created a stable place for itself in America's economy. In fact, advertising has become a business *necessity*. Procter & Gamble, the packaged goods giant and the nation's largest advertiser (as of 1984), wouldn't dream of launching a new laundry detergent or disposable diaper without massive advertising; nor would Apple try to sell a new computer nor Eastern Airlines offer flights to a new destination without a carefully planned, national advertising campaign. Advertising is built in to the American (and the world's) economy and it's here to stay.

Dynamic, booming, highly visible, highly professional, respected, desirable, and crucial to business and culture—the advertising industry was not always like this, not by a long shot. Its origins in this country were actually quite humble, even a bit shady. It used to be, back in the eighteenth and early nineteenth centuries, that the only advertising media were newspapers and broadsides, posters and pamphlets that circulated through the towns. "Nice" respectable companies did not, for the most part, advertise at all: it was considered a bit vulgar and implied the company had fallen on hard times (why else would it stoop to the embarrassment of advertising itself?). Volney B. Palmer gets the credit of being America's first advertising agent, back in 1843 when he set up shop in Philadelphia. Palmer was really an agent for the newspapers, not the advertisers. He solicited orders from advertisers, sent in the copy (which the advertisers wrote themselves), and collected payment. Out of the money paid to the newspaper publisher for the space, Palmer extracted his commission. In a sense, Palmer and other early agents were hardly more than salesmen/errand boys: they knew the periodicals and the rates they charged, they haggled with advertisers to get the highest prices and with the newspapers to get the lowest, they delivered the copy, and they were not above fudging the actual rates so they could jack up their commissions, which were running as high as forty percent.

The first advertising agencies were one-room offices with an agent, a man who kept track of the rates charged by newspapers, a bookkeeper, and perhaps an office boy or two. There were no account executives, no copywriters, no art directors, media planners, researchers, etc., etc. The first products to receive national advertising with big budgets were those notorious hoaxes of the nineteenth century—patent medicines. What with the questionable goods being advertised, the questionable character of advertising agents, and the constant fighting and mudslinging between agents and publishers, advertising was hardly a "glamour" field, and in fact barely even a respectable field, when it started out.

Enter Francis Wayland Ayer, upright, clean-living, honest, and smart, who founded N W Ayer & Son in 1869 (still going strong in 1986 as the nation's eighteenth largest agency) and, by bringing some order to this chaos, reformed the business and set it on its modern course. Ayer did away with a lot of the fighting and mistrust with one broad and significant stroke: he offered an open contract in which the rates charged by the newspapers were explicitly stated, and he set his own commission at 12.5%. Ayer thus became the advertiser's agent, and as such he began to offer "extras" such as art and copy and, in time, business-building advice. A man of unimpeachable moral rectitude, Ayer helped clean up the image of advertising and broaden its appeal to many more types of businesses. It was N W Ayer that launched the first one-million-dollar ad campaign for National Biscuit Company's unforgettably named Uneeda Biscuit. *[For more about the history of advertising, see* The Mirror Makers *by Stephen Fox (Wm. Morrow, 1984).]*

In the 1890s the newspapers got together and agreed to grant the agency commission only to genuine advertising agencies. In time, 15% became established as the standard commission, and it remains so today in all media. Advertising agencies continue to finance their work largely out of this 15%. When you read, for example, that Young & Rubicam had worldwide billings of $3.2 billion, it means that the agency purchased $3.2 billion worth of advertising in various media on behalf of its clients, and out of this the various media paid it a commission of 15% or about $480 million. That, with some variation (some agencies use the fee system—charging the client a predetermined, set amount for the services performed), is how the advertising industry still operates.

Practically everything else about advertising has changed unrecognizably in the past one hundred years. Perhaps the most obvious change is in the media available to advertisers. Today, television dominates the advertising scene: it gets by far the most national advertising spending (national advertising constitutes about 56% of the nation's total advertising; newspapers continue to be by far and away the largest local advertising vehicles). The commercials that run on the air stir up the most excitement and controversy, require the most money to produce, and involve the greatest number of people to create—hence providing the most job opportunities. *[For an in-depth look at making a television commercial and the various people involved, see Chapter Six.]* Television is also the most diverse medium, with cable a small but growing factor alongside the established networks and local stations (known as "spot" TV in the business).

Magazines account for the next largest chunk of today's national advertising spending, and as with television, the magazine scene is undergoing rapid changes that translate into more opportunities for advertisers. The trend in magazines, as one agency chairman told me, is from "mass to class" and to an ever greater number of specialty magazines appealing to small but committed (and affluent) market segments. Then there's radio, outdoor advertising (which includes billboards, posters, skywriting), and direct marketing, the increasingly important and explosively growing area of sales direct from company to consumer, usually through the mails or over the phone. Most direct marketing is done by mailing brochures, catalogues, "special offers" to potential buyers, though any medium can be used. (In his book *Ogilvy on Advertising*, David

Ogilvy calls direct marketing "my secret weapon in the avalanche of new business acquisitions which made Ogilvy & Mather an instant success," and he strongly recommends it as the most valuable experience a person starting out in advertising can get as well as one of the best ways to break in.)

As the media have expanded, so have the types of products and services advertised, and with this has come a diversification in the types of advertising agencies. Though the big consumer agencies dominate the field and are also the best known to the general public (and most sought after by job applicants), agencies exist that specialize in everything from pharmaceuticals to travel. Other areas of agency specialization include finance, recruitment (advertising job openings at companies to job seekers), trade (advertising to people within a given industry, through trade magazines, for example), entertainment, and politics.

The advertising agency scene is lively, thriving, and spread out across the country [*see the following chapter for a discussion of where the agency action is today*], but it remains a fairly small business in terms of employment. The entire American agency work force totals around 175,000 people, which is one reason why competition to get in can be so fierce. However, many more advertising jobs are available in the advertising and marketing departments of companies that advertise (the client side), and still another source of advertising jobs are the media that publish or broadcast the ads or commercials. These media company jobs primarily involve selling space or time to the agencies. *[For discussions of client side and media jobs, see Chapters Twelve and Thirteen.]*

When you start tracking down every one of those nearly $100 billion spent on advertising, you discover that millions of people have somehow been involved. Millions of jobs were needed to spend this money and, in a sense, all of these were advertising jobs. But only in a sense. Let's face it, the creative director inside J. Walter Thompson in New York who devised the "Aren't you hungry?" TV campaign for Burger King (his name is Jim Patterson and you can meet him in the next chapter in a profile of this old but exciting agency) is a lot more critically involved in the advertising process than the manager of the new Burger King branch in your local mall who buys a page announcing the grand opening in the local advertising circular. Not to mention the fact that his job is a lot more interesting. Advertising agencies are really the vital center of the advertising industry: they control the creative flow, they set the tone, they are where the truly exciting action is. Though they may not have the greatest number of advertising jobs, they offer the greatest variety of jobs and the jobs most directly tied to the making, planning and placing of the ads.

These are also the jobs that most people want. So that's where we'll start.

PART TWO

ADVERTISING AGENCIES: WORLDS UNTO THEMSELVES

Advertising agencies. Where are they? What are they? How do they
work? Which are the biggest? Which are making the biggest
waves? Where are the jobs? What are the jobs?
Approaching the world of advertising agencies can be quite daunting
when you have all these questions ringing in your head. You just want a
job—but who had any idea agencies were so complicated? At your first
interview at a large agency, you'll ride up the elevator and see the lights
flash on for the different floors, each with a different department:
Creative, Account Management, Executive, Production,
Media, Research. . . . What's it all about?
The next nine chapters have the answers.

THE AGENCY SCENE:
WHERE THE ACTION IS

There are advertising agencies practically everywhere. The variation in size, personality, style, and opportunity is astonishing. For a quick insight into just how astonishing, go to your local library and get hold of the *Standard Directory of Advertising Agencies*, familiarly known as the Agency Red Book. This handy volume, published in February, June, and October and updated monthly, is indispensable for the job hunter. It lists some 4,400 ad agencies, providing such crucial information as billings, total employees, address and phone numbers, top executives, and major accounts. Here you can discover that Hawaii has some fourteen agencies, while the listings of agency names alone for New York City run to ten pages of tiny type in triple columns. Turn to the J. Walter Thompson section and you'll see that Thompson has full service offices in seven U.S. cities, branch offices in eighteen other U.S. cities, and overseas offices in some forty countries, including Thailand, Bahrain, fourteen in Britain, and two in Greece. Flipping a bit farther back in the Agency Red Book, you can learn that there are two U.S. agencies with the initials Y&R—Young & Roehr, Inc. in Portland, Oregon, with seventeen employees and approximate annual billings of $10,250,000, and Young & Rubicam, Inc., the nation's largest agency, with 8,800 employees worldwide and, according to *Advertising Age*, world billings for 1984 of over $3 billion. This should give you some idea of the range of what's out there.

While it's true that there are advertising agencies just about everywhere there is advertising, it's not true that there are decent agency job opportunities wherever there are agencies. Young & Roehr in Portland with its seventeen total employees is just not going to have a lot of openings in the coming months. They might land a big new account and hire someone lucky enough to be there at the right time—but that's about it: one hired. The odds are a lot better of finding a job where a lot of jobs already exist. Consider the fact that the nation's top twenty-five agencies employ some 88,830 people worldwide, while agencies ranking twenty-six through fifty employ about 10,581 people worldwide. These top twenty-five agencies also command 71% of world gross income.* So much for manpower and money. As for geography, of the top fifty agencies, thirty-seven have their headquarters in New York, three are headquartered in Chicago, two in Detroit, two in Los Angeles, two in Dallas, one in Pittsburgh, one in Minneapolis, one in Boston and one in Indiana. Most of these big agencies have branch offices in other cities, but the headquarters are invariably where the big power, big bucks, and big and exciting jobs are concentrated.

This should put the agency picture in focus a little bit. There are agencies all over the place, but only half a dozen American cities are advertising centers with major agencies and good job opportunities. Of these advertising centers, there is only one capital city—New York—that towers over all the rest. And, just as agencies themselves are concentrated in New York and these other key cities, agency income is concentrated in the big shops. Where income is concentrated, jobs are concentrated. And this trend toward concentration is, if anything, accelerating as big agencies swallow up little ones and giants merge with giants (two huge mergers made the headlines in mid-1985.: D'Arcy MacManus Masius Worldwide with Benton & Bowles and Bozell & Jacobs with Kenyon & Eckhardt, knocking out two of the current top twenty-five and consolidating agency resources even further).

This doesn't mean that you can't and won't land a job at one of those fourteen small agencies in Hawaii, or anywhere else. But it does mean that if you're serious about getting an agency job, and especially if you're trying to break into your first job, you'll stand a better chance if you concentrate your search where the action is. Unfortunately, even *that* doesn't mean you'll breeze right in, no matter how talented you are. Breaking in, as you'll hear many more times than you care to, is notoriously tough. It's tough in New York. Tough in Los Angeles. Tough in Chicago. But it's a whole lot tougher in Hawaii.

Below you will find vital information on the agency scene as it looks now in the U.S. There are nutshell summaries of the action in the major advertising centers, profiles of a few agencies that are making news, and then listings of the top fifty agencies. This should orient you. In the following chapters we cover the departments within an agency with in-depth discussions of what the jobs entail, interviews with people who hold these jobs, and advice on how to get them. A fact to remember at the outset: the agency scene is volatile. Hot shops cool off. Business trends change rapidly. Today's vortex is

Statistics reprinted with permission from the March 28, 1985, issue of Advertising Age. Copyright 1985 by Crain Communications, Inc.

tomorrow's backwater. Keep abreast of developments in *Advertising Age, Adweek,* and the business press. Focus your search on where the action is happening.

NEW YORK

There is no getting around it: New York holds the uncontested title of advertising heavyweight champion, not only of the U.S., but of the world. New York may not be your idea of paradise, but it's advertising's mecca. The nerve center. The major league. Corporate headquarters. Financial capital. Madison Avenue and Wall Street—need one say more?

If you want to get into advertising, you're eventually going to bump up against the stubborn fact of New York. This is not to suggest that New York is the *only* place you can enter advertising. There are lots of jobs elsewhere. There is plenty of great advertising produced elsewhere (some claim the best ads today are coming out of California; others say Minneapolis). But no place touches New York in terms of sheer volume—of agency income, jobs, influence. As Amil Gargano, chairman, president, and creative director of the widely respected New York creative shop Ally & Gargano, recounted during a recent interview *[see Chapter Four on the creative team]*: "In the first couple of weeks after I arrived in New York from Detroit, a photographer said to me, 'In the time of the Romans you live in Rome; in the time of the Americas you live in New York.' I thought, yeah, that's true, that's exactly why I'm here."

That's exactly why lots of people are there. Thousands of bright, hungry, talented people stream into New York each year from places like Detroit. All of them are eager to make it, to break it, to rise fast. For every job opening, there are bushels of people— good, qualified people—fighting to get it. Competition is fierce. Yes, New York is where the main action is—but no, it's not a secret. While New York offers fabulous opportunities, getting a crack at them can be a long, brutal struggle. Brutality and struggle also characterize a good deal of life in the city. Thanks to a score of cop shows, the whole world knows about the crime, grime, and frenzy that make the streets of New York vibrate. Also notorious are the city's skyrocketing rents (always a notch or two above salary levels, which do run high, but not that much higher than those in other advertising centers), the relentless pace of work and play, and the myriad hassles of daily life. All ad executives who have worked in New York and then left it will tell you the same thing: the agency business is just as pressured, fast paced, and demanding in other cities, and you work just as hard, but the rest of your life is so much more pleasant that it's possible to enjoy your work more. On the positive side, they'll point out that their New York experience opened doors in Dallas, Chicago, Los Angeles—and, yes, even Hawaii. Wherever you go next, New York agency experience makes it easier to get there. It's impressive, hence marketable. People all over the world acknowledge that New York is a super place to train. A solid grounding in packaged goods marketing at a big New York agency is the account executive's ticket to the city of his/her choice. Even if you're only there for a few years, New York looks wonderful on your resume. Keep this in mind when you're pounding those treacherous pavements. New York may not be easy, but it's worth it.

Another advantage of New York is the variety, both in the types of accounts to be found there and in the types of agencies. Packaged goods, travel, service, liquor, cigarettes, fashion, media—they're all here, except for maybe automobiles, concentrated in Detroit, and computers, for which a good deal of advertising is done in California and Boston. As for the agencies, take your pick: there are the giants like Young & Rubicam, Ted Bates Worldwide, Saatchi & Saatchi Compton. There are the giants on creative streaks: Ogilvy & Mather International, J. Walter Thompson, BBDO International (see profiles of the last two below). There are the solid marketing agencies that are beefing up their creative: Grey, Benton & Bowles, D'Arcy MacManus Masius. There are the creative firecrackers of yesteryear—Doyle Dane Bernbach; Wells, Rich, Greene—that continue to produce strong advertising, and the creative firecrackers of today—Scali, McCabe, Sloves; Della Femina, Travisano & Partners; Lord, Geller, Federico, Einstein; Ally & Gargano; Ammirati & Puris; Waring & LaRosa; Backer & Spielvogel. Not many of them are located on Madison Avenue anymore; but together, they still constitute Madison Avenue, the driving force of American advertising.

Stories occasionally appear in various magazines that New York has lost its creative touch, that the most vibrant advertising is coming out of smaller cities, that the layers of corporate hierarchy have smothered the city's spark. Chiat/Day, based in Los Angeles (though it has a New York office), won accolades a few years ago and remains in the spotlight with its breakthrough Nike and Apple computer ads; Fallon McElligott Rice (see profile) is the darling agency of the moment, and it's in Minneapolis. But don't let that blind you to reality. Creativity can and does happen anyplace. But there can only be one center and that continues to be New York. If you want to be where the action is, be there.

Chicago

Chicago, America's second city, is also the #2 advertising agency center in the country. Chicago's advertising community is old, established, and prospering, but there's still a very large step down from #1. According to the *Advertising Age* 1985 Agency Profile issue (March 28, 1985), of the top 162 agencies in the nation, those situated in New York command some $5.3 billion of income; Chicago's second place is a "mere" $686 million. Then there's another large jump down to Detroit with $135 million and Los Angeles with $110 million.★ So, as long as it's not stacking itself up against the Big Apple, Chicago looks pretty grand.

With that said, we might point out that Chicagoans feel no great need to compare their city with New York. "In advertising, we Chicagoans don't take a back seat to anyone," a native Chicago executive told me. Today, the agency business in Chicago is healthy; the advertising coming out of Chicago is "better than it has ever been" according to Patrick McKeon, a senior vice president, director of media at Bozell & Jacobs/ Chicago; the mood in the advertising community is positive and upbeat. That's the good news. The not-so-good news is that not too many agencies are hiring right now, especially at the entry level. "Though business is very, very good right now," McKeon says, "agencies are running leaner. I'm glad I'm not trying to get in right now. It's very tough. Hiring of trainees has been cut back; true, everybody hires beginning people once in a while, but it's a lot harder than it used to be." It's a different story , however, if you're already working in an agency and want to switch jobs. "The door opens magically if you have experience."

A few executives voice a bit more optimism, pointing out that breaking in to advertising today is certainly easier than it was during the recession of the 1970s. But all agreed that breaking in was hard. Then, again, breaking in *anywhere* is difficult. "It's tough to crack," Ralph Rydholm, executive vice president, executive creative director of J. Walter Thompson/Chicago, pointed out, "but not that much tougher than New York."

In terms of focusing on specific Chicago agencies, the rule that the bigger the shop, the better your chances of getting hired is probably a good one to get you started. Towering above the rest is Leo Burnett Co. (see agency profile), with over $1 billion of U.S. billings and some 1,400 employees in Chicago alone. Burnett has a great training program (difficult to get in to but worth trying), a great track record, and some great new business. J. Walter Thompson, with some $450 million in billings and about 720 Chicago employees, is the city's #2 shop. Rydholm described the feeling in the Thompson Chicago office as "dynamic" with lots of new business coming in and a strong creative current running. Other agencies that are prospering in Chicago now include Needham Harper Worldwide (older and larger than the New York headquarters); Ogilvy & Mather; Bozell & Jacobs; Foote, Cone & Belding; Tatham-Laird & Kudner; and the midsized agency Grant/Jacoby.

Everybody agrees that the Chicago school of advertising (Leo Burnett, its inventor, described its essence as "sod-busting delivery, loose-limbed stand, and wide-eyed perspective") is a thing of the past. Creatively, there is no longer a real split between the advertising styles of New York and the midwest, though perhaps Chicago accounts continue to skew a bit more toward food companies, which traditionally prefer a warm, wonderful family approach in their ads. Creative breakthroughs and originality are as much prized in Chicago as anywhere in adland.

If you work in an ad agency, there is no getting away from pressure, tension, and a compulsion to succeed—and this is just as true in Chicago as in New York. "Hours are not that much more humane than in New York," one agency executive told me, "the pressure to achieve is just as tough, but perhaps we're just a bit more relaxed here. Maybe it's because getting to work in the morning is not such a battle. People don't come in quite as pissed off. Also, we're less paranoid than New Yorkers—who almost seem *proud* of their paranoia." Another executive, who has worked in both New York and Chicago, felt that "the Chicago work atmosphere and work ethic are more under control and people can get more done in a shorter span of time."

Pay stacks up pretty well against New York salaries, though there are fewer "superstar salaries" than in New York. Keep in mind, when comparing salaries of *any* city to New York, that the cost of renting an apartment and just plain living in Gotham will quickly eat up those extra bucks.

CALIFORNIA

Advertising is not just thriving in California—it's booming. Part of the reason is that business is booming (it's growing at a faster rate than the nation's economy), and where business booms, advertising booms too. But it's more than big bucks, it's big brains that are stirring things up on the Coast. *Newsweek* magazine ran a story (March 4, 1985) about the West Coast ad scene under the headline: "The Advertising Game Tilts Toward the West—California Agencies Set the Creative Pace." The article pointed to the stunning creative work coming out of Ketchum Communications in San Francisco; Chiat/Day (already a legend in its own short time for its Nike running shoe and Apple Computer ads) in Los Angeles; Foote, Cone & Belding (San Francisco's largest agency, winning attention for its music-video-style "501 Blues" spots for Levi Strauss); keye/donna/pearlstein, an eighty-person creative hot shop in Los Angeles; and BBDO/West in L.A. and San Francisco. The *Newsweek* reporter concluded that "the most talked-about ads today are coming from California" and that, as a result, top talent is gathering there. In fact, California agencies are growing at twice the rate of New York agencies. As one San Francisco account supervisor told me: "There is an increasing awareness that agencies on the West Coast are not little satellites, but autonomous and thriving in their own right." A media director at Ogilvy & Mather/Los Angeles went a step further when he joked: "Our motto is, 'We are a Los Angeles agency with a branch office in New York.'"

The good news for job hunters, of course, is more opportunities, especially in Los Angeles, which by most accounts is the nation's #3 advertising city after New York and Chicago.

Not only are the job opportunities expanding on the Coast, but once you land a job out there, you may well find it a more stimulating place to work. One L.A. executive said people tend to be less pigeonholed on the Coast—departments are structured more loosely, rules less rigidly applied, levels less evident, people running the agencies more accessible. Don't, however, be fooled by California's "laid-back" reputation. The pressure is every bit as intense, the pace of work as fast, and the standards as high as in New York or Chicago. And so, for the most part, is the pay. It's the lifestyle, not the workstyle, that can be mellow.

Other Los Angeles agencies that people are talking about include Dailey & Associates, with 245 employees; Ogilvy & Mather; Needham Harper Worldwide; Foote, Cone & Belding (with 350 employees it is the largest in Southern California); and DYR. In August '85, the Texas-based Tracy-Locke joined the flourishing L.A. agency scene with a full-service office.

San Francisco has important branch offices of BBDO; Cunningham & Walsh; D'Arcy; Dancer, Fitzgerald, Sample; Foote, Cone & Belding; Ketchum; Grey;

McCann-Erickson; Ogilvy & Mather; J. Walter Thomspon; and Young & Rubicam. Breaking in to an agency in San Francisco can be tough because the scale is somewhat limited. If you can't land an entry-level job, think about gaining some experience in New York or Los Angeles and then making a move. Word is out that there are jobs open for middle-level media and creative people.

DETROIT

Detroit's substantial agency business has grown up around Motor City's major industry—automobiles. But cars, while big business, are by no means the only business in Detroit, or in Detroit agencies either. Many of the shops in and around the city—in Southfield, Warren, St. Joseph, and Bloomfield Hills—are doing well with footwear and appliance accounts, as well as service businesses and retail. Cars, however, remain the core.

Detroit agencies divide into two types—the home-grown shops and the branch offices. Of the home-grown, the biggies are Campbell-Ewald, long associated with General Motors and particularly Chevrolet; Ross Roy, which has a good mix of accounts including Chrysler, Detroit Edison, Howard Johnson, and K Mart; and William B. Doner. Of the three, Doner is currently the hottest creatively. This good-sized agency (annual billing in the $179 million range) is especially known for its retail accounts, including W.R. Grace, Highland Appliance, and Zellers Stores, and they've also got Arrow Co., Blue Bell, Carling National Breweries, The Detroit Free Press, and Marriott Hotel Corp. business. The quality of the work is widely acknowledged to be superb.

New York and Chicago-headquartered agencies with thriving branch offices in Detroit include BBDO, Leo Burnett, N W Ayer, D'Arcy, J. Walter Thompson, Young & Rubicam, Saatchi & Saatchi Compton, and McCann-Erickson. For the most part, these Detroit offices handle the automotive accounts of the parent agency. For example, J. Walter Thompson/Detroit does all the work on Ford cars, while J. Walter Thompson/New York takes care of Ford trucks.

Breaking into an ad agency in Detroit can be tough for the simple reason that there aren't that many positions available, a problem compounded by the fact that agencies are running with leaner staffs. Balancing this, however, is a genuine commitment to giving newcomers a chance. One Detroit-based creative director told me: "All major agencies here feel a responsibility to move people into the business and help train them. We try to hire young people whenever we can because we've seen how valuable they can be." If you're lucky enough to land an entry-level job with a Detroit agency, you'll probably be working incredibly hard for incredibly little money—but if you're good, you'll make it.

Detroit has a reputation as kind of a depressing place to live, and many people shudder at the very thought of moving there, but this reputation is emphatically undeserved according to both natives and transplants. It's a great place to raise a family, with reasonably priced homes, beautiful suburban neighborhoods, good schools, and unmatched recreation opportunities. As one Detroit executive said, "When people come here and look around for the first time, the typical reaction is 'Holy cow! I didn't know you had all this out here.'" Another executive who had worked in Detroit for a number of years and then went on to New York said, "I'd move back tomorrow—and my wife feels the same way." So if you have an offer to work in Detroit or you're dying to be where the action is in automotive advertising, don't go by the city's reputation. Give it a chance; go out and see for yourself.

Dallas

Dallas is hot, Houston is not. This about sums up the agency scene in Texas right now. The fact is, business is great in Dallas at the moment and lousy in Houston, which is still suffering from the aftereffects of the oil bust. And generally, where business booms, agencies boom right along with it. So, if you're hoping to land a job in advertising in the Lone Star State, cross Houston off your list (yes, there are agencies there, but they're firing, not hiring) and set your sites on Dallas.

The Dallas agency horizon is dominated by three hefty shops: Bozell & Jacobs/ Southwest, with billings in the $280 million vicinity; Tracy-Locke/BBDO, billing about $240 million; and the Bloom Companies with over $154 million in billings. Dallas's up-and-coming midsized agency is the Richards Group, which expects to bill in the $80 million range in 1985.

Dallas may not yet be an advertising center on the order of New York or Chicago or Los Angeles, but it's no backwater either. The three major agencies are all frequently invited to take part in competitions for major national accounts, which means that they're vying for business with the big shops—and they're doing their share of winning. Growth is dramatic, one executive told me, with new business coming in regularly. B&J/Southwest has an impressive client list that includes American Airlines, Greyhound Corp., and Republic Banks of Texas. Tracy-Locke won a Clio for its Frito-Lay Tostito–brand tortilla chip TV campaign. Bloom's clients include Schering-Plough, Liggett & Myers Tobacco Co., and Block Drugs. The Richards Group has a growing reputation for impressive creative work.

As in most places, Dallas offers better opportunities for people with experience than for newcomers. Competition can be fierce for entry-level jobs, but they do exist. You'll just have to look longer and harder to get one. Insiders who have migrated from New York insist that Dallas agencies are "as professional or more professional than New York shops" with comparable pay and hours.

BOSTON

From backwater to mainstream in less than ten years—that's the news on the Boston agency scene. With the advertising industry growing at a rate of 39% a year and agency billings fast approaching the $1 billion mark, Boston has turned itself into an advertising dynamo.

How did it happen? The answer, while complex, can probably be summed up as computers, fresh talent, and lots of determination. Silicon Valley is not the only computer center in the U.S.; Route 128 which rings Boston bills itself as "America's Technology Highway" and houses a thriving high-tech business. Boston agencies got in on the local technology boom on the ground floor, and they're riding it as high as it will go. Hill, Holliday, Connors, Cosmopulos has done fabulously well with Wang Computers, which grew from a tiny account in 1977 to a $40 million international account. HHCC's success with Wang put this agency ahead of HBM/Creamer, which for years had been Beantown's #1. Now HHCC with 411 total employees has offices in New York and abroad, they're hiring big names to staff their new branches, and they're growing at a rate of more than 50%. HHCC is on the hunt for new talent—new people with new ideas—and they're willing to pay for it.

While HHCC's success is perhaps the most dramatic in Boston, it is not the only show in town. HBM/Creamer is settling down to business after a shake-up period following the merger of the two agencies (Boston-based HBM and New York-based

Creamer) that constitute it. Ingalls Associates and Arnold & Co. are also on the move. From 1983 to 1984, Ingalls increased billing from $60 million to $85 million and beefed up staff from 175 to 240. Ingalls, which has an impressive intern program, hires people right out of college, especially imaginative people who can take an unorthodox approach, and trains them up fast.

A notch below these Boston big four, there is a handful of small creative shops that are also expanding at a clip. Among the more noteworthy of these are Harold Cabot & Co.; ClarkeGowardFitts; Rizzo, Simons, Cohn (which has New Balance business); Cosmopulos, Crowley & Daly; Emerson Lane Fortuna; Mullen Advertising in Beverly Farms; and Kelley & Wallwork. There is also a good-sized branch of Kenyon & Eckhardt in Boston.

Most satisfying to Boston ad executives is that the local agencies are winning business away from the big New York shops by coming on strong with brash, original advertising. Boston, however, is obviously not going to topple New York and Madison Avenue in the near future. But the fact remains that in a remarkably short period of time it has managed to put itself on the map as the #2 advertising center in the Northeast. Boston has a reputation as an easy place to live but a tough place to find work, especially for young professionals. No one is claiming that it's easy to break into the Boston ad game, but it's a lot easier than it used to be. Take the example of Nancy Goodfellow, now an account supervisor with HBM/Creamer on Reed & Barton, S.D. Warren, and in the agency's design group. Goodfellow, who had (brief) New York agency experience, came to Boston on a whirlwind fact-finding mission in 1984 to size up the agency scene. She set up a number of interviews, and things really clicked at HBM/Creamer; two days later the agency offered her a job. Goodfellow comments: "I work harder and longer than I ever did in New York. It's very fast-paced here in a professional way and there is more than enough work for everybody."

For the moment, anyway, this is an advertising boom town. Try to catch Boston while its star keeps rising.

IAMI

Miami may not spring immediately to mind in connection with advertising agencies, but in fact Florida's sunshine city is a happening place in adland. Business is growing, new blood is coming in from cities to the north and islands to the south, and suddenly, perhaps thanks in part to the success of the "Miami Vice" TV show, people are recognizing Miami's inherent style, a compound of deco decadence and business street smarts.

At the top of the Miami agency heap is Beber Silverstein & Partners, which the two founding women partners, Elaine Silverstein and Joyce Beber, have managed to turn into something of a phenomenon in a mere thirteen years. With offices in Miami, New York, and Washington, billings around $55 million and over 105 employees, Beber Silverstein has entered the ranks of the top ten in the Southeast. Now the agency management is saying "come on down" to top Northeast creatives and executives from all over who want to get in on the hot Florida action. Clients include Bacardi Imports, Citicorp Savings, Pfizer Inc. (Coty's Sophia fragrance and Musk for Men), the Helmsley Palace, and the National Organization for Women. Smart and aggressive are the operative words in describing this agency on the move.

Other top Miami shops include McFarland & Drier Advertising, known as a more buttoned-down establishment shop rather in the Madison Avenue mold (its founders are refugees from the Big Apple); Mike Sloan, Inc., a small shop that packs a big creative punch; Tinsley Advertising, and Ryder & Schild.

FOUR AGENCIES IN THE NEWS: PROFILES

BBDO

What makes BBDO run? Fabulously creative, top-notch management, and phenomenal growth for starters. In terms of growth, the numbers speak for themselves: in the past fifteen years the agency has turned itself from basically a domestic operation to a truly global one, with 120 offices in thirty-eight countries.* In the past five years, net income has nearly doubled, rising from $13.6 million in 1980 to $22.6 million in 1984. *New York* magazine has called the agency "the darling of Wall Street" and cites its excellent management and consistent profits. But BBDO's really big surprise is its new, improved creative. It's no exaggeration to say that BBDO is undergoing a creative revolution all its own, and the preeminent evidence of this phenomenon are those Pepsi commercials that no one can stop talking about. Michael Jackson and Lionel Richie have made Pepsi the "choice of a new generation," and these super-entertain-

In the spring of 1986, after this book had gone to press, BBDO entered into an agreement with Doyle Dane Bernbach and Needham Harper Worldwide to merge into a single mega-agency, as yet unnamed.

Modern art for your kitchen: BBDO creative is now at Adland's forefront.

ing, big-budget commercial extravaganzas have made BBDO the choice of *Advertising Age* as Agency of the Year for 1984.

The Pepsi spots are not the only creative breakthroughs coming out of the New York-based agency. Commercials for Dodge cars, Black & Decker tools, Campbell Soups, Pierre Cardin fashions, and GE have also been cited for creative excellence. Visa is a major client that has just jumped on board.

What happened? How did BBDO go from being the "gray grandmother of advertising," respected most for its marketing and research capabilities, to its current wild, exciting, creative turbulence? Credit for this changeover goes to three leaders: Bruce Crawford, who recently left the post of agency chairman to become general manager at the Metropolitan Opera; Allen Rosenshine, president–chief executive officer of BBDO International; and Phil Dusenberry, vice chairman and executive creative director. Crawford pushed the agency ahead in two directions—he greatly expanded the international operations and he set about to revitalize the creative product at home. Crawford put Rosenshine, who had risen up through the ranks as a copywriter, in

Two campaigns that show off BBDO's strength in print.

charge of the creative facelift, and Rosenshine brought in Dusenberry. Dusenberry gathered together the best creative staff he could get his hands on and fired them up with his own energy and determination to make new advertising. In the words of Tom Clark, agency president and chief operating officer, "Those creative people are superstars and that's why we've got the work we do today. It's sensational stuff." Clark described the working environment inside the agency as "unstructured" and characterized BBDO as "an agency that takes the business seriously but doesn't take itself too seriously." *[For more on the management and philosophy of BBDO, see the profile of Tom Clark in Chapter Ten.]*

BBDO began as George S. Batten Company back in 1891; today BBDO International (the other initials are for Roy Durstine, Alex Osborn, and Bruce Barton, advertising legends all), is ranked by *Advertising Age* as the fifth largest U.S. agency, with world billings of $2.3 billion and a total of 4,472 employees in its various offices. Within this global structure, there is a smaller unit called BBDO Inc., which encompasses the New York, Detroit, and Minneapolis offices, and it was this division (with billings of $617.5 million) that *Advertising Age* honored as Agency of the Year. The overall agency also has major U.S. offices in Chicago (Wrigley is a big account), Los Angeles, and San Francisco with BBDO/West; BDA/BBDO in Atlanta (Delta is a major account); along with a slew of subsidiaries including Tracy-Locke/BBDO in Dallas, Denver, Philadelphia, and Los Angeles; small but intensely creative Waring & LaRosa in New York; Doremus & Co. (the nation's largest financial advertiser in New York, Boston, Chicago, Los Angeles, San Francisco, and Washington, D.C.); Quinn & Johnson/BBDO in Boston; and Franklin Spier, book publishing specialist located in New York. BBDO abroad includes offices in South America, Australia, Europe, the Middle East, and Asia.

While BBDO's breakthrough creative is what's making headlines, the agency maintains superb standards in media, account management, and research. There is a formal training program in account management for which nine or ten people a year are accepted at the New York office out of a pool of many thousands. The highly structured program gives an assistant account executive two nine-month assignments, one in packaged goods and one in some other area. Hiring is done on a rotating basis depending on openings. BBDO/New York also has an informal training program in media, with weekly lunch-time classes at which representatives of the various media functions and major agency departments explain what they do. Currently, the program has about thirty entry-level people in it. Apply through the Manager of Training and Development.

LEO BURNETT COMPANY

If there's one agency that epitomizes advertising in Chicago, it's the Leo Burnett Company, which celebrated its fiftieth anniversary in 1985. While the "Chicago school of advertising" with its larger-than-life photos, clear and sincere headlines, and wholesome feel may be a thing of the past, the Burnett agency which pioneered this approach is very much a thing of the present. With world billings over $1.7 billion, Burnett currently ranks as the ninth largest agency in America in gross income. Despite its size and prestige, Leo Burnett remains a home-grown Chicago product: it is the only major U.S. agency with a full-service office in Chicago and Chicago only. There are service and production branches in Los Angeles, Detroit, and New York, and offices around the world, but Chicago not only runs the show, it *is* the show.

Perhaps more than any other giant agency, Burnett reflects the philosophy and style of its founder, legendary adman Leo Burnett, who got things going on the strength of one account in 1935. "Go for the heartland" sums up the approach taken by Burnett who, despite increasing fame, power, and fortune, never really stopped being a copywriter until his death in 1971. Burnett had a way with pithy mottos and dicta, one of the best known of which was his instruction to creatives to look for the "inherent drama" present in almost every product and service. These creatives over the years have found or created drama with such characters as Tony the Tiger, Charlie Tuna, the Marlboro Man, the Pillsbury Doughboy, and Morris the Cat. Some say the Burnett approach verges on (revels in) the corny; others suggest that there's a certain sameness to many of the campaigns. But the main thing is, it works. "We have one criterion for superior advertising," Burnett chairman Norman Muse told *Advertising Age*, "and it's sales." Such clients as Kellogg Co., Philip Morris, United Airlines, Pillsbury, Maytag, Allstate Insurance, and Star-Kist tend to agree: they've all been with Burnett for years, and many continue to use the original campaigns that Burnett devised for them. Newcomers include McDonald's, Beatrice, and Kraft.

Loyalty, so rare in the agency business, characterizes not only Burnett's clients (half of the agency's twenty-eight clients have remained loyal for twenty or more years) but its staff as well. The top executives in most departments, aside from creative, have risen through the ranks. Ninety percent of the agency's top brass has started off in the agency's fine training programs. "Conservative" and "inbred" are words often used to describe Burnett employees, who now total 3,838, with 1,575 in the U.S. Burnett has a certain mystique based on the good-old American values it continues to embrace and endorse in its ads. Perhaps there's a certain romantic naiveté at the core, but it's a naiveté that meshes brilliantly with business savvy. Many Burnett alumni speak glowingly of their years at the agency, and it gives insiders a nice warm feeling to know that most promotion is done from within

Getting to be a Burnett insider is another matter. The agency receives some 5,000 resumes each year for the fifty entry-level positions in the client service development program. The way to score, says Kathie Hoppe, vice president associate recruitment director, is to demonstrate your leadership potential. Leadership, Hoppe stresses, is more important than top grades from fancy schools. The Burnett Company takes great pride in its training program, which has been going on for twenty-five years and is one of the most comprehensive in the industry. Trainees with MBAs or previous work experience start in the client service department on one brand; those right out of college spend some time in the media department learning the ropes. Within two years, trainees become assistant account executives.

For more information about Leo Burnett Company and some of its clients, see the August 1, 1985, issue of *Advertising Age*, which celebrates the agency's fiftieth birthday with in-depth coverage.

FALLON MCELLIGOTT RICE

One of today's most talked about and written about agencies is not in New York, not in Chicago, not in Los Angeles, or even Dallas or Miami, but in Minneapolis. It's not quite right to say that Fallon McElligott Rice put Minneapolis on the advertising map, because there were and are other substantial agencies in town, including BBDO, Bozell & Jacobs, Campbell-Mithun, and Grey, but this redhot shop certainly brought this midwest city to national prominence as its own star rose. And its star rose very high, very fast. FMR was named *Advertising Age* Agency of the Year in 1983 when it was just two years old; at the last Art Directors Club annual awards it made off with eighteen awards, including three golds. An even more substantive coup was wresting the prestigious *Wall Street Journal* account from BBDO in January, 1985, a feat that brought in $4 to $5 million in billings and untold publicity. Now, every other week it seems there's a mention in the trade press or the advertising column of *The New York Times* of a new account landed by FMR. This agency is taking off because of its superb creative output—and despite anything you'll hear about marketing depth or full-service capacity, great creative remains the rarest and most valued commodity in advertising. FMR proves that when you're hot you're hot, no matter where your main office happens to be located.

FMR was the brainchild of two Minneapolis advertising executives, Patrick Fallon, its thirty-nine-year-old president who had directed marketing at the Minneapolis agency Martin/Williams, and creative director Thomas McElligott, forty-one, who had been with Bozell & Jacobs's Minneapolis office. The reason they wanted to start their own agency was not new: they wanted to do their own work their own way; but the creative product *was* new—new and tremendously effective. Their TV work for Minnesota's Gold'n Plump Poultry showing live chickens in combat gear (helmets, parachutes) created a sensation. Their work for the *Wall Street Journal*, including print ads using old photos of immigrants and the theme line "The daily diary of the American dream," is both eye-catching and moving. Says creative director McElligott, "All our work is breaking its neck to be different." His agency currently enjoys a reputation as the best print shop in the business.

FMR now has annual billings of about $45 million and employs over seventy people, more than twenty-four of them in the creative end. If business continues to boom, as it gives every sign of doing, they're going to need to draw on a larger pool of talent than Minneapolis can supply. McElligott is looking for "people who are emotionally dedicated to turning out great stuff and who are willing to pay the price. And the price is that they're going to have to be really hard on their own ideas." *The New York Times* says that FMR is "driven to become a major force in advertising," and driven young people are exactly what it will need to keep pushing.

J. WALTER THOMPSON COMPANY

The words "creative," "vibrant," "youthful," "dynamic," are not the first ones that spring to mind at the mention of the name J. Walter Thompson. Even people who don't know much about advertising know about JWT—or *think* they do. Thompson is that huge, stodgy, frumpy shop that's been around forever and got stuck in its ways back in the fifties.

Think again. Yes, Thompson is huge—it's got 188 offices around the world in nearly forty countries and a total of 8,174 employees and world billings for 1984 of $2.7 billion. And yes, Thompson, founded in New York back in 1864 by, you guessed it, James Walter Thompson, is old. But in the last five years or so, Thompson has come unstuck—very unstuck—from its old ways and won a name for itself as one of the hottest creative shops around. And along with a skyrocketing reputation has come skyrocketing business. The biggest plum to fall to Thompson of late was the Miller High Life account, which it won in a much-publicized creative competition with N W Ayer, Burnett, Jordon, Case, Taylor & McGrath, and Chiat/Day. Other new accounts include Goodyear, Eagle tires, Showtime cable TV movie channel, and Warner-Lambert. And then there are the good old accounts—Kodak (with Thompson since the 1880s), Ford, Lever Brothers, Burger King, Nestle, and Pepsi-Cola.

Billings at the New York office, which leads the Thompson hot streak, jumped from $350 million to $580 million in just one year. The Chicago office, not far behind with $450 million (for years it was the #1 JWT office, though New York has always been the headquarters), has picked up important new business in the Sears "Discover" card and the Lowenbrau account, a $25 million piece of business that it won in a creative shootout with such celebrated creative hot shops as Chiat/Day and Backer & Spielvogel. Winning creative shootouts has become rather a common event at the "new" Thompson, certainly a lot more common than it was at the old Thompson. When you're hot you're hot, as they say, and advertisers are bowled over by Thompson's

Jim
Patterson

Jim Patterson, executive creative director
J. Walter Thompson/New York, "likes being
surrounded by terrific people."

reel. A typical reaction is, "Hey, I didn't know Thompson was doing stuff like *this*!"
Really new vivid stuff for Kodak, Toys 'R Us, and Burger King.

Burger King—those were the magic words at Thompson, and that's where the turn-
around began. Back in the seventies, America's #2 burger chain told Thompson to go
a little crazy with the ads. Jim Patterson, executive creative director of the New York
office, came up with the "Aren't you hungry?" campaign, and things kind of took off.
Suddenly Thompson creatives realized they could be creative. They took the ball and
ran with it. Patterson, a wise, gentle, quiet-spoken creative leader, who writes award-
winning espionage thrillers in his "spare" time (6 to 8:30 A.M.) has been given a lot of

credit for turning the New York creative team around. Patterson, in turn, credits his staff with making his job rewarding: "What I like best about my job," he told me, "is being surrounded by absolutely marvelous, loving, terrific people. That's what makes me come to work in the morning." Patterson works in close collaboration with Steve Bowen, the general manager of the New York office and the other leader frequently credited with the successes of that office. Their leader is Burt Manning, chairman of J. Walter Thompson/USA, who pushed for a reemphasis on the creative product.

Getting out the best product naturally translates into attracting the best people, and JWT has been aggressive in going for top talent, especially new talent. The agency has excellent training programs for creatives, account managers, media, and research, and an excellent attitude toward new staffers. An art director I spoke to who had just come on board from another large agency raved: "This agency really values *people*. It treats you like family. At the end of the day, people get together in the company bar and socialize. You are rewarded for what you do. And there's great quality control. There's this feeling of 'let's do it right. Let's do it *once* and make sure it's the best.' " Thompson's dedication to attracting new talent is evidenced by the full-page ad they ran in newspapers in November, 1984, with the headline: "Write If You Want Work." About 1,100 people completed this copy test and to date, several people have been hired as junior copywriters as a result of their answers. Such openness to new people, new ideas, new experiences is rare, even in an industry like advertising that thrives on the new; but it seems to be one of the hallmarks of Thompson today. Everyone I contacted at the agency was delighted to talk with me and delighted to be working at this agency. Says Patterson: "We hire only one kind of person—incredibly talented and incredibly nice." It shows. There's a spirit in the air that fairly sings of pride in work and happiness in results. If ever there was a time to work at Thompson, it's now.

Aside from New York and Chicago, the major Thompson offices in the U.S. are in Detroit (which handles the important Ford work), San Francisco, and Los Angeles. There are also smaller offices in Atlanta and Washington.

THE TOP FIFTY ADVERTISING AGENCIES IN THE U.S.

This listing is intended as a service, not a bible. The agency ranking (based on 1985 figures for gross world income) will change, new agencies will jump up into the top fifty as current agencies fall off the list, merge with each other, or decline. In fact, there have already been some startling changes since these figures were issued. Even before it's half over, 1986 is shaping up as the year of the agency merger as a series of mega-mergers turns the agency scene on its head: BBDO, Doyle Dane Bernbach, and Needham Harper joined forces to form a single mega-agency, as yet without a name; and the merger-hungry London-based Saatchi & Saatchi first snapped up Dancer Fitzgerald Sample (now known as DFS Dorland) and then, breaking all records, acquired Ted Bates for $450 million—and became by far the world's biggest agency network. The top fifty line-up is volatile, to say the least.

These top fifty agencies make exciting headlines and offer exciting jobs—but there are lots of exciting jobs at lots of exciting smaller agencies, agencies that will never make it to the top fifty and thank their lucky creative stars for it. So don't take this line-up as the last word in your job hunt. Take it rather as a jumping-off point. It's good to know the names of the biggies, and to know a little bit about their major clients—it makes you feel like you're already inside the world of advertising. And since there's a decent chance you'll be applying to and interviewing at one of these shops (or one of their branch offices), it's good to have the address and phone number of the headquarters. Given how things change, though, it would be wise to check this information before writing. The agency of your choice may have been merged out of existence even as you read this.

I've included the names of a few key clients for each agency to give a feeling for what the agency is all about, but remember, clients change agencies even faster than agencies change their ranking. Also, large companies generally divide their products up among a number of agencies, which is why the same company may appear as a key client of more than one agency. Updates on client/agency affiliation and on agency mergers and agency address changes can be found in the Agency Red Book, as well as in the agency profile issues of *Advertising Age* and *Adweek*. The indispensable Agency Red Book also lists addresses of agency branch offices and top personnel in agency departments.

1. Young & Rubicam
   285 Madison Avenue
   New York, N.Y. 10017
   212-210-3000
   Key clients: American Home Products, AT&T, Canada Dry, Colgate-Palmolive, Disney Pictures, Disneyland, Dr Pepper, General Cigar, General Foods, Gillette, Gulf Oil, Holiday Inns, Johnson & Johnson, Kentucky Fried Chicken, Kodak, Kraft, Lin-

coln-Mercury, Metropolitan Life, Peter Paul Cadbury, Time, Inc., Union Carbide, U.S. Postal Service.

2. Ogilvy Group
  2 E. 48th Street
  New York, N.Y. 10017
  212-907-3400
  Key clients: American Express, AT&T Information Systems, Avon Products, British Tourist Authority, Campbell Soup Co., CBS Inc., Chesebrough-Pond's, Ex-Lax, General Foods, Hallmark, Hellman's, Hershey Foods, International Paper, Kimberly-Clark, Lever Brothers, Mattel, Pepperidge Farm, Peugeot, Polaroid, Trans World Airlines.

3. Ted Bates Worldwide
  1515 Broadway
  New York, N.Y. 10036
  212-869-3131
  Key clients: American Cyanamid, AT&T Consumer Products, Avis Rent-A-Car, Colgate-Palmolive, General Foods, Home Box Office, Mars Inc., Maybelline, Panasonic Co., Schweppes, Warner-Lambert.

4. J. Walter Thompson Co.
  466 Lexington Ave.
  New York, N.Y. 10017
  212-210-7000
  Key clients: Beatrice Companies, Benetton, Burger King, Christian Dior, Ford, R.T. French Co., Gerber Products, Goodyear, S.C. Johnson, Kellogg Co., Kodak, Lever Brothers, Lowenbrau, Miller Brewery, Nabisco, Nestle, Pepsi-Cola, Quaker Oats, Reader's Digest, Rolex Watch, Showtime/Movie Channel, Warner Lambert.

5. Saatchi & Saatchi Compton Worldwide
  625 Madison Avenue
  New York, N.Y. 10022
  212-754-1100
  Key clients: American Motors, British Airways, Cunard Line, IBM, Johnson & Johnson, Paine Webber, Procter & Gamble, U.S. Steel.

6. *BBDO International*
   383 Madison Avenue
   New York, N.Y. 10017
   212-415-5000
   Key clients: Almaden Vineyards, American Cyanamid, Black & Decker, Campbell Soup Co., Delta Airlines, Dodge, Dow Jones & Co., Du Pont, Frito-Lay, General Electric, Gillette, Lever Brothers, National Distillers, PepsiCo, Pillsbury, Polaroid, Quaker Oats, Scott Paper, Stroh Brewery, 3M Co., Visa, Wrigley.

7. *McCann-Erickson Worldwide*
   485 Lexington Avenue
   New York, N.Y. 10017
   212-697-6000
   Key clients: American Express, AT&T, Beatrice Foods, Coca-Cola, Eastman Kodak, Exxon, Gillette, General Motors, Heublein Inc., Johnson & Johnson, Nabisco, Nestle, Pabst Brewing, R.J. Reynolds, Shearson/American Express, Sony Consumer Products, Texas Instruments.

8. *D'Arcy Masius Benton & Bowles* (formerly D'Arcy MacManus Masius Worldwide and Benton & Bowles)
   909 Third Avenue
   New York, N.Y. 10022
   212-758-6200
   Key clients: Anheuser-Busch, A&P, AT&T, Cadillac, Corning Glass, Equitable Life, General Foods, General Motors, Mars Inc., MCI Communications, J.C. Penney, Procter & Gamble, Texaco, U.S. Air Force.

9. *Foot, Cone & Belding Communications*
   401 N. Michigan Avenue
   Chicago, Ill. 60611
   312-467-9200
   Key clients: American Can, Carnation Co., Citibank, Clairol, Clorox, Adolf Coors, Co., Corning Glass, Doubleday, Hughes Aircraft, Johnson Wax, Kimberly-Clark, Kitchens of Sara Lee, Levi Strauss, Thomas J. Lipton, Mazda, Pacific Bell, Sears Roebuck, Sperry.

10. Leo Burnett Co.
   Prudential Plaza
   Chicago, Ill. 60601
   312-565-5959
   Key clients: Allstate Insurance, Beatrice Foods, General Motors, H.J. Heinz, Keebler, Kellogg, Kraft, Maytag, McDonald's, Nestle, Phillip Morris, Pillsbury, Procter & Gamble, RCA, Schenley, Star-Kist Foods, Seven-Up, Union Carbide, United Airlines.

11. Grey Advertising
   777 Third Avenue
   New York, N.Y. 10017
   212-546-2000
   Key clients: American Broadcasting Co., Bloomingdale's, Borden, Bristol-Myers, Canada Dry, Canon USA, Clairol, General Foods, BF Goodrich, Mitsubishi, No Nonsense Fashions, Panasonic, Procter & Gamble, RCA, Remington, Revlon, Swift/ Hunt-Wesson, Toys 'R Us.

12. Doyle Dane Bernbach International
   437 Madison Avenue
   New York, N.Y. 10022
   212-415-2000
   Key clients: American Airlines, Borden, Bristol-Myers, CBS Broadcast, Celanese Fibers, Chanel, Clairol, General Mills, GTE, Heinz, IBM, Michelin Tire Co., Mobil Oil, Murjani, Nabisco, Joseph E. Seagram, Volkswagen.

13. SSC&B:Lintas Worldwide
   One Dag Hammarskjold Plaza
   New York, N.Y. 10017
   212-605-8000
   Key clients: American Brands Inc., Amstar Corp., Carnation Co., Coca-Cola, Good Humor, Johnson & Johnson, Lever Brothers, Thomas J. Lipton, Timberland, Van Munching & Co.

14. Bozell, Jacobs, Kenyon & Eckhardt (formerly Bozell & Jacobs and Kenyon & Eckhardt)
 40 West 23rd Street
 New York, N.Y. 10010
 212-206-5000
 Key clients: American Airlines, Air France, AT&T, Avis, Bally Mfg., James B. Beam Distilling, Beatrice, Blue Cross & Blue Shield, Borden, Bristol-Myers, *Business Week,* Coca-Cola, Dalton Book Sellers, Dino de Laurentiis, General Mills, Greyhound, Holiday Inns, Honeywell, Jaguar Cars, Jockey International, Lee, Lipton, New York Telephone, Prudential-Bache Securities, Union Carbide, Union Pacific Railroad.

15. Marschalk Campbell-Ewald Worldwide
 1345 Avenue of the Americas
 New York, N.Y. 10105
 212-315-8360
 Key clients: Braun USA, Coca-Cola, Fanny Farmer, General Motors, Gillette, Mutual of New York, Sony.

16. Needham Harper Worldwide
 909 Third Avenue
 New York, N.Y. 10022
 212-758-7600
 Key clients: American Cancer Society, American Honda Motor Co., AMTRAK, Anheuser-Busch, Campbell Soup, Clorox, Embassy Pictures, Frito-Lay, Fortune Magazine, Frigidaire, General Mills, Kraft, McDonald's, Ramada Inns, RCA, Rubbermaid, Sears Roebuck, State Farm Insurance, Xerox.

17. DFS Dorland Worldwide (formerly Dancer Fitzgerald Sample, Inc.)
 405 Lexington Avenue
 New York, N. Y. 10174
 212-661-0800
 Key clients: American Automobile Assoc., American Cyanamid, Bell & Howell, Ciba-Geigy, Consolidated Edison, CPC International Best Foods Div., General Electric Co., General Mills, Lorillard Div. of Loew's Theatres, Nabisco, Procter & Gamble, Republic Airlines, Royal Crown Cola, Toyota, *U.S. News & World Report,* Wendy's, Western Union.

18. N W Ayer
   1345 Avenue of the Americas
   New York, N.Y. 10105
   212-708-5000
   Key clients: ABC Network News, AT&T, Avon, Chemical Bank, Club Med, E.I. du Pont, Gillette, J.C. Penney, Toshiba, TV Guide, U.S. Army Recruiting.

19. Wells, Rich, Greene
   9 West 57th Street
   New York, N.Y. 10019
   212-303-5000
   Key clients: Ford, Hills Bros., Max Factor, MCI Mail, Miles Labs, Pan American World Airways, Philip Morris, Procter & Gamble, Purolator Courier, Ralston Purina.

20. William Esty Co.
   100 E. 42nd Street
   New York, N.Y. 10017
   212-697-1600
   Key clients: American Home Products, Chesebrough Pond's, Genesee Brewing Co., MasterCard International, Nabisco, Nissan Motor, Texaco, Travelers Corp, Union Carbide.

21. HCM
   866 Third Avenue
   New York, N.Y. 10022
   212-752-6500
   Key clients: Alfa Romeo, Beatrice, Columbia Pictures, Grumman, IBM, Jack In The Box, McGraw-Hill, Mita Copiers, Spiegel Retail.

22. Ketchum Communications
   Four Gateway Center
   Pittsburgh, P.A. 15222
   412-456-3500
   Key clients: American Honda, Bank of America, Ciba-Geigy, Pacific Bell, Pillsbury, Swift/Hunt-Wesson, Westinghouse Electric Corp.

23. *Backer & Spielvogel*
    11 W. 42nd Street
    New York, N.Y. 10036
    212-556-5200
    Key clients: Campbell Soup, Helene Curtis, Hyundai Motors, Miller Brewing, NCR Corp., Paddington Corp., Philip Morris, Quaker Oats.

24. *C&W Group* (formerly Cunningham & Walsh)
    260 Madison Avenue
    New York, N.Y. 10016
    212-683-4900
    Key clients: AAMCO, American Brands, Inc., American Home Products, Bank of New York, Beecham Products, CBS, Moet Hennessy, Panasonic, Procter & Gamble, Sterling Drug.

25. *Scali, McCabe, Sloves*
    800 Third Avenue
    New York, N.Y. 10022
    212-753-8000
    Key clients: Bloomingdale's, Hertz, Maxell, Nikon, Perdue, Ralston Purina, Revlon, Saks Fifth Avenue, Sharp Electronics, Time Inc., Volvo.

26. *Campbell-Mithun*
    222 So. Ninth Street
    Minneapolis, Minn. 55402
    612-347-1000
    Key clients: General Mills, Honeywell, Kimberly-Clark, Kraft, Land 'O Lakes, Pentax Corp., Quaker Oats, Schwinn Bicycle Co., 3M Co.

27. *TBWA Advertising*
    292 Madison Avenue
    New York, N.Y. 10017
    212-725-1150
    Key clients: American Dairy Association, Anheuser-Busch, Cartier Inc., Chock Full O' Nuts, Condé Nast (*Gourmet* magazine, *GQ*), Hebrew National, Granada TV Rentals, Mohawk Data Sciences, Monsanto Co., Ralston Purina.

28. *HBM/Creamer*
   1633 Broadway
   New York, N.Y. 10019
   212-887-8000
   Key clients: A&W Beverages, Alcoa, BASF Systems, Ciba-Geigy, Colgate-Palmolive, Foot Joy, General Mills, Gulf & Western, Molsen, Nestlé, New American Library, Palm Beach Inc., San Giorgio, Scott Paper, Sheraton Hotels, Stride Rite.

29. *Ross Roy Inc.*
   2751 E. Jefferson Avenue
   Detroit, Mich. 48207
   313-568-6000
   Key clients: Ameritech, Chrysler Corp., Detroit Edison, Dunn & Bradstreet, Eagle Electric, Howard Johnson, K Mart, Michigan Bell, Texaco, Upjohn Co.

30. *Chiat/Day*
   517 S. Olive Street
   Los Angeles, Calif. 90013
   213-622-7454
   Key clients: Apple Computer, Barney's New York, Breakthrough Software, Clairol Inc., Disney Channel, Drexel Burnham Lambert, General Electric, Mitsubishi Audio Systems and Electric, Nike, Porsche, Suntory.

31. *DYR Worldwide*
   1114 Avenue of the Americas
   New York, N.Y. 10036
   212-869-8350
   Key clients: Canon, Del Monte, Disneyland, Don Q Rum, Fazi Battaglia, Harveys Bristol Cream, Heublein, Kirin Beer, U.S. Suzuki Motors.

32. *Tracy-Locke*
   P.O. Box 50129
   Dallas, Tex. 75250
   214-969-9000
   Key clients: Best Products, Chrysler Corp. Dodge Division, Frito-Lay, Imperial Sugar, Mountain Bell Technologies, Pepsi-Cola, Phillips Petroleum, Princess Cruises,

Taco Bell, Texas Monthly.

33. Geers Gross Advertising
   220 E. 42nd Street
   New York, N.Y. 10017
   212-916-8000
   Key clients: American Cyanamid, G. H. Bass, Bristol-Myers, Cuisinart, General Mills, Hearst Corp., Hebrew National, IBM, Kraft Dairy Products, Ralph Lauren, Random House, Schenley Laboratories, Toys 'R Us, Warner Communications.

34. Della Femina, Travisano & Partners
   625 Madison Avenue
   New York, N.Y. 10022
   212-421-7180
   Key clients: Beech Nut, Book-of-the-Month Club's Quality Paperback Book Club, Bulova Watch, CBS, Coca-Cola, Cointreau, Walt Disney Pictures, Dow Chemical, Metromedia Telecommunications, New York Mets, Pacific Southwest Airlines, Rolls Royce, Westinghouse Broadcast Corp.

35. Wunderman, Ricotta & Kline (a direct marketing agency)
   575 Madison Avenue
   New York, N.Y. 10022
   212-909-0100
   Key clients: Black & Decker, L. L. Bean, Book-of-the-Month Club, CBS, Ford, General Foods, Grolier Enterprises, IBM National Distribution Div., Johnson & Johnson, Kodak, Time Inc., Time-Life Books, USA Today.

36. Leber Katz Partners Advertising
   767 Fifth Avenue
   New York, N.Y. 10153
   212-705-1000
   Key clients: American Stock Exchange, Campbell Soup, Citicorp, Condé Nast, Eastman Chemical Products, Lenox Inc., Newsweek Magazine, Pepperidge Farm, R.J. Reynolds, Scott Paper Co.

37. Laurence, Charles & Free
   261 Madison Avenue
   New York, N.Y. 10016
   212-661-0200
   Key clients: American Brands, Bristol-Myers, Coca-Cola Foods, Diner's Club, Dreyfus Corp., Hearst Corp., National Distillers, Uniden Corp.

38. Hill, Holiday, Connors, Cosmopulos
   John Hancock Tower
   200 Clarendon Street
   Boston, Mass. 02116
   617-437-1600
   Key clients: Aer Lingus, The Boston Globe, Cluett-Peabody YouthWear, Ford Motor Co., Gillette, John Hancock, Jordan Marsh, Lotus Development Corp., Puma, Ritz Carlton, Spalding Sports, Wang Laboratories.

39. Admarketing
   1801 Century Park East
   Los Angeles, Calif. 90067
   213-203-8400
   Key clients: Dakota Farms Cheese, Disney Channel, Georgia-Pacific's Household Chemical Division, Hartfield Zodys, Los Angeles Raiders, Wilsey Foods.

40. McCaffrey & McCall
   575 Lexington Avenue
   New York, N.Y. 10022
   212-421-7500
   Key clients: ABC TV, American Express, Air Canada, Avis, Citibank, European American Bank, Exxon, Hiram Walker, Mennen, Mercedes-Benz, National Coffee Assn., North American Phillips Corp., Pfizer Inc.

41. Jordan, Case, Taylor & McGrath
   445 Park Avenue
   New York, N.Y. 10022
   212-906-3600
   Key clients: Aetna Life & Casualty, Bausch & Lomb, Duracell Corp., Hanes Hosiery, Lorillard, Nestle Co., Norcliff-Thayer, Procter & Gamble, Tonka Corp., Welch

Foods, Westinghouse Broadcasting.

42. Tatham-Laird & Kudner
625 N. Michigan Ave.
Chicago, Ill. 60611
312-337-4400
   Key clients: Adolph Coors, Jack Daniels Distillery, Del Monte, Domaine Chandon, Kimberly-Clark, Miles Laboratories, Procter & Gamble, Quaker Oats, Ralston Purina, R.J. Reynolds, Velamints.

43. W.B. Doner & Company   *co-headquarters:*
   26711 Northwestern Hwy.   *2305 N. Charles Street*
   Southfield, Mich. 48034   *Baltimore, Md. 21218*
   313-354-9700   *301-338-1600*
   Key clients: American Home Video, Arrow Co., *Baltimore Sun*, Blue Bell, Carling National Breweries, Control Data Corp., Detroit Buick Dealers Assn., Favorite 5 Buick Dealers, W.R. Grace, Highland Appliance, Little Caesar's Enterprises of Farmington, Mich., Lone Star Brewing, Marriott Hotel Corp., McCormick & Co., Orange Julius, Zellers Stores.

44. Lord, Geller, Federico, Einstein
   655 Madison Avenue
   New York, N.Y. 10021
   212-421-6050
   Key clients: Charles of the Ritz, IBM Personal Computer, *New Yorker* magazine, *Scientific American* magazine, Sony, Steinway & Sons, WNBC-TV.

45. Ally & Gargano
   805 Third Avenue
   New York, N.Y. 10022
   212-688-5300
   Key clients: Bank of New York, Dunkin' Donuts, Federal Express, Andrew Jergens Co., Karastan Mills, Polaroid, Saab, Sony, Time Inc., Union Carbide.

46. Doremus & Co.
   120 Broadway

New York, N.Y. 10271
212-964-0700
Key clients: Bank of America, Bank of Montreal, Forbes Magazine, General Electric, E.F. Hutton, Irving Trust, Kidder Peabody, Lazard Frères, Manufacturers Hanover Trust, Paine Webber, Salomon Brothers, Tenneco, Union Pacific.

47. Sudler & Hennessey Inc.
   1633 Broadway
   New York, N.Y. 10019
   212-265-8000
Key clients: Ayerst Laboratories, BASF Wyandotte Corp., Beech-Nut Nutrition, Dupont Pharmaceuticals, General Foods, Johnson & Johnson Health Care, Lever Brothers, Olin Chemical, Parke-Davis, Whitehall Laboratories.

48. Keller-Crescent Co.
   P.O. Box 3
   1100 E. Louisiana Street
   Evansville, Ind. 47701
   812-464-2461
Key clients: Firestone Steel Products, General Electric, Hardee's, Luber-Finer Division of Champion Laboratories, Magic Chef, Mitsubishi, Northern Laboratories, Petrochem Corp., Wavetek Indiana, Wayne-Dalton Corp.

49. The Bloom Companies
   7701 N. Stemmons
   Dallas, Tex. 75247
   214-638-8100
Key clients: Anheuser-Busch, Block Drug Co., Bojangle's Restaurants, 800-Flowers, General Electric, Mobil, Schering-Plough Corp.

50. MCA Advertising
   405 Lexington Avenue
   New York, N.Y. 10174
   212-661-5491
Key clients: Avon, Heinz, Lorillard Div. Loew's Theatres, Marketing Corp. of America, Ralston-Purina, Stroh Brewery, Tambrands.

THE CREATIVE TEAM

"You know, you sometimes sit there and say, 'Yeah—I get *paid* for this!' Going and shooting commercials is terrific fun, going to music sessions is great. The people in the business are terrific—the directors, the editors, the music people, the guys in the videotape places. It's great, but it's not easy. You're *always* thinking about it. It's real hard work and real long hours. *Real* long hours."

SENIOR ART DIRECTOR with a
major New York Agency

Though everyone in an advertising agency has some connection (if ever so distant) with ads, the creatives are the people who actually invent, write, design, realize, and produce them. They work with ideas—words, images, and the endless details involved in getting even the simplest print ad made. They also work with pressure—the constant pressure to keep coming up with something new. To the outside world, their jobs may seem wonderfully exciting: they travel to exotic and beautiful places, they collaborate with top directors and models, musicians and media personalities, and the ads they create are seen and heard by millions of people all over the world. On the inside, these same jobs can often seem grueling. "The glamour aspect is vastly exaggerated," one creative director told me. "Nothing is that glamorous when you get up close to it." Creatives tend to agency-hop; many say they have to in order to get ahead. They often work long and erratic hours. They can, if they've got the talent and luck, rise fast. And when they do, they get paid for it—as much or more than any other department in the agency. Is it any wonder, then, that these are probably the most difficult advertising jobs to land?

Difficult—but not impossible. While the refrain "there are no jobs for creatives" is one that you'll get more than sick of hearing when you're trying to break in, the truth is there *are* jobs for creatives. They're terribly scarce and brutally competed for, but they exist. And for the most part, they go to the people who have the abiliity and don't give up.

THE CREATIVE PERSONALITY

Advertising people in general have some pretty bizarre reputations, and perhaps the most bizarre of all are reserved for creatives. The image is: egos rampaging like a herd of bulls; impossible prima donnas screaming, "Do it MY way!"; hysterical geniuses atwitch with eccentricity. You hear stories of creative director tyrants whose staffs cower before them. Stories of copywriters and art directors who do their best creative work on the beach—or locked in some conference room at 4 A.M. Stories of creatives who've threatened to jump from skyscraper windows if the client wouldn't approve the ad. Fistfights in the halls. Furniture smashed up. Madison Avenue madness! And then there are the child wonders, kids not five years out of college who storm the industry with a barrage of creativity, who get recognized and lavishly rewarded overnight, and who burn out by the time they hit twenty-nine. Some of the stories are even true *[for an interview with grown-up boy wonder Ed McCabe, who's still going strong as president and worldwide creative director of Scali, McCabe, Sloves, Inc., see page 81]*. Perhaps some of these stories used to be truer in the sixties during the heyday of the creative revolution than they are today. (Jerry Della Femina, one of the creative revolutionaries, offers a very funny insider's look at the advertising world in those days in his book, *From Those Wonderful Folks Who Gave You Pearl Harbor* (Simon & Schuster, 1970); for a look at some of the breakthrough advertising that came out of the creative revolution, see *When Advertising Tried Harder: The Sixties: The Golden Age of Advertising* by Larry Dobrow (Friendly Press, 1974).

But advertising, as everyone I spoke to pointed out to me, is not *really* like that anymore. Hardnosed business practices and scientific research have reined in a lot of the creative excesses of the sixties and also, it would seem, some of the excesses of the creative personality. The creatives you meet in advertising today look more like professional people and less like urban guerrillas. "It's a tough business, not a playground," is the way one creative put it.

But it's still a business unlike any other. And being an advertising creative still means thinking and sensing and communicating in a way unlike any other. "*Erratic* is a key word to describe the industry," a creative director told me. "It attracts people who thrive on that quality." "What's great about advertising," said a young enthusiastic art director at J. Walter Thompson/New York, "is you can be yourself. You can be crazy if you want to. So long as you're creative and you sell, you can be anything."

The consensus seems to be: while the wild times of the sixties are definitely over, advertising creatives are still a long way from investment bankers. While there is no one definable creative personality type (and surely never was), there are lots and lots of creative people who are excited by advertising and who make exciting ads. Yes, a lot of them may be a little crazy (or driven or demanding or extreme), but most of them seem to show it more in their work than in the way they behave day to day. They know who they are, and they know what makes them different.

THE CREATIVE DEPARTMENT

At most agencies today, creatives work in teams. A copywriter and an art director will be paired up. Or a creative director will have a creative group consisting of copywriters, art directors, and producers for TV commercials. Or there will be a kind of loose system in which copywriters and art directors work on accounts on an ad hoc basis. The size and composition and structure of the team varies with the agency, the account, and the nature of the ad. But the team aspect is pretty much universal. Bill Bernbach, the fabled creative director of Doyle Dane Bernbach and a key leader of the creative revolution, is credited with doing away with the old system whereby a copywriter would sit down and write an ad and then turn it over to an art director to design. Creating advertising today is above all a collaborative process. There's no rigid division of labor: an art director may be the one who comes up with the headline and a copywriter with the visual. Ideas flow freely back and forth. Many an ad is thrashed out in a meeting or even an informal conversation among team members. As Tony Zamora, executive art director at William Esty Company in New York, describes it: "In this agency, we sit the art director down with the copywriter; we have the problem and we create the solution together. In many cases, if it's done properly, we don't know who wrote the copy or who came up with the visual. It's a give-and-take situation and one of the nice things about it is that you are bouncing two minds together, and hopefully coming up with one very successful idea." In *From Those Wonderful Folks Who Gave You Pearl Harbor*, Jerry Della Femina calls this experience "a crazy chemistry": "Suddenly the two of you think alike . . . There is an electric feeling in the room and this is what the business is all about as far as the creative person is concerned."

While it's true that the magic moment of creation may be a team endeavor, there are still certain clear responsibilities associated with each job in the creative department and fairly distinct career paths within each job. Though creatives work in teams, they apply as individuals for specific jobs. No two creative departments look exactly alike in size or structure, but for the most part all of them have copywriters, art directors, producers, and creative directors. Here is what each of these jobs entails, and the various levels that each is commonly divided into.

COPYWRITER

Obviously, a copywriter writes the ads—the headlines and "body copy" of the tantalizing spreads that light up the pages of magazines, the words that appear on billboards, the lines that actors and announcers say on TV commercials. But writing advertising copy is not quite like writing articles, poems, books, or screenplays. First of all, there's the client to worry about and something called the "creative strategy." Craig Wensberg, a dynamic thirty-three-year-old senior copywriter at William Esty whose products include Myers's Rum, Vaseline Lip Therapy, and Milkbone Dog Biscuits, puts it this way: "The strategy is often dry and bland and somewhat technical from a marketing point of view and it's my job to make that compelling, interesting, and, if I'm lucky, humorous."

Even before he begins to write anything, Wensberg will sit around with his creative director and art director and sometimes an account person and brainstorm. It might look as if they're doing nothing but chatting, but actually a lot of the creative foundation of an ad is laid in these meetings. Part of what they're doing is thinking themselves into the product; part of it is coming up with different approaches for translating the strategy into an ad. Some of these approaches will be brilliant; some will be awful; and some will *sound* awful but actually have a germ of truth. It is these germs of truth that the copywriter will work up into an ad.

At some point, Wensberg will sit down at his typewriter and wait for the muse to strike. And when it does, whether it's 7 o'clock in the morning or 7 o'clock at night, "you just sit there and write your brains out."

But the copywriter's job by no means stops there. In the case of a television commercial, the copywriter and art director will decide together on music, theme lines, format, special effects. Once they have put the ad into comp form or the commercial into a storyboard, they'll bring it to the creative director, who will probably suggest some changes. Once they've all agreed, they'll take it to the account person, who will probably suggest some further changes. There may be mild disagreements—or fullscale battles. Whatever the case, the copywriter has to be flexible enough to roll with it and patient enough to keep revising his or her work (or see others revise it).

Once the agency side has agreed on the comp or storyboard, they've got to get the client side to agree to it, and this too is part of the writer's job. For a major new piece of work, a formal presentation meeting will be arranged, at which the writer will really try to sell the client on the ad. You sing, you act—and inevitably, you revise again and meet again and revise again and . . . The process can go on for months or even a year. The finished ad, or the board the client agrees to buy, will often look unrecognizable to the writer who was in on it from the start. And that's the other major difference between advertising writing and most other forms of writing: it's fundamentally a collaborative effort. The image of the ruggedly independent writer, holed up in isolation with his or her typewriter, simply does not apply to advertising.

In the case of a television commercial, the writer remains involved right up until the commercial is finished and ready to be sent to the networks: he or she is in on preproduction, the "shoot," the editing. *[For more about how a TV commercial is made, see Chapter Six.]*

J. Walter Thompson, one of the biggest advertising agency networks in the world, recently offered some fascinating insight into the qualities they're looking for in copywriters. They took out a full-page ad in *The New York Times* (Friday, November 30, 1984) with the headline "Write If You Want Work." It was a test for copywriters, with questions such as: write a song for "hitmaker Poppy Putrid" about moldy pizza, rancid butter, and flat beer and also make it a love song; compose a speech out of pictures and symbols welcoming a delegation of Martians to Central Park; make a can of baked beans sound mouthwatering; tell in 100 words how you would sell a telephone to a Trappist monk who is under a strict vow of silence.

Clearly, you've got to have a way with words—but it's more than that. You must be clever, quick, visually oriented, and culturally tuned in. You have to be able to think on your feet in a fairly wide range of situations. You have to have a knack. Probably some of our finest novelists and journalists would fail miserably at the Thompson test, while some of the most successful copywriters never got much recognition as writers until they sat down and wrote their first ad.

POSITIONS AND PAY

The entry-level copywriting job is called *junior copywriter*. As one copywriter described it, "You write the stuff that no one else wants to write, but it's the only way you're going to learn." Several writers commented that titles in the advertising field are somewhat nebulous. Junior writers may be doing a lot more work than senior v.p.'s. The best thing a junior writer can do is diversify: work on as many different products as possible. "What you've done," says Craig Wensberg, "the accounts you've worked on, what your reel has produced on it, is more important than the title that you leave an agency with."

Like all those in entry-level advertising jobs, junior writers are expected to work hard for "no money" (though salaries vary widely, $15,000 is a figure that many quote). As one moves up from junior copywriter to *copywriter* and *senior copywriter*, the responsibilities increase and the pay jumps up. Generally speaking, the higher you go as a writer, the more conceptual and less executional the job becomes. Copywriters in the middle ranks make between $35,000 and $50,000; senior writers make between $50,000 and $100,000. Fortunately or unfortunately, agency-hopping remains one of the best (perhaps only) ways to get big salary boosts and promotions. Advertising does not reward the loyal company man or woman: if you sit tight, so will your pay increases.

At the big agencies there will usually be a *copy director* (or supervisor or chief) who oversees the copywriters, assigns work, and supervises the flow. He/she will also work on the choice campaigns.

BREAKING IN

The consensus is: you can't talk your way into a copywriting or art directing job. You *must* have a portfolio (or spec book) of sample ads that you've either done for another agency or worked up on your own. One creative director put it succinctly: "I would never hire anyone who didn't show me work. I don't expect to see finished storyboards, but if someone comes in and says, 'I want to be a copywriter—what is that?' I'm not going to spend a whole lot of time with them. In fact, the interview is over." The more ideas you have—and the wilder and more original they are in many cases—the better impression you'll make. *[For more on how to put a spec book together and on tips for creatives seeking jobs, see Chapter Fourteen.]*

Almost all creative directors agree that street smarts, instinct, a gut feeling for what is happening in the world and the culture around us are more important for creatives than fancy degrees from high-class schools. Of course having both is probably ideal. None of them advises majoring in advertising. Aside from having the knack to write and come up with ideas, you have to be able to communicate articulately, synthesize and evaluate material, manage time and eventually other people. For that, a liberal arts background is probably the best path.

If you can't break into copywriting for one of the big, general consumer agencies, think about such options as direct mail (a hot field at the moment) or pharmaceutical advertising. Susan Blackwell, a copy supervisor with Sudler & Hennessey, one of the most prestigious pharmaceutical agencies, jumped into copywriting from a decade-long career as a pharmacist. Though she didn't know anything about advertising (even what a spec book meant), she began to network, talking with just about anyone who might be of help. Eventually she got in to see a copy director at a pharmaceutical agency who helped put her book together and provided her with introductions to a number of creative directors. Then "it was a matter of knocking on doors until somebody had an empty desk." Blackwell landed her first job after a six-week intensive search. This was in 1982. Since then she's changed jobs twice, managing to double her salary in the process.

Craig Wensberg, an English and theater major in college during the early seventies, "didn't feel quite stalwart enough to struggle through the rejections of being either a struggling actor or a struggling novelist." So he settled on advertising as a happy medium between financial security and creative fulfillment. Wensberg started his search in Boston and "wasted a good four months making the rounds with a rough portfolio of speculative work and being told by a number of creative but too-small agencies that they simply couldn't afford to hire me. So against my better judgment and my will, I started coming to New York. This was in 1976-77. After three months of knocking around here, begging a bed, floor space wherever I could, and living on a *very* slender budget, I found a job at Grey Advertising, where I spent the next five years."

Based on his own experience, Wensberg strongly recommends job hunting in a major advertising city: "Unless you try to start in an advertising center like New York, Chicago, or Los Angeles, maybe even Atlanta, you're in for a long haul. The handicap is immeasurable."

ART DIRECTOR

The job of an art director at an advertising agency, like that of copywriter, is a lot more varied than the title alone would indicate. Martin Lipsitt, executive vice president and creative director at middle-sized New York agency Calet, Hirsch & Spector, puts it this way: "When you first become an art director, you don't have to talk, you just have to create. You don't have to explain anything: you just have to *feel*. But that's not true. You really have to learn to *direct* and to be able to implement your ideas." Lipsitt, who has been in the business over twenty-five years, working his way up to his present position through the art departments of various agencies, clearly speaks from experience.

Tony Zamora, head of the art department at William Esty and in charge of hiring, makes a similar point: "When you hire somebody, you have to look not only at the work but at the potential of that person. Would he be someone you could send to a client? How does he work with other people? It isn't just: can you draw? The average senior art director in this agency handles about $40 million worth of business a year, and that's quite a lot of responsibility. Everyone we hire has to be groomed to be an art director and has to be able to take on that responsibility."

Though chances are the "typical" art director will be doing a mix of many different things on a "typical" day, for convenience of discussion we might divide the work into three categories: conception, presentation, and production. One senior art director with the international division of one of the nation's largest agencies handles primarily a soft-drink account, a huge account with advertising appearing all over the world. For an international client, the agency creates something called "pattern" advertising: commercials are made by the New York team (shot almost exclusively abroad) and then they are sent to more than 150 countries all over the world for music and voice-overs to be added in the language of the country. Obviously, working on an account of this type will involve a great deal of traveling and a much wider range of focus. You have to get ideas that will work not just in Oklahoma and Maine but in Thailand, Brazil, and Italy. Here's how the senior art director describes what she does:

"The international group has about twelve creative people, which is pretty slim for the amount of work that's done out of here. We're writers, art directors, and television producers. When the client starts planning their commercials for the next year, they'll give us a pretty good briefing about what they want. Then we go back and work on concepts: We work in teams and with the group head and we'll all sit around and hash out ideas. In the beginning it's concepts—you have rough ideas and you write them down. You get your ideas at home, in the shower, wherever. So you sort of talk out these ideas and you start doing up some rough concept boards, which are really just one visual to give you the idea of the commercial. Then you get it presented here, maybe do a storyboard, present it to the client, and if it gets approved, then we go into production.

"The beginnings of it are just the germ of an idea. And the art director is critically involved, particularly on this account where it's a very visual account. You're not writing dialogue. There are visuals and music."

The art director, she explains, is involved in every step of producing a commercial, from casting to editing: "When the commercial is being shot, you have to be involved with the director: How's it going to be shot? What do you want it to look like? The line of each frame is critical. My greatest love in this job is the actual production and especially the editing. You are *integrally* involved in that." Though many creatives travel a certain amount, particularly to California for shoots during the winter months, the creatives on this international team may be overseas for months, doing commercials just about anywhere in the world where the soft drink is sold, which is just about everywhere. "You can't really have big egos here," she says. "You have to be able to pick up and go. You have to be real flexible and you have to think pretty quick."

The hours an art director works can be as unpredictable as the nature of the work. Doing a commercial, Tony Zamora points out, will usually run a twelve-hour day. Sometimes you'll only be able to get the 11 P.M. slot at a busy editing or videotape transfer house and so you'll be working through the night. Other days it's 9 to 6. When the agency is pitching a new account, it can be two solid weeks of working until midnight.

The underside of the creative excitement, for art directors and all creatives, is the pressure and unrelenting pace. "You can get really sick of it," one art director commented. "You say to yourself, 'Why am I doing this? Who needs this?' There are very few people who stay in this business their entire lives." At the higher levels, the pressure can become even more intense because there are fewer and fewer positions available as you move up the pyramid. It's not a business for resting on your laurels—ever.

The underside of travel—even to lovely, tropical islands or sunny California—is that it disrupts your life. An art director may have to spend three months in California at a stretch, and that can be rough on a family or a sane social life. "After your second trip out there in the summer, it loses its glamour," comments Tony Zamora.

Never boring but never easy seems to sum up the life of many an art director working in advertising agencies today.

POSITIONS AND PAY

Those entering the art department of an ad agency without any previous work experience may be hired as an *assistant art director* or a *bullpen artist* (also called *layout artist*).

Essentially, you're the "pair of hands" of a senior art director, responsible for layouts and mechanicals (a pasteup of type and art that is used in making a printing plate). The higher up you go in an art department, the more conceptual and less hands-on your job becomes. Thus when you start out, chances are you won't actually be designing ads but will be assembling the elements of an ad designed by your superiors. The job of an assistant art director may also involve a fair amount of work that has nothing at all to do with art: being a gofer, tidying up the art department, etc.

Junior art director, the traditional next step up, will also spend a lot of time on pasteups and mechanicals. Art departments are seldom rigidly regimented, and often your responsibilities depend more on circumstance, luck, and talent than on your job title. One art director got her first real job working at Ogilvy & Mather in New York and, because it was more a design group than an advertising group, she had to jump in and learn how to art direct fast. Marty Muller, an art director with J. Walter Thompson in New York, says her first job as an assistant art director at Grey Advertising was a "sink or swim" situation: since she was hired to fill a slot left by a senior art director, she had to learn quickly. And she did. Six months after landing her first job, she was made an art director.

Art director and *senior art director* have responsibility for coming up with the ideas for ads and for seeing that their ideas are carried out. Their jobs usually involve a good deal of client contact as well as contact with the other departments of the agency. It's often the case that as you move up in an agency art department, you'll get more television and less (or more major) print work.

The *executive art director* heads up the art department and makes sure it works smoothly. He decides who on his staff works on what ads, he's in charge of hiring and firing, he's the key person at major presentations, and it's his responsibility to see that the art department works within its budget. Though part of the job is administrative and supervisory, executive art directors also work on the conceptual end of important ads. "Coming up with the ideas," in the words of one executive art director "is the *best* part of the business. It's something I don't want to lose touch with."

Art directors at the various levels command about the same salaries as copywriters at commensurate levels. As with copywriters, the pay tends to start off fairly low and then jump rapidly once you've established yourself.

BREAKING IN

Like copywriters, art directors must have a portfolio of their work in order to be considered for a job. One art director had a fine arts degree from a liberal arts college; she was a painter but she went back to school to get some graphics and design background and "to have a portfolio that would be more than just landscape drawings." Without this additional experience and the expanded portfolio, she never would have landed her first art director's job at Ogilvy & Mather.

Marty Muller grew up in Michigan, spent two years in college in Detroit, and then decided to go into art. Her mother insisted she be able to support herself, so she enrolled in the advertising program at Syracuse University, where she won top honors and got together a portfolio of her work. Brimming with confidence, she came to New York "young and naive and without knowing a single person." She slept at the YWCA and started taking her book around and getting polite rejections. So then she tried a different approach: she looked through the advertising awards annuals and got the names of creative directors and art directors who had worked on winning campaigns and she wrote them glowing letters about how much she admired their work. "I lied like crazy," she admits, but it got her interviews. She would flip through *Advertising Age* and see which agency had won a new account and then she'd get on the phone and ask to speak to the creative director who would be handling it. "I had no connections but I wasn't scared to call anyone—and they all talked to me." In August, 1980, she landed a job at Grey Advertising; this was one of the places she had left her book and been given the old line about "we'll get back to you." They did get back, however, four months later with a job offer.

PRODUCER

It's the job of an advertising agency's television producer to see that the commercial gets made, and this involves a tremendous amount of coordination of people, equipment, and ideas. "Ultimately, we're responsible for the sum of the parts," is the way one producer explains it. Though the producer is not usually the one who comes up with the original concept of the commercial, he or she is intimately involved in how the final commercial will look and sound and "feel." Of the team that makes the commercial, the producer is the one who is up on the latest developments in film and tape technology, and this technical expertise often has a tremendous impact on the creative product. Producers perform daily, perhaps hourly, juggling acts as they deal with the thousands of details involved in putting a commercial together. It's a job for people who are flexible, meticulous, and superb at following through.

Patty Wineapple is a hard-working producer at Grey Advertising with a good deal of experience under her belt. She has won a Clio for work she did on a Highway Safety anti-drunk driving ad, and products she has produced commercials for include Raisin Bran, Canada Dry Mixers, No Nonsense, Shoprite, and Vitalis. Wineapple explains what being a producer at Grey entails:

"We work in triumvirates here—there's a copywriter, an art director, and a producer and we work as a team. The copywriter and art director develop the concept, and then it's brought to me. I see it in storyboard form, unless it's some special kind of project where an art director has an idea and he doesn't know if it can be done. Then he'll consult me to ask if I think it will work.

"I'll decide [from the storyboard] whether or not it's produceable—whether it works as a commercial. Often my job is to enhance the project if possible. I will then be responsible for hiring a production company, which is the director and his support group. I bid the job [usually this means contacting three production companies, explaining what the commercial is, comparing their cost breakdowns, and choosing one to shoot it]. I meet with the casting department and they set up auditions. I then supervise all aspects of the production until the film is completed. I don't make all the decisions by any means, but what I do is create a forum for ideas to be exchanged so that we can reach a unified point of view. I think that's the most difficult part of producing: to get everybody to agree on one thing.

"The legwork is another aspect of the job. I'm responsible for setting up all the meetings. And I'm in charge of the budget, which is a very key piece of producing: making sure we can produce it for that and staying within the budget.

"We also decide who will do the music. Grey is unique in that we have a music department here—there are three composers at Grey who write. But we do not necessarily use them exclusively.

"[Before the commercial is shot] we have pre-production meetings with the client, and that is an enormously important meeting. We discuss exactly what we're going to do: we talk about music, we talk about casting, we talk about how it's going to be shot, special propping. Everything is submitted to the client for their approval. The choice of director remains a creative decision.

"[When the commercial is actually being filmed], my function is to make sure we shoot what we've sold. Often there's some terrific creative spontaneity at the shoot and you don't want to squelch that, assuming you're not behind schedule and you're not running into more money. Another function of the producer is to be the line of communication to the director. Hopefully people who have ideas and suggestions will address them to me and I will communicate them to the director. I try to set things up so that only the director speaks to the actors, because if they get barraged with commands, they become overwhelmingly confused and then performances suffer.

"After we've shot the commercial we have to screen dailies and edit the spot. We pull takes and the editor and I sit and put the commercial together. During post-production we record the voice-overs, often post-score the music; we then screen it for the agency hierarchy and soon after that screen it for the client, continuing the process from there to completion."

As you've probably gathered, Wineapple does not spend much time sitting at her desk. There's a lot of running around town and there is major people contact, which is one of the things she most enjoys about the job.

Though her job sounds like fun, and some of it *is* fun, Wineapple cautions against getting too starry-eyed about it: "I think the thing to keep in mind is that it's about five percent film and ninety-five percent business. This is not always the business to be in to stretch your creative muscles in the way many people think. The business has changed dramatically since the sixties. We're now in a business, like Wall Street, like banking. Budgets matter a lot. It's tough on your nervous systems. The stress factor is very high."

The other thing Wineapple cautions against is using the job as a springboard into television or film. Though the skills involved in producing a commercial or producing a television show or movie may be the same, it's not easy to move from one area to another. You tend to get "typed" and if you want to switch, you may have to go back to the beginning.

The responsibilities of producers vary tremendously from agency to agency At Grey, where Wineapple works, producers are integrally involved in the creative process of getting commercials made. But at some shops they're basically high-class messengers: they set up meetings and edit sessions but they don't really participate creatively. And they don't get paid as much as "on-line" producers.

POSITIONS AND PAY

The entry-level broadcast production job is called *production assistant* or *production coordinator*. The old adage about working long hours with endless patience and dedication and for very little money applies here too. Basically, the production coordinator works under producers and does all the support work: setting up casting sessions and meetings, filling out paper work, organizing tape transfer, accompanying producers throughout the process of making a commercial so they'll be on hand to assist with details and also so they'll learn. The next level up is *junior producer*; usually junior producers are given radio spots, test commercials, and animatics (rough animated commercials used for testing concepts) to produce. As a junior producer gains experience, he or she may be given lower budget TV projects to handle.

Usually above the level of producer there is a *group head*, who administers the department, assigns the work, and also produces projects of his or her own. Often there will be a single person who heads up the department.

On the subject of breaking in, Wineapple has this to say: "Entry into production is very difficult. I think film school is really the best avenue. A working knowledge of the medium does not hurt. Though you can learn a lot on the job, I really think it helps if you understand film and tape before you start working. Ultimately, all of what you do has to wash technically."

Salary levels for agency producers run a notch below those for copywriters and art directors.

CREATIVE DIRECTOR

The position of creative director is possibly the most sought-after, talked-about, and culturally influential in all advertising. It is, preeminently, a mover and shaker job. Creative directors lead the agency's creative department (and in some cases head up the agency itself). They set the creative pace and tone and style. And sometimes they become culture heroes in their own right. Everyone knows about Bill ("We try harder") Bernbach of Doyle Dane Bernbach who spearheaded the creative revolution of the sixties with unforgettable ads for Volkswagen, Alka-Seltzer, Avis, Levy's Jewish Rye Bread, and many others. And creative director David Ogilvy has also become a legend in his own time: he started Ogilvy & Mather almost from nothing in 1948 and through stunning advertising and extraordinary hustling helped turn it into the fifth largest agency in the world. Ogilvy has also done pretty well for himself: working out of his chateau at Bonnes in the south of France, he remains active in the worldwide business of his agency.

Two of the hottest and most highly regarded creative directors working today are Amil Gargano and Ed McCabe. See below for interviews.

Of course, not all creative directors achieve quite the fame and fortune of a Bernbach or an Ogilvy. But all of them are crucially involved in the creative product of the agency. Just as film directors don't actually appear in the films they direct but are responsible for the performances of the actors, the way the story is told, the look and feel and overall impact of it, so creative directors may not actually conceive and produce the individual ad campaigns, but they are ultimately responsible for how the advertising communicates.

Neil Calet, co-chairman and co-creative director of Calet, Hirsch & Spector: "The best part is helping develop young writers."

Neil Calet, co-chairman and co-creative director of Calet, Hirsch & Spector, gave me perhaps the best summary of the role of the creative director when he said: "First in importance is to create the best possible department of talented, productive, creative people; to set the highest standards of quality; to gather the writers and art directors who will do the best possible job for the clients—best in quality and best logistically. Picking and attracting the best people is important. But once the staff is in place, it's my job to maintain the morale of the department as well as the creative standards of the agency. The best part, though, is helping develop young writers. At least a dozen creative directors and agency owners started as junior copywriters at Calet, Hirsch. In a way, I've been creating my own competition, and I love it."

A creative director is also a business person in a service business, and as such he or she must be ever responsive to the needs of the client. A creative director is also, frequently, a manager who helps run the agency. That means strategy planning, budgets, new business, keeping the big picture in focus. When the creative director is also chairman, president, or chief executive officer, he or she really runs the whole show, merging creative and fiscal responsibilities. It's a big job that comes only with major experience and ability. Like all positions of power and leadership, the creative director's job is not one that you can set your sights for and be pretty sure of attaining if you stick it out long enough. However, while you can't necessarily "work your way up," there are a number of paths that creative directors traditionally follow, and there are rungs on the ladder that mark one's progress.

Most creative directors enter the business as art directors or copywriters. They show promise and they'll be promoted: senior art director, senior copywriter. They produce winning ads and display a sense of leadership and they'll be made head of a creative group of other copywriters and art directors. The title now may be creative supervisor or associate creative director. It could take ten years to get there—it could take five, depending on the individual's drive, ambition, talent, and luck.

Seldom is the climb up to creative director slow and steady. Often it involves agency-hopping. Neil Calet had risen to the position of copy chief, took a job at Interpublic as assistant creative director, and then came back to Calet, Hirsch & Spector as creative director and partner. Penny Westerbeck, a senior vice president and creative director at William Esty, started as a junior writer at J. Walter Thompson, moved to D'Arcy MacManus and Masius as senior writer, spent nine years at Grey Advertising where she rose to the rank of vice president and creative supervisor. And then she made the move to Esty. A number of creative directors move into the position by starting their own agencies. And then, of course, there are the exceptions to all of these patterns—the boy and girl wonders who turn the industry upside down and become creative directors in their twenties. It happens.

It's true that creative directors work hard at what they do and work hard to get there; it's equally true that the rewards are also substantial, both creatively and financially. Salaries for full-fledged creative directors at large agencies will be between $75,000 and $150,000 and can go much, much higher. The money at the very top, as one creative director told me, is unlimited. Power, prestige, pressure, high pay and high profile, creative acumen, and business savvy—these are the qualities that make the job of creative director one of the most demanding and fulfilling in the advertising business. Let's meet two creative director heavy hitters and see what they have to say about it.

AMIL GARGANO
Chairman, President, CEO, and Creative Director
Ally & Gargano

There is a distinct irony in the fact that Amil Gargano never intended to go into advertising. "I entered the business in 1955 in what I thought would be a temporary job," he explains. "I took it because I was trying to become an illustrator having abandoned the idea of becoming a serious painter." The temporary job was working in the bullpen at Campbell-Ewald, a Detroit-based agency specializing in automobile ads. Gargano did layouts and mechanicals for $55 a week. Under the circumstances it was, he says, "pretty hard to get excited about the advertising business." So what happened? Two things: a promotion to art director gave him the chance to work through some of his own ideas, and the creative revolution that was just getting under way fired his imagination. As Gargano himself puts it: "My whole perception of advertising changed drastically and I became very excited about the potential of advertising when I saw what was going on in an agency like Doyle Dane [in the late fifties]. The possibilities served as a great stimulation for me." This was also the time that the role of the art director opened up into a full creative partner in making the ads. Gargano realized that he could do great work in advertising and do it in a way that met his own exacting personal standards. He was hooked.

Gargano came to New York in 1959 and three years later, he and partners Carl Ally and Jim Durfee won the Volvo account, and on the basis of that founded their own agency, Carl Ally, Inc. Right from the start it was a creative powerhouse, small but committed to excellence and originality. That commitment has not flagged a bit over the years. Gargano has been on board for all of the agency's ups and downs. In 1978 the name was changed to Ally & Gargano. *Advertising Age* made Ally & Gargano its Agency of the Year in 1982, the same year Amil Gargano was elected to the Creative Hall of Fame sponsored by The One Club. The agency and the man are on a wave of success that keeps on building. Recent television spots for Federal Express and Dunkin Don-

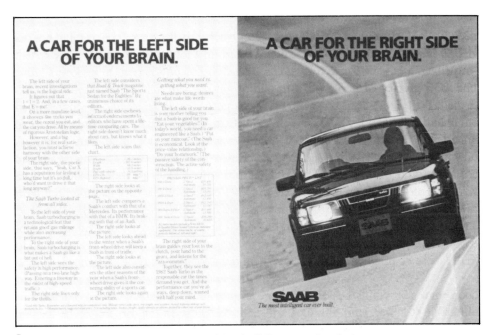

Informative, authentic, and useful—the qualities Amil Gargano strives for in Ally & Gargano's advertising.

uts, vivid, funny, yet somehow wise commercials, have won attention, praise, and sales. The agency has also had stunning success with print ads for Saab, The Travelers Insurance Company, Timberland footwear, and Karastan carpets—ads that consumers relate to and advertising people pin awards on. Ally & Gargano stock is even a hot item on the stock market.

Now that Carl Ally has retired from the agency, Gargano holds a raft of titles (some of which he plans to divest himself of) and all the lines of power emanate from his office. But Gargano carries his power lightly. Quiet-spoken, thoughtful, and rather modest, he has a reputation for generosity and for creating a superb working environment for his staff. But while he may be gentle in his manner, he is also fierce in his pursuit of excellence. You get the feeling that Gargano is his own sternest judge and harshest critic. He has to please himself first. And what pleases Amil Gargano just happens to be some of the strongest and most impactful advertising being produced today.

Q: Your titles at Ally & Gargano include chairman, president, chief executive officer

Some of us have more finely developed nesting instincts than others.

Karastan

Some recent memorable print ads from Ally & Gargano.

THIS IS FOR ALL THE PEOPLE WHOSE FAVORITE CLOTHES ARE A 10-YEAR OLD PAIR OF JEANS, A FADED FLANNEL SHIRT, AND THE CREW NECK THEY WORE IN COLLEGE.

You finally have the shoes to go with those clothes: a pair of Timberland® handsewns.

Timberland's aren't made to just look good fresh out of the box. They're made to look even better a few years down the road.

Our handsewns are made with only premium full-grain leathers. They're soft and supple when new and, like any fine leathers, they get that beautiful aged look as they get old.

We use only solid brass eyelets, so they won't rust. Nylon thread on all stitching and chrome-tanned rawhide laces because they last longer. And long-wearing leather or rugged Vibram® soles because they're unbeatable for resistance to abrasion.

The final ingredient: Timberland's genuine handsewn moccasin construction. (We're one of the few companies still practicing this art.) This results in shoes so comfortable, and so well made, that you'll hold on to and enjoy them year after year.

Few things in life improve with age. A pair of Timberland handsewns are two of them.

Timberland 🌲

and creative director. Is it unusual to have so many different titles and functions at once?

A: Yes. I suppose what makes it a little bit unusual is that I've always been on the creative side: I started out as an art director. Since the day we started the agency, back in the summer of 1962, my title has been creative director and it's the thing that I feel the greatest affinity for and enjoy the most. But about five, six years ago I became president, and then chief executive officer and chairman came just a few months ago [late in 1984]. My first consideration for '85 is to spread some of this responsibility around.

Q: Does your job involve a lot of juggling of all of these responsibilities?

A: If you're in the advertising business and your responsibility is chief executive officer, I think that it's impossible to exclude certain areas of the company. If you do, then you're not fulfilling your job. Certainly there is the business of your clients, there's the welfare of your people, there's the persistent monitoring of your advertising to ensure a standard that you find acceptable, that consumers find acceptable. The work you create for your client is your primary mission. Everything stems from that. You've also got to make sure that the company runs profitably so that you can reward your people. Having gone public a year ago, we also have a responsibility now to outside shareholders. The chief executive officer of an advertising agency has to be involved in these major activities.

Q: Since your background was as an art director, did you have to acquire your expertise in running a company along the way?

A: Yes, that's right. It was never my intention to run an advertising agency. My goal as a young man was to make ads when I got in the advertising business.

Q: Do you miss that aspect of it?

A: Sure I do.

Q: Can you give me a rough idea of how you spend your time on a typical day? Is there even such a thing as a "typical" day?

A: It varies enormously. I'll spend time with clients in meetings; I'll spend time talking with the people here about what we're trying to accomplish as an agency and listen to what they're trying to accomplish as individuals. There's a lot of interpersonal dialogue that goes on. So it's the review of the work, working with people and working with clients—but the mixture varies. Sometimes you may spend an entire day working only with your own people never seeing a client and sometimes you'll spend an entire day working with clients spending little time with your own people. And then there are new business presentations, resolving compensation agreements, establishing an international advertising capability, etc., etc.

Q: Does all the creative work pass through your office before it goes on to the clients?
A: The strategies and the major campaigns I want very much to be a part of. I don't see all of the work that goes through, but I see the work where a client's major dollars are being spent.

Q: Everyone always talks about Ally & Gargano as one of the "hot" and creatively influential agencies of today. How did it get to be so hot?
A: I'd like to think that from the day we started we were a hot agency because we had a very special point of view and I don't think we've violated it over the years. We may have bent it out of shape a little bit from time to time, but what we've always tried to do is to be honest with ourselves; honest with our clients; avoid deception in our work; create advertising which contains informative, authentic, and useful information of real benefit to consumers. And then present the message interestingly. In short, we simply follow what we believe is the right thing to do.

Q: When you came to New York in 1959 it was the time of the so-called creative revolution. Was it really as much of a revolution as people say? Was there really a feeling of ferment in the air?
A: Oh indeed, unquestionably. There was a remarkable change taking place in this business.

Q: What changed?
A: The ground rules changed. The ground rules began to shift from a service-dominated business to a product-dominated business. Creativity became the product. The creative revolution alerted agencies and, more important, clients to the fact that the work agencies create is *the* essential ingredient. Good creative work could rapidly change consumer opinion which would then translate into sales and then net profit. And that's what made the whole thing exciting. And it didn't have to be some slow, long-term build: success happened in many cases overnight. This was the real magic

that fueled creative people, that stimulated an enormous amount of energy. But in the other extreme, there were also an enormous amount of abuses that this revolution fostered—the presumption that creative people could do what they damn well pleased. Disciplines were either ignored or not understood by a lot of people, and there was an inordinate amount of self-indulgent, self-absorbed, egocentric work that I think fell far from the rank of good advertising.

Q: Has there been a swing back from that in recent years?

A: Oh, there was certainly a counter-reaction once clients got their fill of the excesses and the economic times got tough. During the seventies people began to pull back considerably and decided they'd had enough of this stuff; let's start getting more practical, more businesslike, so that the abuses that occurred at one end of the creative revolution occurred at the other end by virtue of putting rigid contraints on people, becoming much more dictated to by research, becoming acutely concerned about production budgets. So the face of the business turned cautious and conservative and far less exciting.

Q: Do you think the pendulum is swinging back now toward the creative?

A: It appears to be the case, but I can only speak for this agency; for it was never the case that we abandoned it. If you keep at it and pursue what you do well and you don't abuse that hard-earned trust that clients give agencies, you'll wind up with a product you feel proud of and consumers and advertisers feel good about too.

Q: Would you say that is your personal philosophy of advertising?

A: I think so. I think you have to feel good about yourself in order to make other people feel good about the work you're doing.

Q: Coming to New York marked a real turning point in your career. Would you still advise young people to come to New York?

A: I can't think of another place I would prefer to work over New York. That is not to say that good advertising can't be done elsewhere, because there is work being done that is quite exceptional in other places throughout the country, in unexpected regions of the United States. It depends on what one's goals are. But as a photographer once said to me the first couple of weeks after I arrived in New York: "In the time of the Romans you live in Rome; in the time of the Americas, you live in New York." I thought, yeah, that's true, that's exactly why I'm here.

Q: Is advertising in your opinion a glamorous field, or do you think the glamour aspect of advertising has been overstated?
A: I think it's simply not considered. It's funny, glamour is a word that people use who aren't in the business. When I hear it, it always sounds incongruous. Nobody ever says, "Gee, isn't that a glamorous opportunity." Nobody who's in the business talks that way. I never think about it that way. It's an interesting job; that's it. That's what most of the people I work with think. Maybe the perception [of glamour] is much greater on the outside than it is on the inside. Maybe if you're working in a job that's tedious and unchallenging, you may look at advertising and wind up with that term. Because advertising is *never* boring; frustrating, demanding, stressful, stimulating— but never boring.

Q: Advertising has the reputation of being a very high pressure field. True?
A: Unquestionably.

Q: How do you deal with that?
A: I'm not sure I do deal with it very well. I just accept it. Ultimately what you say to yourself is, "Am I happy with what I'm doing?" It's a high pressure business. It has its emotional rewards and it pays well. It makes inordinate demands on your psyche, on your stomach lining, on your families, on your personal time, and almost everything that's important to you in your life. But you try to keep matters in perspective so that you don't destroy what's important—including yourself.

Q: Let's talk about advice for people trying to break in: What are some of the qualities that you look for in young people trying to get into the creative side?
A: There are a lot of qualities that you look for. You look for somebody with obvious talent, to begin with. Somebody who has a keen awareness. Do they sense what's going on around them? Do they seem to be fine-tuned to a wide variety of interests? I've always believed that people who are extremely sensitive and aware of what's going on around them in the world tend to be able to communicate very well. I look for people who are confident and honest with themselves and with the people around them. Whether you're gregarious or introspective, it doesn't matter much. Excellence comes in different guises. There are a lot of disparate personalities in an advertising agency.

Some of the most creative people I've met have been extraordinarily quiet and inhibited, but they're able to sense a way of touching other people. And you look for that kind of quality. There's something about gifted people—you see work that they've created and it strikes a universal chord. It is often some fundamental piece of truth they have identified and you say, "Yes! that is exactly the way it is." It isn't their use of clever language or exotic visuals, it's their depth and character that shines.

ED McCABE
President and Worldwide Creative Director
Scali, McCabe, Sloves, Inc.

 Boy-wonder copywriter of the late sixties and seventies, Ed McCabe has grown up to become a self-described "man-wonder" of the eighties and also something of an industry legend. McCabe has won just about every advertising award there is, including the honor of being youngest person ever elected into the Copywriter's Hall of Fame (this was in 1974 when he was thirty-five). Scali, McCabe, Sloves, the agency McCabe helped to found with four partners in 1967, is also something of a prodigy. In less than twenty years it's grown from zero in billings to nearly $300 million with offices in Canada, Mexico, England, Germany, and Australia. Some of its major accounts include Volvo (Volvo and McCabe both left Carl Ally—now Ally & Gargano—to try their fortunes with the fledgling Scali, McCabe, Sloves; both are still there, happy and successful), Perdue Farms, Maxell Corporation, Hertz, and Ralston Purina. And new business is pouring in. Scali won *Advertising Age* Agency of the Year in 1974. But it's not just the billings or the growth or the client list or the awards that make Scali one of the most talked-about agencies around; it's the quality of the advertising: tough, sharp, hard-hitting, some might even say go-for-the-jugular. But the main thing is it works: McCabe himself thought up the idea of Frank Perdue as the tough man with the tender chickens, and it helped turn the company from a rinky-dink poultry farm to a multi-million dollar household word, with sales increasing 525% from 1968 to 1984. Volvo's North American sales have doubled since

Frank Perdue and his chickens, a big creative breakthrough for Ed McCabe and for Scali, McCabe, Sloves.

1976. And as their clients' business booms, Scali, McCabe, Sloves keeps right on booming with them.

McCabe, who dropped out of high school at the age of fifteen, sort of dropped into advertising by chance. He started out working in the mailroom of a Chicago-based agency because it was the only job he could get. Once McCabe decided that copywriting was what interested him, he went after it with characteristic impatience and determination. He succeeded with equally characteristic flair. He was in on the founding of Scali before he turned thirty; and it was his wonder-boy reputation as much as anything else that got business rolling. It's sort of the all-American success story, except

Volvo was Scali's first client and they're still making the profits go round and round.

that tough, scrappy, and outspoken Ed McCabe is not exactly your apple-pie-style hero. McCabe may very possibly be as hard-hitting and hard-driving as the advertising he writes. In a cover story about Scali, McCabe, Sloves that ran in *The New York Times Magazine* in 1976, McCabe was described as "a driven man," a demanding perfection-ist whose staff once presented him with a whip. In a brief interview in his New York office, I found McCabe as ready to laugh as he was to fire off pointed remarks about the advertising business, the creative personality, and the advertising myths. Though the whip was not in evidence, McCabe really didn't seem to need it.

Q: When did you first decide to go into advertising?
A: I never decided to go into advertising. I was looking for a job: I was fifteen years old, I was a high school dropout, and an employment agency sent me to an advertising agency. They'd sent me to a number of companies that wouldn't hire me, so they said, "We'll send you to an ad agency—they'll hire *anybody*." And that's how I started. I started in the mailroom.

Q: So how long did it take before you were writing ads?
A: About two years. I was in the mailroom. Then I worked in the art department. I worked in the traffic department. And after about a year and a half, I decided that of all

Hertz, another long-standing success story for McCabe and his creatives.

With Affordable Weekly and Weekend rates, everyone can afford the reliability of Hertz.

Hertz

The "1 way to rent a car."

the people in an agency copywriters had the most fun. So I was helping out in the traffic department and I found out which copywriters were way behind in their assignments. I would go to them and say, "Now look, I know you're really overdue on this trade ad and that you're having an affair with such-and-such girl in the media department and that you'd like to have lunch with her. Why don't you do that instead of working through lunch on this horrible, dreary trade ad and let me try it because I'm trying to learn something about the business. The worst thing that could happen if it doesn't work out is that you'll have to work tonight, which you'll probably have to do anyway. And the best thing is I'll have learned something and you'll have one less pain in the neck."

Q: Has that kind of approach worked for you in other situations later in your career?
A: Luckily, I haven't had many other situations where I've had to be quite so desperate.

Q: How about when you started Scali, McCabe, Sloves—was there a lot of desperation then about starting out? Was it scary?

A: Yeah, it was pretty scary. It wasn't my idea. Sam Scali and Marvin Sloves wanted to start an agency and were looking for someone to do it with them. At the same time, I was at Carl Ally, and I got into an argument with him over something and I just decided what the heck. So I recommended myself. I was twenty-seven at the time. We had some money we'd been able to put together through friends and we scraped together whatever we had ourselves, so we had enough to last a year. But we had a pact—altogether there were five of us who started it—we had a pact that we would jump one a week out of the window, so that there would always be somebody behind to answer the phone. We never got to the point where the first one had to jump.

Q: When did things really take off?

A: We were in business two months with not much going on. We had landed a public service account and I was pitching an automobile account when another automobile account called us. And that was Volvo, which we subsequently got, and it remains one of our biggest and our oldest accounts.

Q: Was Perdue one of the big breakthroughs for you?

A: No. Perdue was a little, tiny account. It was a big *creative* breakthrough: we were able to make a lot of noise with it. It was an account that allowed us to do a very good job and create visibility.

Q: What are some of the other ads you consider breakthroughs?

A: I would consider most of our work right along breakthrough. I think Hertz was probably a breakthrough in that it was a big, important account that we got at a time when we were still fairly small. Volvo was a breakthrough because it was our first account, and for years we've done advertising that everybody talks about. We had Barney's for a while and that created a lot of visibility for us. I think the secret is you have to do it with as many of your accounts as you can.

Q: Based on your experience, is there any advice you have for people who want to start their own agencies today?

A: Yeah. Probably not to.

Q: Why not?

A: I think it's a lot different business than it was when I started in it. The cost of office space is astronomical. Unless you have a *huge* account (like Backer & Spielvogel with $60–$80 million), I think anybody with the brains to do well in advertising could use their brains more profitably in another business.

Q: Do you think small is better for a creative agency?
A: No. I don't think big is better either. I think good is best.

Q: Your agency has the reputation of being really hot creatively. Is that the kind of reputation you'd like to have?
A: I would like our reputation to be an honest reflection of what we are. I think we're very good in handling only products that we believe in and only good quality products. I think we're very good in that we don't handle products that are harmful to people's health. We don't take cigarette advertising. I think we do very good work and I think we do honest advertising that doesn't mislead consumers. What we're really talking about is an agency that does a first-rate job and has the courage of its convictions when it comes to dealing with its clients and its employees.

Q: Do you still work on ads or is your job now mostly running the agency?
A: Well, it's mostly running the agency, but I still do some ads. I'm starting to do more and more advertising and less and less running. You get to the point where you feel that the psychic return of having others do things as a result of your prodding, cajoling, and teaching is not sufficiently rewarding to justify the effort. And that's what I came to and I decided I'd be better off just doing more of my own work.

Q: Is there any way you could describe a typical day?
A: No. Luckily none of them are typical. That's what makes this business interesting.

Q: Do you work incredibly long hours?
A: No. I work incredibly intense normal hours.

Q: What aspect of the job do you find most exciting and rewarding?
A: Being terrific at it.

Q: I'd like to ask you about the myth of the creative personality as a kind of eccentric, egotistic prima donna. What do you think about that?

A: I think it's true. I think any creative people tend to be eccentric because if they're truly creative they tend to be very impatient with uncreative people and their inability to see things the way they do.

Q: What are some of the qualities that you look for in people trying to get hired at your agency?
A: I tend to look for people who aren't normal. In my time I've hired ex-priests, cab-drivers, short-order cooks—all as copywriters who had no prior experience as copy-writers, and they all worked out very well. I look for street smarts and an intuitive sense of what people want and what they're all about. A sense of reality that you can't teach someone. Then I look for a gift of communication, which sometimes can be referred to as glib—but that's only one aspect of it. It's an ability to boil a lot of complicated issues down in a very simple and impactful way.

Q: Do you think people in advertising have to be able to handle a lot of pressure?
A: Absolutely.

Q: Is it worse for creatives?
A: In one respect it's worse for creatives because of the fact that so many people who have no ability or talent have a say in what you do. And that's a terribly frustrating thing. On the other hand, it's less frustrating than being in account management or some other areas of the agency where there is nothing concrete that you can hold up as indicative of what you do. The creative person can at least at the end of the year look at the ads and commercials that he's created—and that is in some respect a measure of his worth.

ACCOUNT MANAGEMENT:

IN THE THICK OF IT

In *Ogilvy on Advertising,* David Ogilvy, attempting to define the role of the account executive, recounts a conversation he overheard between two people on an airplane:

"What business are you in?"
"Engineer. You?"
"I'm an account executive in an ad agency."
"You write the ads."
"No, copywriters do that."
"That must be a fun job."
"It's not that easy. We do a lot of research."
"You do the research?"
"No, we have research people for that."
"Do you bring in the new clients?"
"That's not my job."
"Forgive me, but what *is* your job?"
"Marketing."
"You do the marketing for the clients?"
"No, they do it themselves."
"Are you in management?"
"No, but I soon will be."

"Trying to describe to people what you do," one management supervisor told me, "is the biggest joke in the industry." First of all, no two days are ever alike—the nature of the work keeps changing all the time. Second, the cast of characters keeps changing. Since you represent the client to the agency and the agency to the client, you're dealing with all the major players in the advertising game. Third, the work itself is hard to get a handle on because it tends to be more conceptual than material. At the end of the month, the creatives can screen their commercials or flash their finished print ads, the media people can whip out the media plan, research people can display weighty reports—but the account person, who has been intimately involved in all of these projects along with a good deal more, has nothing tangible to show for his or her efforts. Though in some physical, material sense they may not actually *do* anything, they *are* everywhere and must *know* about everything. Clearly, it's not an area for people who prefer a narrow focus, instant results, and complete predictability in their work.

In the structure of the agency, account management is at the center. Bill Gross, a thirty-one-year-old vice president with J. Walter Thompson in New York, explained this with an analogy, "Looking at it very simplistically, if you drew a wheel, account people would be at the center of the wheel in agency organization. Coming off as spokes from that center would be the creative department, the media department, research department, and then the tactical people—traffic, billing, and accounting."

From this position at the center, the account person manages the client's business within the agency—but this only accounts for part of the job. The person in account management also enters into a kind of marketing partnership with the client. He or she is thus partially a coordinator and partially a marketing consultant with an expertise in communications. This marketing aspect of the job is very often overlooked or misunderstood, even by other agency people. As Denny O'Hearn, an account supervisor at Grey Advertising, pointed out: "A media person might think all the account guys do is come down and ask when they're going to see the media plan. They don't see that we're here at 10 o'clock at night working on marketing plans with the client, identifying marketing problems, coming up with business-building ideas. In a large sense, we're a trusted partner with our client. We really have to understand their business. They use us as a resource."

Understanding the client's business involves a good deal more than reading a few trade journals or chatting with the client over lunch. Account people will routinely visit the factories where the products are made, immerse themselves in the technical aspects of the business from production to distribution, talk with consumers, visit stores. Madeline Lewis, who started in advertising as an assistant account executive at Benton & Bowles and now holds the position of vice president and management director (same as management supervisor) at Foote, Cone & Belding, has worked on products ranging from hand lotion to dog food, shampoo to sunglasses. With each new product comes a new group of consumers to think about, new uses, new packaging potential, new distribution patterns. Lewis, like so many people in account management, has had to shift

Madeline Lewis, up-and-coming vice president and management director at Foote, Cone & Belding/New York.

gears frequently and rapidly in order to acquire the crucial expertise in each new product. But then, constantly shifting gears is something that many account people enjoy most about their jobs.

Bill Gross characterized one of his key functions within J. Walter Thompson as "getting from the agency the highest quality end product, which is advertising, for the client." This sounds simple enough, but it translates into a massive process of planning, explaining, reviewing, presenting. Invariably, the process of coming up with an advertising plan and devising strategy involves tons of meetings. Ann Paustian, an account supervisor with Foote, Cone & Belding in San Francisco, described it this way: "When we need a new advertising campaign or need to refurbish an existing campaign, we'll go to the client [in her case, the client is Pacific Bell] with a recommendation. It then becomes a joint decision between the account team and the client: together we'll agree to the strategy. There may be three or so meetings to get this approval of strategy. Next we'll give them a timetable. While the creative team usually plays some role in the strategy development process, they aren't usually formally involved until there is final approval of the strategy. At that point, we'll meet with all creative team members to explain the strategy at a kind of kick-off session. This is to make sure everybody is singing from the same sheet of music. After that, we try to leave them alone for a few weeks, to give them plenty of breathing room for creative development."

Then there are more meetings at which the early ads are discussed, revised, redirected if need be so that they will be on strategy, and then discussed and revised again. Often, nudging creatives in one direction or another requires the utmost tact and delicacy. It's all part of the job.

Once there is consensus on the agency side, the work is shown to the client at a presentation meeting. The bigger and more important the piece of work being presented, the more formal the presentation meeting will be. The account group sets up the meeting, explaining what is going to be shown and what research data went into it. Though the creative (or media or research person, depending on the type of presentation) actually will present the work, the account person is there to make sure the client is absolutely clear on what is being said. He or she acts as the liaison.

An account person also plays a key role in the production aspect. Bill Gross explains: "Let's say the client says, 'Nice approach, go ahead and film it,' then I become somewhat of a cost controller. I work with creative people to make sure that we're giving the client the right value for their production dollar. Once the commercial expenditure is approved, an account person goes to the shoot, often to be with the client. The client wants to be there to make sure their funds are being well spent and an account guy goes to make sure that all the agreements are adhered to."

The same type of involvement holds true for the media plans. The account person, who has been in on the marketing strategies from the start, knows the kind of people they're trying to sell to, where they live, what they do, how old they are, even what kind of values they have (the term used now to describe this kind of in-depth profile is "psychographic"), and he knows how many times a week or a year he wants that person to buy the product. The account manager will discuss these broad parameters with the media planner, who will then determine how to implement them most effectively through a specific media plan. As with the creative end, it's a give and take in which the account person has an eye both to the particular focus of the job and to the big picture. As one associate media director told me, "If the account person really knows his product, he may come up with something that you didn't think of because he has the ability to step back and see things in perspective."

Madeline Lewis gave me a good illustration of how the account managers work hand in hand with the other departments at Foote, Cone & Belding in a kind of core group. When she first came to work at the agency in 1984, she was assigned to a product that was having a lot of problems. It had been rushed into test market and, as a result, some of the decisions about its positioning (the personality of the product—the image the advertiser wants to convey of what it does and whom it's for), its packaging, its name, and the advertising suffered from being pulled together too quickly. Lewis was asked to take a hard look at the product and try to reposition it. But she wasn't working in a vacuum: "I was working closely with the key research, creative, and account people on the business. After some upfront thinking, my boss and I sat down with Jack Young, the agency president, and Len Sugarman, the creative head, and David Budner, the head of research, and thrashed it out. We got into a room together and figured out what was the best way to go and there was a real roll-up-your-sleeves, hands-on attitude. There was a true *exchange* of ideas, whether it was packaging ideas from the creatives, copy ideas from the research people, or whatever. It was wonderful! When you have the openness and richness of people exchanging different ways of thinking about things, the ideas get much better."

Most people in account management work on one or more ongoing brands (or products) as well as brands that are in the development stage. Working on the development stage of a new product is something that gets a lot of account people fired up. You're sailing into unknown waters, not only in terms of what the advertising will be, but with the very basic elements of the product: how will it be packaged, how much should it cost, in what sort of stores should it be sold? Your client relies on you to help with all of these questions. In a sense, you're really helping to create the product. And the potential for success is unlimited.

Even more exciting is pitching a new account. One account supervisor described this as "the sexy part of the job. Everyone gets real psyched and works really hard." Essentially, you have to crash-course an industry you knew nothing about last week and in an extremely limited period of time come up with a presentation and analysis of how you would approach the advertising and marketing. The pressure can be enormous, not only because of the time factor, but because millions of dollars of new billings may be riding on winning that account. Though some big agencies have new business departments, many shops don't. What happens is you drop everything and go crazy. And winning that new account, of course, can be one of the great highs of the job.

Tight deadlines and competition for new accounts are not the only sources of pressure on account people. There's a certain pressure built in to the position of being a go-between. As one account manager put it, "Not only are you sometimes feeling beat-up by the client and having to answer to them, you also sometimes take the frustration and the anger of the creatives and the service groups. There are some days when you're getting it from all sides and you feel like a goddamned punching bag." And another person who climbed fairly high through the account management ranks in a short period of time reflected on the future: "I'm not sure I want to be an ad person all my life. This business really sucks you dry. It's incredibly demanding because you're trying to please people all the time and it's really a fast-paced business. I think that's why it's such a young industry. People simply get burned out. And there are times when I think, 'I'm not going to be able to do this for years longer.'"

Advertising *is* a young industry. You'll come across many account people who made it to the level of account supervisor and management supervisors in their late twenties and early thirties. While it was exhilarating to see these people in such demanding and responsible jobs, it does make you wonder: what happens when you hit forty? "We laugh about this sometimes," one management supervisor confided nervously. "We look around and think, 'Where do these people go when they get burned out in their forties?'" The days of the bloodbaths and mass firings may be over, but there are still plenty of anxieties lurking in account management departments.

Since account people work in close collaboration with the client, it's crucial to the job to establish a good working relationship. In most cases, the agency's account services department is organized to mirror the client's marketing department, with the agency jobs falling in between client jobs. So the structure may look something like this:

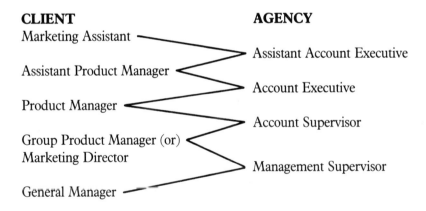

CLIENT   **AGENCY**

Marketing Assistant

                                   Assistant Account Executive

Assistant Product Manager

                                   Account Executive

Product Manager

                                   Account Supervisor

Group Product Manager (or)
Marketing Director

                                   Management Supervisor

General Manager

The client's marketing departments will usually be broken down into product groups (or brand groups) which really run one line of the business. At the head of the group is the group product manager or marketing director who manages a number of products, then the product (or brand) manager in charge of one particular product in that group, and reporting to him or her the assistant product manager and marketing assistants. People at each of these levels will work most closely—often on a day-to-day or hour-to-hour basis—with the agency people at a corresponding level.

For example, Denny O'Hearn, an account supervisor at Grey Advertising, works on Post Cereals, which is part of the General Foods account. He has a couple of brands, among them Honeycomb, and some development work. When O'Hearn is wearing his Honeycomb hat, he'll be in touch with the Honeycomb product manager on all the daily details of the business and with the group product manager on higher level decisions. O'Hearn describes the relationship as "formal informality": "Because General Foods is only forty minutes away in White Plains, New York, you don't have to fly out once a week for formal meetings. We can see each other every day or once a week or we can handle something over the phone. General Foods has a very easy-going group. They're all people about my age. It's really a situation where, when we have a problem, we put our heads together and solve it."

For account people whose clients are not forty minutes away, there can be a good deal of travel on the job. And there is also travel to commercial shoots. When O'Hearn worked on the Kool-Aid account, he used to spend as much as a month at a time in Los Angeles for winter shoots. Ann Paustian, an account supervisor with Foote, Cone & Belding/San Francisco, says she spent practically the entire fourth quarter last year in Los Angeles seeing commercials through production. Many account managers also travel for consumer research and to keep abreast of all phases of their client's business.

As an account person, you may go on some exotic shoots, rub shoulders with celebrities (occasionally), and spend some time in sunny climates, but chances are you won't be living it up in four-star restaurants on the client's money. The wining and dining aspect of the job seems to be pretty much a thing of the past. "The old three-martini lunch is just nonexistent today," according to Madeline Lewis. Though she stresses that it's important to get to know the client on a personal basis, the contact is most often in someone's office or over a sandwich and a cup of coffee. As one account supervisor told me: "You whip down to the client for lunch, but then a crisis arises while you're there and you end up having a ten-minute bite in the company cafeteria. So much for glamour!" The fact is, advertising has become a more serious business and most clients are keeping closer tabs on their advertising dollars; they'd rather see the money going into great campaigns than great champagne.

Account people do put in long hours, but their hours seem a bit more predictable than the erratic schedules kept by creatives. Also, the hours often become more regular and reasonable the higher up you go. A young, ambitious assistant account executive may be working early every morning, late every night, and weekends; this is a position in which people are proving themselves and flexing their muscles. The account supervisors and management supervisors I spoke to try to keep their working day from about 8:30 to 6:30 or 7, though when they're pitching new business or working on a rush project they may be at the office until 9 or 10 for several nights running. Madeline Lewis gets to work at 7 or 7:30 A.M. because she "desperately needs those two hours of quiet time. I'm so interrupted with phone calls and people that it's virtually impossible to get writing and reading done on a normal day." But getting in early allows her to leave the office by 6:30, and also gives her time to play squash. She sums up: "You put in heavy, heavy hours at the lower levels and then you hopefully try to lead a still hard-working, but somewhat saner life as you go on."

Lewis was not alone in pointing out the need for quiet time for reading and especially writing. People in account management stress that writing is a major part of their jobs. They write up presentations and internal memos, selling documents about marketing plans, letters to the client with recommendations for how to improve business, and reports on the endless numbers of meetings they engage in with clients. An account person is sort of like a swinging door through which information passes back and forth between agency and client. And writing is one of the prime ways of communicating this information. Though being creative is not their frontline responsibility, account people will often have to use their imaginations in selling ideas to the client and in representing the client's point of view to the agency. And at the lower levels, there are countless reports to put together tracking sales, spending, media ratings, market share, etc.; in short, numbers-crunching distilled into crystalline prose. The writing that account people do at all levels is not the kind of zippy, catchy prose that copywriters specialize in, but clear persuasive business writing that shows an equal facility with the technical and the intuitive sides of advertising.

The same sort of businesslike clarity and persuasiveness seem very often built in to the characters of people in account services. Being in the middle of the sometimes stormy partnership between agency and client requires a good deal of diplomacy and tact and the ability to lead without bossing. Account people are not supposed to be eccentric egomaniacs or temperamental creative geniuses—it's simply not part of the job description. And in fact, the account managers I spoke with were some of the most charming, articulate, and confident people I've ever encountered. They seemed calm with their responsibilities and pressures and they inspired trust in their abilities. The feeling was that when they said, "I'll take care of it," you could stop worrying about it. Just the kind of feeling that clients with several million dollars worth of advertising like to have when they call their agency.

POSITIONS AND PAY

ASSISTANT ACCOUNT EXECUTIVE

The entry-level account services position is assistant account executive, an ideal vantage point from which to see everything that goes on in the department and thus to learn. The AAE's job has variously been described as executional, administrative, implemental, or, more colloquially, as gruntwork. What it boils down to is carrying out the myriad details of the business and following through. If the client wants a comparative study of their product versus the other competing products on the market, the AAE digs up the numbers, sets up the charts, and submits the work for the account executive's review. If the color proof of a magazine ad has been misplaced and the client has to see it the next day, the AAE goes down to the art department and gets another. If the client wants to see a graph of the advertising budget broken down in six different ways, the AAE will get on the computer and feed in the information. If there's a big presentation meeting at the client's on Wednesday, the AAE will spend a good part of Monday and Tuesday running around gathering facts, figures, reports, and creative pieces. It's legwork, analysis, orchestration, putting together studies, keeping timetables and records, making budgets, getting invoices signed, and keeping track of just about everything. One AAE described the job as "cranking things out and getting things done." Another commented, "You really have to be willing to roll up your sleeves and sit down and do a lot of dirty work." When everyone else in the account management department is sitting in meetings theorizing about how to break into new markets, the AAE is probably writing up a competitive spending report with one hand and dialing the phone with the other.

Usually an AAE will report to one AE and thus will be involved in one product or brand that is part of a larger account. At some agencies the AAE is enrolled in a company training program and rotates through various agency accounts. Typical assignments last six to nine months, and you may have two or three of these before you are promoted to AE. At a big agency, an AAE will earn anywhere from $15,000 to $20,000 a year.

ACCOUNT EXECUTIVE

As you move up the ladder in account management, the jobs become more conceptual and less executional. You're spending more time thinking about ways to improve the client's business and less time tending to the day-to-day details of servicing that business through the agency. Also, as you move up, your perspective on the business broadens. For example, the AAE will write up a report showing month-by-month spending on the brand; the AE will review the report, compare the numbers with those of previous years, and draw conclusions about the health of the business. The account supervisor or management supervisor might glance through the report and use it as one piece of datum in his or her thinking about spending trends.

The AE is the key function person on a given business and as such is in charge of the day-to-day management of the product and for keeping in daily (sometimes hourly) touch with the product manager on the client's side. Typically, the AE will be running one ongoing brand and also have a few related products in the development stage. The AE divides his or her day between meetings with other people in the department, meetings with other people in the agency—media, creative, research—phone calls and meetings with the client, and writing up memos, presentations, and notes on all these meetings. A lot of the job is reactive; the AE may be reviewing work with the AAE when the client calls to discuss a change in the plans for the presentation meeting at the end of the week. The AE will then have to call the agency art director about two of the creative pieces that are to be presented, dash down to the media department to go over revisions to a proposed media plan, and report back to both the account supervisor and the client. Very often the AE's job is a juggling act. *[For a more in-depth look at what the AE actually does on a "typical" day, see the special section "A Day in the Life of an Account Executive."]*

Salary range for an AE at a large agency is $25,000 to $40,000.

ACCOUNT SUPERVISOR

Like the AE, the account supervisor heads up day-to-day operations, but chances are that he or she will be running two to four ongoing products along with some development work, as opposed to the single, basic product that the AE oversees. As a result, there is absolutely no way that the AS can keep track of *all* the details of all the businesses. That's where the supervising comes in. Two or three AEs report directly to the AS, so he or she will be intimately acquainted with the businesses these people are running and will know what to handle him or herself and what to delegate. Because you're responsible for a larger chunk of the business, you're more aware of the big picture. For example, Denny O'Hearn, an AS at Grey Advertising, works on the Post Cereals business, which is part of the General Foods account. O'Hearn is in charge of several ongoing Post Cereal brands as well as some development work on brands that are in the test market stage. He is one of six AS's assigned to the General Foods group and has three AEs reporting to him, each one working mostly on one major brand. O'Hearn points out that the more experienced the AE is, the less involved the AS has to be in his or her business and the more time the AS can spend on guidance, troubleshooting, and strategy. But invariably, details come up that require the AS to jump in. On the client side, the AS works most closely with the marketing director and the product manager. In many cases, the AS is the key client contact person on a given account and as such must be up-to-date on all aspects of the business.

Salary range for an AS at a large agency is $35,000 to $65,000.

MANAGEMENT SUPERVISOR

Another step up the pyramid is the management supervisor, who may have two or three account supervisors reporting to him or her. Very often, the management supervisor will oversee a number of different products from unrelated accounts. For example, Madeline Lewis, a management director (Foote, Cone & Belding's title for management supervisor), works on Corning Sunglasses and Lipton's Sunkist beverages. The management supervisor is less involved in the day-to-day running of the business than are the AS and AE and more involved in strategy planning and providing marketing counsel to the clients. Ideally, concepts are his or her major focus while the AS and the AE attend to business. The management supervisor is also the primary intermediary between agency management and the account group; on the client side their contacts are the general manager and the marketing director. Since their focus is quite wide, the management supervisors are able to keep an eye on the overall profitability of the accounts they're involved in and the benefits of the business to the agency. They monitor the expenses and the budget of the account group, consult with other department heads about assigning work, review major creative work and major marketing reports before they are presented to the client, and make sure their staff is working well together. While there is only one step separating the account supervisor and the management supervisor, it is often rather a large one. When you reach this position, you can really pat yourself on the back: you have arrived.

The salary range for management supervisor at a large agency is $55,000 to $90,000.

ACCOUNT DIRECTOR and GROUP ACCOUNT DIRECTOR

At the pinnacle of account management departments, the air becomes thin and heady with power and the positions are few and far between. The structure here varies a good deal from agency to agency, but at the larger shops there is often someone called the account director (or management representative), who has charge of one big account and probably a good chunk of another. For example, at a really big agency, the management supervisor would have a piece of the giant packaged goods business and possibly a few food products; his boss, the account director, would oversee the entire packaged goods operation and perhaps part of the technology company and he might have two or three management supervisors reporting to him. Above that, there is a position known as group account director, and this person would oversee the packaged goods, all of the technology company and baby food products. This is one of the top agency positions, and the person holding it would really be as much concerned with agency management and new business development as with actually running the accounts. In rough figures, if the agency had five group account directors, there would be about ten account directors, fifteen management supervisors, twenty-five account supervisors and fifty account executives.

Salaries for account directors at a large agency range from $78,000 to $125,000, and for group director from $150,000 to $175,000.

 # A DAY IN THE LIFE OF AN ACCOUNT EXECUTIVE

What exactly does an account executive *do* all day? Why is it so difficult to explain this job in general terms? Some would say that the reason you can't explain it is that they don't actually do anything. Those who know better say it's because they do so much and it's all so different. Well, let's go behind the scenes and find out. The account below, while based on an actual day spent following an account executive around, is something of a composite picture: most of the events recorded really happened, and the rest *could have* happened. The names of agency personnel, products, clients, and the agency itself, as well as the nature of the products, have all been changed to protect confidentiality.

Adlai Ernestsale (AE for short) is a twenty-five-year-old account executive with the Adland Agency, a large reputable shop headquartered in New York. AE, who has an MBA from a fine business school, launched a major job-hunting campaign upon graduation, and, after two months and nearly two dozen interviews, landed a job as assistant account executive with Adland. The agency had just the mix he was hoping for: solid marketing and a growing reputation for creative innovation. The promotion to account executive came in a little over a year. AE is currently working on the Sexy Soap brand, part of the giant Peculiar Packaged Products (PPP) account, and he's been spending more and more time of late on several PPP development products, including Talc 'N Chew, a flavored edible baby powder now in test market. AE sees two or three years of hard work ahead of him at Adland and then, if all goes well, a promotion to account supervisor.

Here, then, is a day in the life of Adlai Ernestsale . . .

TUESDAY, MARCH 5, 1985

8:07: AE arrives at Adland's midtown Manhattan offices before receptionist but after Arnold Solidman (his AS) and Mel Sonicboom (his MS). AE, with danish and coffee, sits at desk and spends a few quiet minutes going over his project lists and jotting notes to himself about the coming day's activities.

8:35: AE turns his attention to Thurday's presentation meeting over at the PPP office, a meeting that will focus on new developments in the Sexy Soap brand. As of yesterday afternoon, MS informed him that the brand manager also wants to see the test commercials and layouts on Talc 'N Chew, so AE has to get all of these pieces together pretty fast.

9:00: AE calls the PPP brand manager about Thursday meeting, and leaves message with secretary. Calls art director in Adland's Creative Department, but no one picks up. Continues jotting notes on project lists.

9:20: MS pops in to go over some questions about Talc 'N Chew test market campaign and mentions that there will be a 10:00 meeting of staff in his office. AE to inform Alicia A. Estimate, the AAE for the group.

9:25: Brand manager from PPP returns call and lengthy conversation ensues about the test marketing ideas for Talc 'N Chew. AE emphasizes the importance of getting the campaign off with a bang, but product manager seems to need more reassurance about some of the specifics. At 9:45, AAE comes in and waits for AE to wind up call. At 9:50, AE begins to pace. Finally hangs up at 9:52 with reminder about agenda of Thursday meeting.

9:53: Before going over project lists with AAE, AE makes quick call to Research Department about setting up an idea-generating session to develop new product ideas for PPP. Research person is out on honeymoon, so meeting must be postponed.

9:55: AE and AAE go over project lists together, discussing such topics as the special "scent strip" magazine ad for Sexy Soap, the Talc 'N Chew concept boards, and revised commercials that will be shown at Thursday meeting, and the mechanical for the new Sassy Soap ad, a variant of Sexy Soap that has just gone on sale. AAE to follow up in getting hold of these pieces by Thursday.

10:04: On the way to meeting in MS's office, AE and AAE discuss latest development in signing up famed women's mud wrestling team to appear in Sexy Soap ads. AAE says it's all falling into place.

10:05: Meeting of account group in MS's office covers these topics:
- Is new Sassy Soap brand campaign going to fragment image of Sexy Soap and ultimately hurt sales?
- PPP wants to start selling "beauty-size" bars of Sexy Soap, formerly sold only in bath and family sizes. Does this make sense given buying patterns of their market?
- AAE goes over report she's written on typical Sexy Soap user; MS makes comments.
- AS asks AE how pieces are coming together for Thursday meeting. AE goes over his morning conversation with brand manager about test market campaign. MS agrees that it's important to launch Talc 'N Chew with a big bang and capture large market share right away.
- MS asks AE how progress is coming on Sexy Soap tracking study (a report based on interviews with consumers on how they are perceiving the brand and how they use it). AE to try to bring this report up at Thursday meeting but must run it by the account director first.
- AS and MS go over alternate media plan for Sexy Soap and agree that they need to get higher quality spot television, maybe not prime, but something better than fringe. AE to pursue with media planner.
- AS asks AE how the idea-generating session for new products is shaping up and tells him to schedule it even if the research person is on her honeymoon.

11:15: Meeting ends, AE heads down to Art Department to try to get Aida the art director to change concept board on Talc 'N Chew that he desperately needs for Thursday meeting. She is out of office.

11:30: Calls PPP brand manager to set up idea-generating session.

11:35: Goes over notes from meeting with account group, jotting down things he must follow up on. Calls media planner about changes discussed at meeting.

11:40: AAE brings in overtime invoices for rush work for Talc 'N Chew. AE glances through them and signs.

11:45: Phone calls to assistant brand manager on Sexy Soap, media assistant on question concerning plan; tries to get Aida art director again—still no luck.

12:12: Jots a few notes on his analysis of the Sexy Soap tracking study and drops it off at office of research director. Wants to get her input before running it past account director.

12:20: Personal call.

12:40: Lunch in Adland cafeteria.

1:45: AAE comes in to report her progress on the scent-strip ad for Sexy Soap and to ask AE's advice on the competitive spending report (a report that shows how Sexy Soap is doing compared with similar soaps on the market).

1:50: AS drops in to say he'll be at PPP office most of afternoon; asks if AE has any matters to bring up with client.

1:57: AE reminds AAE that there are three major reports she must prepare this week: budget, Nielsen, and spending; he explains priorities and reminds her to keep the format simple and the big picture in focus. The budget report will show how much advertising money they plan to spend per quarter and will include updates on how much was actually spent in previous quarters.

2:30: Calls Aida once again about Talc 'N Chew concept board and leaves message. Getting nervous about this piece.

2:33: Sits down to write up condensation of report on the progress with development products, but . . .

2:34: Brand manager calls to go over format of Thursday meeting. Brand manager thinks it might be a good idea for him and AE to meet separately before presentation to go over scent-strip ad and other related issues on Sexy Soap.

3:07: Calls the PPP product manager in charge of development products and discusses scheduling of idea-generating session.

3:10: AAE returns to go over print estimate for new Sexy Soap ad, but AE tells her to hold off on this. Asks her to follow through on getting several mechanicals from Art Department.

3:15: Heads down to office of research director to get her comments on his analysis of the tracking study prepared for Sexy Soap. Research director compliments AE on doing a fine job but suggests a few changes in the way some of the charts are broken down. They agree that focus should shift to fifteen- to thirty-year-old women who perceive Sexy Soap as an all-purpose nonluxury soap.

4:06: AE heads down to cafeteria to get a soft drink. Returns to office to get down to some writing, but then remembers that he should go to Art Department and take a look at the proof of magazine ad for Talc 'N Chew. He and AAE go down together to check it out. The creatives insist they can (and will) do better, but time constraints are tight. AE says that this is fine for Thursday meeting.

4:40: AE drops proofs off on desk and goes back to art department to see if he can finally get Aida to change that concept board. She's on the phone. He tells her to please call him as soon as she can.

4:50: Returns to office and calls assistant product manager re technical problem having to do with paper stock on scent-strip ad. He will get back with answer soon.

4:55: Leaves message for in-house commercial editor who worked on test spot for Talc 'N Chew. Wants to see how commercial looks before showing at Thursday meeting.

5:00: Settles down to writing, when phone rings—his wife calling to make plans for that evening.

5:10: Commercial editor calls to check on schedule for presentation meeting.

5:11: Media assistant stops in office for quick question.

5:16: Finally connects with Aida about making changes on those concept boards. She agrees to get it done by Thursday. AE breathes huge sigh of relief.

5:30: AE and AAE go up to commercial editor's office, and the three of them head over to conference room with TV set. Editor plays the two spots he's edited for Talc 'N Chew: one called "Bubbles" shows happy baby grabbing handful of product, chomping on it, and blowing bubbles while Mom changes diaper; one called "Gagging" shows split screen with baby on left licking regular baby powder off hand and gagging/spitting/crying; on right side of screen, happy baby eats Talc 'N Chew and smiles for camera. AE thinks they look good, but wonders if the product isn't a tiny bit too green. Editor shrugs and promises they can fix it.

5:40: AE and AAE discuss paper stock for Sexy Soap scent-strip ad. Must discuss with product manager tomorrow and iron it out. AE concludes that it looks like they're in good shape for Thursday's presentation meeting. And they still have another day!

5:45: AE finally settles down to his writing, working on confirmation of agreements with client and a few reports.

6:35: Heads out to elevator, subway, and home.

BREAKING IN

The first question anyone interested in breaking into account management work must consider is whether or not to get an MBA. There are two schools of thought on this issue. One school says that the MBA mania is over. Yes, there was a time, in the late seventies and early eighties, when it was practically required to have an MBA in order to get hired into an account management department. As Bill Gross summed up: "In those days, you were a second-class citizen if you didn't have an MBA." But now the fashion has changed. The MBAs, some say, proved to be too expensive and too demanding. They felt they were somehow "above" doing the running around and detailed grunt work required of AAEs, and they complained because their business school classmates on Wall Street were making more money. Account supervisors and management supervisors found that people with plain old BAs were hungrier and more eager to learn, and that people with a few years working experience in whatever field were catching on quicker to the special demands and the pace of account work. So this school concludes: forget the MBA. If you're bright, sharp, good at communicating and writing, and can show that you're familiar with business (either through impressive summer jobs or some experience working in another field), you're going to make the right impression and get hired.

The other school of thought says: Agreed, the MBA may no longer be necessary, but it can't hurt. Practically everyone on the client's side has an MBA; it's a degree the clients value, and what the client likes the agency is bound to like too. Anyway, fashions change and the MBA may very well come back into vogue at the agencies. The word of caution here is: If you have an MBA, make sure you don't come on too arrogant in an interview. Even if you were at the top of your class in school, you're going to start at the bottom in the account services department. Nothing is more of a turn-off in a job seeker than a haughty, know-it-all, superior attitude. And it is precisely this attitude that has soured a lot of account people on MBAs. Enthusiasm for advertising and a genuine willingness to jump in and work hard win you the most points. If you can combine these qualities with an MBA, fine. Just don't assume that the degree is going to open advertising doors all by itself. Maybe it once did, but it doesn't today.

From all accounts, it's easier to land a first job in New York than in any other city for the simple reason that there are more jobs available at the entry level (and every other level too) in New York. Ann Paustian, who is with Foote, Cone & Belding/San Francisco, points out that "San Francisco agencies don't have the luxury of hiring massive numbers of AAEs because they're so much smaller. In fact, we tend not to hire at the assistant level." Paustian got her basic training in New York before she made the move to San Francisco, and she recommends this path to job seekers. Nothing beats a solid grounding in packaged goods marketing at one of the big New York agencies. It's a springboard to a whole range of opportunities.

If you really want account work but simply can't break into that first job no matter how hard you try, think about getting hired at an agency media department and then making the crossover once you've gained some experience. This is a classic route, and it was the one followed by Denny O'Hearn and Bill Gross. Both of them were job hunting during the height of MBA mania and, though both were excellent candidates, they were turned down at interview after interview because they didn't have the magic degree. After three frustrating and fruitless months, O'Hearn shifted his focus from account services to media, and he got hired at one of his first interviews. This was at the media department of BBDO, where he spent nearly two years, moving up from assistant planner to media planner. Then he made the move to Grey as an AAE. In his three and a half years at Grey, O'Hearn has been promoted from AAE to AE to AS. He attributes this rather rapid rise in part to his media experience, which gave him an expertise in one important advertising function.

In Bill Gross's case, once he started looking for media work instead of account work, he got five job offers in a single week. Of those, he chose Benton & Bowles, starting at $7500 a year. After a year and a half, he made the move to account work, also at Grey, where he spent five years climbing the ladder to the position of account supervisor. Gross jumped up to the next level by switching agencies, moving from Grey to J. Walter Thompson. Both Gross and O'Hearn went through headhunters when making the transition from media to account management. Headhunters, while useful for this kind of move, will usually deal only with experienced people; they're not going to help you get your first job. *[For a listing of headhunters, see Chapter Fourteen, Getting Hired.]*

If you do decide to try the media route into account management, don't make this obvious at your media interviews. "You have to remember that media is a discipline, not a training ground for account management," Bill Gross advises. "Go to learn that discipline. Media is a very strong credential." Both Gross and O'Hearn speak warmly of their media experience and both feel that it gave them a running start on the fast track of account management once they made the move.

The most fundamental word of advice for landing a job in account services is also the most time-honored: "Be persistent." O'Hearn points out that there are lots of ways to get in, so if your preferred route doesn't pan out, try another. Geoffrey Ramsey, a young AAE at D'Arcy MacManus Masius, is living proof of that. Graduating from New York University in 1981 as a marketing major, Ramsey wanted to get into account work but didn't want to get an MBA. After a three-month intensive search he landed a job as a billing clerk for a small agency in Queens, but the agency folded after he'd been there a year. His next job was for a midsized Manhattan-based agency that was undergoing a process of merger and consolidation. Ramsey, now working as a media/production biller, realized that this was not getting him any closer to account work and became more and more frustrated. After two years there and another brief job change, he landed a job as an AAE at TWBA in October, 1983. The agency enrolled him in the American Association of Advertising Agencies Institute of Advanced Advertising Studies program, a sixteen- to twenty-week "boot camp" for agency newcomers who show promise. Students meet for the courses after a full day at their offices and the program culminates in a competition between various student groups pitching new business in elaborate presentations. In the midst of this grueling program, Ramsey was let go from his job, but he stayed on at IAAS and his group won the competition. One of the judges was an executive vice president at D'Arcy, and Ramsey, an unemployed winner, promptly called on him for a job interview. D'Arcy took him on as an AAE, he's making good money—and he loves it!

Madeline Lewis, management director at Foote, Cone & Belding, has some good general advice for people preparing for their first round of interviews: "You should really do your homework about an agency and try to figure out in advance which are the six or so agencies you most want to go to. Then save those interviews for last. Before you go to these chosen agencies, talk to a million people and get good interviewing experience. I know I really overestimated my ability to interview. I thought—I'm fairly gregarious, good with people, and relatively communicative—and I just figured interviewing would be a snap. Well, it's not. There's a real art to it and you really need to get the experience under your belt of fielding questions and thinking things through. So when you finally do see those six key agencies, you'll come across as knowing what you want and knowing what you're getting into."

THE MAKING OF A
TELEVISION COMMERCIAL

You've probably seen one of them on certain prime-time shows. A well-known celebrity—it might be Christie Brinkley or James Coburn—finds him- or herself in a comically sticky situation with an outspoken fan. Maybe it's a brash woman who has on the same outfit as glamorous model Christie Brinkley and pounces on her in a department store. Or a peppery old lady who can't resist getting in a few digs at James Coburn when she finds herself seated next to him in an airplane. After a few seconds of amusing banter, the dialogue veers toward the real point of the encounter: it turns out the hotshot celebrity uses the same credit card as the fan . . . MasterCard. It's all done with a light touch and a wry humor. The celebrities seem approachable and human, the connection with MasterCard is natural and unforced, the feeling you're left with is: Gee, I bet I could get one of these credit cards and have some fun too. Witty, light-hearted, sophisticated, but somehow also folksy. In short, contemporary commercial making at its most polished and professional.

It all looks so effortless when it flashes by on your television screen in thirty seconds. Just a couple of actors, an extra or two, a simple, realistic setting. But even commercials as straightforward as these require an astonishing number of hours to make and involve a considerable human and financial investment. We've seen in the chapter on creatives how the copywriter and art director collaborate on the words and images that go into a storyboard. In this case, the art director, Patrick Fanelli, and the creative director/writer, Tony Jaffe, of the William Esty agency in New York came up with the idea of using celebrities in "real life" situations to advertise MasterCard. The five celebrities chosen for the thirty-second spots were Loretta Swit, Shari Belafonte, James Coburn, Pierce Brosnan, and Christie Brinkley. But what about all the work that goes on from the time the storyboard is approved by the client to the time the finished spot appears on the air? The casting, the sets, the actual filming, the editing. For this chapter, the William Esty agency and MasterCard International agreed to let me in on the making of these MasterCard celebrity commercials and in particular "Same Card/Coburn," the spot featuring actor James Coburn. Though the Coburn spot went incredibly smoothly compared to some commercial productions, it was still, as we'll see, a tremendously complicated procedure requiring elaborate planning and coordination.

Before we get to the actual process of preparing for, filming, and refining this commercial, let's meet the people involved in the production.

THE PEOPLE WHO MADE THE COMMERCIAL

THE AGENCY

Though Pat Fanelli and Tony Jaffe devised the scenario and wrote the dialogue for "Same Card/Coburn," the person at Esty most directly involved in getting it produced was Woody Walters, vice president and television producer. In his more than twenty-five years of involvement with commercial production, Walters has worked both for

James Coburn with Esty copywriter/creative director Tony Jaffe at the "Same Card/Coburn" shoot.

advertising agencies and for production companies. He gained work experience in Chicago and Atlanta before coming to New York, and in 1968 he joined the television production department of William Esty. He's been there ever since. Over the years he's worked on a wide range of Esty accounts, but in the past three years about eighty percent of his time has been devoted to MasterCard.

The Esty management supervisor for MasterCard is Mr. Len Faupel.

THE CLIENT

The key MasterCard person involved with this particular commercial was Barbara

Esty producer Woody Walters, MasterCard's Barbara Bromberg, and Coburn watching a playback on the video monitor between takes.

Bromberg, vice president/advertising director. Russell Hogg, president and CEO of MasterCard International, also played a role in making certain decisions.

THE PRODUCTION COMPANY

The director chosen to shoot "Same Card/Coburn" was Bob Giraldi, one of the hottest names not only in commercial directing but in the burgeoning field of music videos as well. Giraldi, whose credits seem to mushroom each month, is most recently basking in the glory of the three-minute extravaganza he directed for Pepsi starring pop singer Lionel Richie and featuring 4,000 extras. His work with Michael Jackson, both on a much publicized Pepsi commercial and on the video of "Beat It," which he made in two nights, has become legendary. According to *Playboy* magazine, "Giraldi could easily be the highest paid director in the business."

Giraldi acquired expertise and contacts as an art director at Young & Rubicam before making the move into commercial direction. In 1973, he and his business partner Phil Suarez started Bob Giraldi Productions and, as Suarez says, things took off from day one. Giraldi used to be best known for his work with celebrities and sports figures—he did the Miller Lite spot featuring Rodney Dangerfield and the Schlitz Malt Liquor spots—but in recent years he's gone in more for big-budget, large-scale productions and musical numbers. He directed the Dr Pepper spot in which hundreds of people shout "Try it!" from stadium bleachers, and he's also done commercials for the musicals "Dream Girls," "Evita," and "A Chorus Line."

Suarez calls Giraldi the "Steven Spielberg of videos," and it's not just hype. Giraldi got in pretty much on the ground floor and he's shot to the top *fast* with Jackson, Diana Ross, Pat Benatar, Lionel Richie, Hall and Oates, and many other top names. Though he's gotten a lot of recognition for the video work and had a lot of fun doing it, commercials are still his bread and butter and he still devotes the bulk of his time to making them. "Same Card/Coburn" was a minuscule effort as Bob Giraldi productions go, but he brought to it the swift sureness and bright style that have become his trademarks as a director.

Bob Giraldi Productions has a staff of about thirty people with offices in New York and Los Angeles. The staff includes casting people, wardrobe specialists, assistant directors, estimators, stylists, executive producers, production assistants (one of the best ways to break into this line of work, a kind of do-everything-help-everyone job), secretaries, and accountants. For the Coburn spot, Todd Allan, with Giraldi's West Coast office, acted as producer.

THE EDITOR

Bob DeRise, the editor of "Same Card/Coburn" (as well as the Belafonte and Brinkley spots), practically grew up in an editing room: he's been in this line of work since

Bob DeRise (at right) in the offices of his editing company A Cut Above Editorial Inc. He edited the Coburn spot.

age seventeen. A professional to the tips of his fingers, DeRise got his first job as a messenger with an editing house, soon moved indoors to the shipping room, and graduated from there to become an editing room apprentice, where he rewound film, spliced dailies together, and soaked up the technical expertise and intuitive know-how needed to become a commercial editor. Two years ago, after spending the better part of two decades working as a commercial editor in a number of New York-based editing and production houses, DeRise opened up his own company—A Cut Above Editorial Inc.

Today DeRise, like Bob Giraldi, is at the top of his field, recognized as one of the top five film editors in New York (which, as he points out, is where the action is in commercial editing). DeRise's recent editing credits are studded with the brightest stars in commercialdom: he edited the Michael Jackson and Lionel Richie Pepsi extravaganzas shot by Giraldi as well as the eighteen-minute 1984 campaign film for Ronald Reagan put together by the Tuesday Team of top advertising people; DeRise has put the flash in a number of recent commercials for Kodak, Close-up toothpaste, Mountain Dew, Burger King, and Nabisco.

DeRise's editing house, A Cut Above, has a total of five people working there: DeRise himself, who does all the editing; two assistants, a bookkeeper, and an apprentice/messenger. A typical day for Bob DeRise, who works on a project-by-project basis, starts at 7 A.M. and ends at 9 or 10 at night. DeRise says his favorite part of the job is "getting a commercial in which the director has shot twenty or thirty thousand feet of film and getting a dynamite music track and then going crazy with the footage. Just to put it all together myself."

DeRise does not feel that film school is any advantage in breaking in to commercial editing. The only way to learn is by experience and the only way to get a job is to show a willingness to learn—and to show it with more enthusiasm and energy than anyone else. You start as a messenger or apprentice at $250 a week, rewinding, splicing film, lining up music tracks. Next step up is assistant, for which the scale pay is $450 a week. Editors start at $600 to $650 a week. DeRise himself gets $3,500 for cutting a thirty-second spot. He insists, however, that even he never has enough work. The next big editing project he's looking forward to is another Pepsi extravaganza featuring a top celebrity act, whose name unfortunately he is not at liberty to disclose.

THE CREW

For commercial productions, the crew—the technical people who set up the lights, run the cameras and sound equipment, and perform the hundred other tasks that are needed to capture the images and sounds on film—are hired on a freelance, job-by-job basis. Most directors have a certain crew whom they prefer to work with and they try to line them up for a job by putting them on "first hold." Commercial crew members belong to one of two unions——IATSE (International Alliance of Theatrical Stage Employees and Moving Picture Machine Operators of the United States and Canada), the biggest entertainment union, or NABET (National Association of Broadcast Employees and Technicians).

For "Same Card/Coburn" Giraldi got his preferred crew, including Danny Quinn, director of photography, John Fleckenstein, camera operator, Matt Cantrell, gaffer, and Roger Daniel, sound mixer.

GETTING STARTED: WORDS, SETTING, AND MASTER SKETCH

The master sketch of the cabin with Coburn and Wheeler.

Creative team Pat Fanelli and Tony Jaffe worked together on the concept behind "Same Card/Coburn." Together, they came up with the idea of using Coburn (actually, Coburn had appeared in a previous MasterCard spot and it worked out so well they decided to use him again) and they hit on the notion of putting him on an airplane next to a spry and appealing old lady. They worked out the general concept of the old lady taking Cobourn down a peg by boasting about how *she* uses the same credit card that *he* does: "You don't have to be a big cheese to own MasterCard!" Fanelli did the master sketch of the airplane cabin (see illustration)—in this case, there was no need for the customary storyboard (a frame by frame visualization of the basic action of a commercial) since all twenty-five seconds of dialogue would take place in the same setting and same position (the final five seconds of the commercial show the MasterCard logo while voices sing "MasterCard International").

Here is the dialogue Tony Jaffee wrote for the spot:

Old Lady: I got the same card as you, Coburn.
Coburn: Oh . . . that's nice.
Old Lady: Y'don't have to be a big cheese to own MasterCard!
Coburn: I know.
Old Lady: The same card *you* bop around the South of France with, *I* use to buy wool.
Coburn: Wool?!
Old Lady: So you're not as hotsy-totsy as you think, Mr. Tinseltown.
Coburn: May I buy you a drink?
Old Lady: Anytime, Jimbo.

PRELIMINARY ARRANGEMENTS: HIRING JAMES COBURN

When you're dealing with a star of the magnitude of James Coburn, you don't "cast" him—you negotiate. Before any work could go ahead on the spot, Coburn's people had to be approached, arrangements had to be made and firmed up. Angie Montalbano, casting director at Esty, contacted Coburn's agent for his commercial work, Liz Dalling, head of Special Artists in Los Angeles. The fee they settled on was in six figures: an annual guarantee plus an agreement that any residuals earned in the course of a year would be credited against this amount (it's unlikely that the residuals would surpass this rather hefty sum). If the commercial run was extended beyond a year's time, the contract would be renegotiated and another sizable lump paid out to

Coburn. Yes, celebrities are expensive, but then, when James Coburn appears on the TV screen, people sit up and listen. He's got that magic called "star quality," and it doesn't come cheap.

After agreeing on the guarantee, Montalbano and Dalling figured out possible shooting dates, drew up a formal contract, and got Coburn to sign. The production could now start rolling.

BIDDING THE JOB

The first order of business is to line up a director and production company, and the normal way to do this is to send the job out for bids. The producer, writer, and art director decide on three directors they think would be good for the job; in this case, the choices were Giraldi, Steve Horn (one of the tops in his field, Horn was the director featured in Michael Arlen's book *Thirty Seconds*, a wonderful account of all the steps that went into making one thirty-second spot for AT&T's "Reach Out and Touch Someone" campaign), and Gomes Loew Inc. (a partnership between directors George Gomes and Dick Loew). Woody Walters invited the three directors (or their reps) to a bid meeting at Esty; he gave them each a specification sheet on the commercial and a copy of the master sketch, then he went through all of the agency's requirements on the job—shooting dates, set requirements, casting, props, etc.

After the bid meeting, the directors or reps went back to their offices and, over a period of several days, worked with their estimators and producers on bids on the job. This bid, presented to the agency on the standard AICP form, shows a complete breakdown of costs, including shooting crew, who are hired by the production company on a job-by-job basis, props, wardrobe, set, the amount of film to be used, etc.

Giraldi came in with a bid of $124,600, which was the lowest of the three, and he won. Usually the job goes to the lowest bidder, but not always. Walters points out that "Giraldi was our top choice from the start. He has a very good reputation for shooting humor, for shooting celebrities—and he's a top director in the field. We had not worked with him yet, and everybody was eager to find out what he could do for us." Thus, even if Giraldi's bid had not been the lowest, it's possible that the Esty team could have convinced MasterCard to pay extra money for the person they felt would do the finest job.

As it turned out, Esty and MasterCard liked Giraldi so well that he won the bid for the next MasterCard commercial as well, which featured Christie Brinkley and was shot in the New York department store Bergdorf Goodman. James Moore, who at one time was associated with Bob Giraldi Productions, had directed two earlier Master-Card spots featuring Shari Belafonte and Christie Brinkley.

The agency at this time also lined up Bob DeRise of A Cut Above to edit the spot.

PRODUCTION ESTIMATE TO CLIENT

Sample of the Commercial Production Estimate form used by the William Esty agency.

WILLIAM ESTY COMPANY, INC.   **COMMERCIAL PRODUCTION ESTIMATE**

CLIENT: _____ TV ___ RADIO ___ DATE: _____

PRODUCT: _____ YEAR _____ JOB # _____

DESCRIPTION:

NR	PRODUCER'S CONTRACT PRICE *	$	R9	FILM PRINTS/VIDEO TAPES	$	
LP	PRODUCTION — OTHER		SW	DUPES		
RE	EDITORIAL**		A4	PHOTOBOARDS		
N5	TALENT (inc. P&W)		S2	STORAGE		
B4	TALENT EXPENSES			**TOTAL COMMISSIONABLE COSTS**		
A2	CASTING			AGENCY COMMISSION		
PT	SINGERS (inc. P&W)		XO	OUT OF POCKET EXPENSES		
MU	MUSIC		XP	PAYROLL TAXES		
06	MUSICIANS (inc. P&W)		XQ	COMPETITIVE MATERIAL		
QU	CREATIVE FEES		XS	STATE/LOCAL SALES TAXES		
Q8	ARRANGING FEES		X9	SHIPPING		
RV	RECORDING, MIX, TRANSFER		Z4	OTHER:		
B1	VTR TRANSFER					
TX	OTHER:					
OS	ARTWORK/STATS					
				GRAND TOTAL	$	

BIDS: * _____ $ _____ EDITORIAL: ** _____ $ _____

_____ $ _____ WEATHER CONTINGENCY COST PER DAY $ _____

_____ $ _____

Breakdown is attached showing additional information ____ Yes ____ No

COMMENTS:

CLIENT APPROVAL: BY _____ DATE _____   TVC-39 REV.

After Giraldi was settled on, Walters put together a total estimate sheet *(see illustration)* that he submitted to MasterCard. The total estimate includes the $124,600 figure Giraldi came in with, the fee that A Cut Above would charge for editing, talent expenses (which in this case applies mostly to the actress playing the Old Lady, since Coburn's payment is handled separately. She was paid at scale, a set amount that non-celebrities with speaking parts in commercials get. In this case, scale was $330 plus overtime; however, unlike Coburn, the Old Lady is likely to make a good deal in residuals). Though Coburn's fee is not covered in talent expenses, his miscellaneous expenses such as travel arrangements and accommodations (if needed), limo service, dinners, etc., would be.

Since the commercial was to be shot in Los Angeles, casting (except for Coburn) was handled not by the agency but by an L.A. casting service, and this cost gets included in the estimate. Other costs that the client covers include recording, voice-overs, artwork, titles, duplicates for tapes and cassettes. All of these figures are added up to arrive at the total commissionable costs. The agency adds its commission and then any noncommissionable expenses such as the cost of flying the agency producer and writer to the West Coast and payroll taxes. When all of these were tallied up, it came to a grand total of $167,859: MasterCard must pay this amount of money (plus the six-figure guarantee to Coburn, handled separately) to get James Coburn and a yet-to-be-decided-on Old Lady to chat about their MasterCards on film for thirty seconds.

Before any money changed hands, the client had to approve the estimate. It was the responsibility of Len Faupel, the management supervisor on the job, to present the numbers to MasterCard and to go over any changes they may want. On January 3, 1985, the MasterCard people signed on the bottom line and the preproduction arrangements could now begin, to culminate in a shoot date scheduled for January 22.

CASTING AND LOCATION

After the choice of director, the cast and location used for a commercial are probably the two most important elements for its success—and sometimes the most difficult to get right. Luckily for everyone involved, the casting and location for "Same Card/Coburn" was pretty much of a snap as commercials go. One thing that made it easy was the relative simplicity of the commercial: only one setting was needed, the inside of an airplane cabin; and only one part had to be cast—the Old Lady, since Coburn was obviously the given. There were other actors slated to appear on the set—stewardesses, other passengers—but none of them had speaking roles and thus all were hired as extras at the time of the shoot.

The Giraldi people were responsible for scouting the location, and they got in touch with a company called Airline Film & TV Promotions, located in the Los Angeles area. This company has complete mock-ups of the interiors of various types of airplanes, from executive jets to 747s, as well as airport corridors, lounges, and check-in counters. Their 747 cabin interior was ideal for this commercial and made building a set unnecessary. That took care of the location.

The casting was also arranged on the West Coast since that's where the commercial would be shot. Walters contacted a California casting operation called Baker/Nesbitt and gave them the specs on the Old Lady: she must be sweet but feisty, grandmotherly but hip enough to banter with James Coburn and let him buy her a drink. The casting company sent back a reel of forty or so women whom they interviewed for the job; each Old Lady said her lines into a video camera, and then all of the auditions were assembled on a single reel. Back in New York, Walters, Fanelli, Jaffe, and Giraldi screened the reel and picked out three or four women who looked like the best. Eventually, veteran movie and commercial actress Margaret Wheeler was selected as the agency's top choice: she would be recommended to the client at the preproduction meeting, along with two back-ups in case MasterCard didn't go for Wheeler.

THE PREPRODUCTION MEETING

At the preproduction meeting, in this case held on January 11, the agency and production company go over all the major production decisions with the client, iron out any problems, and make sure all parties are in agreement so that production can begin. Held at the MasterCard midtown Manhattan office, the meeting was attended by all the major contributors to the commercial: Jaffe, Fanelli, and Walters represented the Esty creative team; Len Faupel, Jim Stewart, account supervisor, and Eileen Wynn, account executive, were the account managers involved; Barbara Bromberg held up the client side; and, though Giraldi himself couldn't attend since he was shooting another commercial on the Coast, he sent his producer, Barbara Michaelson, and Aud

Howard, his stylist, who would be discussing wardrobe.

The meeting went smoothly. Since there were three excellent choices for the Old Lady, the only problem was deciding on the best, not settling for a compromise, as so often happens. The participants batted around the relative merits of each and, rather unusually, Russell Hogg, chairman of MasterCard International, came into the meeting and took part in the decision to give the role to Margaret Wheeler. (As we'll see, he was especially pleased with Wheeler's performance when he saw the rough cut).

Usually the agency shows the client a set sketch at the preproduction meeting, but in this case Walters passed around the brochure from Airline Film & TV Promotions to show what their cabin mock-ups would look like. Bromberg thought it was fine, the meeting ended with all parties in accord, and the agency and production house were ready to make their final arrangements, which meant booking flights to L.A., booking the crew, and getting all schedules set.

FINAL PREPARATION FOR THE SHOOT

On Thursday, January 17, Walters and Jaffe flew out to Los Angeles and checked into the Westwood Marquis hotel. With the shoot scheduled for Tuesday, January 22, this gave them a few days to get everything set. Though it's the responsibility of the production company to hire the extras, Walters and Jaffe wanted to check them over. They also wanted to go out to the set and make sure it looked okay.

On Friday afternoon, Walters, Todd Allan, Giraldi's West Coast producer, and Betsy Jones, Giraldi's West Coast stylist, went over to James Coburn's home in Sherman Oaks to run through the commercial with him and to discuss wardrobe. "Coburn was very accommodating," Walters said, "and I enjoyed working with him a lot." The meeting went very well, the stylist came up with a few different blazers for Coburn to wear, and Coburn, charming and relaxed in his own home, even told a few war stories.

On Monday, January 21, Giraldi, Walters, and Jaffe held a final meeting with Coburn to decide about his wardrobe and to settle other production details, such as the props for the stewardesses. Walters and Jaffe went over the copy with Giraldi once again, and Giraldi discussed the shots and angles he was planning. No problems arose on any side, and everybody felt ready for the shoot the next day.

THE SHOOT

Commercial shoots usually begin quite early and run quite late. Overtime is the rule rather than the exception. There's always a certain amount of tension and more confusion than anyone feels comfortable with. "Organized chaos" is the way Walters describes it. Even large studios quickly become jammed with cameras, recording equipment, and bodies either working the equipment, being filmed by it, or standing around monitors watching what's being filmed. And then there's the food—invariably a big spread supplied by the production company, and a crucial component of any commercial shoot. To the uninitiated, much of this whole process can look like a waste of time: at any given moment, any given individual from director to extra may be slouching back on his or her heels, waiting, waiting, waiting (or picking at the buffet) while some piece of equipment is made to function properly, or someone has the dirt removed from his nails, or some piece of the set is moved or removed, or until the camera is positioned at the right angle, or until the take looks *just right*. The repetition can be numbing. The hours seem alternately to fly and to creep by. Even something as seemingly simple as shooting a tube of toothpaste lying motionless on a backdrop can take hours, and when children and animals are involved, despair can set in. But somehow, at some point, the dog wags, the child smiles, the cat arches just when and how they're all supposed to—the interested parties know that they've got what they want on film and, to the relief of all participants, it's a wrap. This is the agony and the ecstasy of a commercial shoot.

For "Same Card/Coburn," the crew showed up at Airline Film & TV Promotions at 7:00 A.M. on January 22, Coburn and Wheeler were due at 7:30, and the agency people at 8:00. Joining Walters and Jaffe were Len Faupel, the Esty management supervisor, and Barbara Bromberg from MasterCard. There was the usual hustle and bustle as crew members prepared the 747 cabin mock-up for filming, got the lights and camera in place, and hooked up the monitors so the agency and client people could see what was being filmed.

The extras were assembled, the actors went into makeup, and Giraldi was ready to start shooting at about 9:00. The extraordinary thing about this shoot was that by 11:15 A.M. it was a wrap. "Outrageously fast" is how Walters described it. "It was over almost before we started. Normally you do an eight-hour day and then you go into overtime." Two and a quarter hours of actual photography is almost unheard of. What happened? How did Giraldi do it so fast? Walters explains: "First of all, there was only one setup—it was two people sitting in a seat—so the nature of the photography was fairly simple as commercials go. Also, the two actors were *very* professional and they fed off each other. The better one got, the better the other got. Within half an hour of takes they were really doing *exactly* what we wanted them to do. The third factor is Bob Giraldi himself—he's very fast. He knows what he wants, he knows what the agency wants, and he gives it to you. Giraldi made several shots at different angles; he made a master shot where they do the dialogue all the way through, both people; he did a single on her all the way through; he did a single on Coburn all the way through so the editor could cut from one to the other. At 11:15, when he turned to us and said, 'It's a wrap, unless there's anything you two guys [Jaffe and I] want to shoot,' we were dumbfounded, but we had everything we wanted. I think in all we had forty takes."

Giraldi also did the next MasterCard commercial, which featured Christie Brinkley, and he polished that one off in four hours. "He's good, there's no question about it," Walters sums up. "Though you don't get a lot of his time, he is very intense in the time he is involved." Clearly, there's a reason why Bob Giraldi is "king" of commercials, as one crew member put it: he delivers everything he promises and lives up to his reputation.

Though the Esty and MasterCard people now had what they wanted on film, the commercial was still by no means finished. Before leaving the Coast, they all took a look at the dailies (the processed film that comes back from the lab), which were ready Wednesday afternoon. Satisfied with what they saw, Walters and Jaffe were ready to fly back to New York on Thursday morning, January 24. They'd been in California nearly a week to prepare for and review the results of two hours of shooting, and they'd spend a good part of another week winnowing and refining this film down to thirty seconds of commercial.

EDITING

Editor Bob DeRise got the film as soon as it came back from California, and by Monday, January 28, he had put together the "first cut." DeRise describes the process like this: "What happens is I get the dailies—the footage the director shot the previous day on location. Normally, the producer, art director, and writer come down here and look at it on the moviola, and we start selecting what we like best. They shoot ten scenes, say, and we select maybe one or two takes from each scene. Then they leave me alone and I make the first cut. They come down the day after and screen the first cut. Most of the time they have their own ideas and want to see it their way, so we go back and forth." In this case, DeRise went over the two hours of film that Giraldi had shot and pulled the best takes from that to make a rough form of the commercial—rough because there is still no music or effects or titles, and the density and color will have to be altered somewhat. But it is the basic commercial in the proper sequence with Coburn and Wheeler enacting the scenario devised by Fanelli and Jaffe. In addition, DeRise added on the final seconds of the commercial, an animated segment showing the MasterCard logo that had been prepared two years before by Sam Alexander of Zepplin Productions. The MasterCard theme music was created by Tony Jaffe working with Joey Levine, one of the top jingle writers and composers in the business. It too had been scored and recorded for previous commercials, so there was no new creative work or editing needed.

Despite the simplicity of the basic situation of "Same Card/Coburn," DeRise, Jaffe, and Walters spent the better part of two weeks fiddling with it. DeRise comments: "Walters and Jaffe came here *a lot*. I cut a lot of versions of it—I think it went through six or seven. This was the first MasterCard spot with on-camera sync dialogue, which is very hard to put together, especially if it is a comedy situation. It was the two actors sitting on a plane, and there were only four angles—there was a two-shot, where you see Coburn and Wheeler, there was a shot on her, there was a shot on him, and then there was an over-the-shoulder shot. Working with these four angles wasn't difficult, but they kept on changing it, trying different ways. Ultimately, the 'feeling' of it, the speed, is up to me."

AGENCY REVIEW AND CLIENT APPROVAL

Finally, on February 7, the Esty people and Bob DeRise agreed on a cut of "Same Card/Coburn," and DeRise put the commercial on cassette. Now Walters was ready to screen the spot for the creative and account people involved with MasterCard, as well as for Chuck Cilo (Esty executive vice president and chief creative director) and Gor-

MASTERCARD INTERNATIONAL

"SAME CARD / COBURN"

COMM'L. NO.: IAMC 5243

OLD LADY: I got the same card as you, Coburn.

JAMES COBURN: Huhhh? Oh. . .that's nice.

OLD LADY: Y'don't have to be a big cheese to own Mastercard!

COBURN: I know.

OLD LADY: The same card you bop around the South of France with, I use to buy wool.

COBURN: Wool.

OLD LADY: So you're not as hotsy-totsy as you think, Mr. Tinseltown,

COBURN: May I buy you

a drink?

OLD LADY: Any time, Jimbo.

SINGERS: MASTERCARD

INTERNATIONAL.

The finished spot.

don Bushell (Esty chairman of the board and chief executive officer), who attended because this was a fairly important spot for a very important client. Cilo, Bushell, and the others chose the version they liked best and requested some minor changes, which were promptly carried out. By the next day, Friday, the Esty team was ready to screen "Same Card/Coburn" for the MasterCard people. Chairman Russell Hogg and other MasterCard top brass attended the screening, and naturally there was some tension in the air. "Client approval" is as precious to agency people as rave reviews to the actors and producers of a Broadway show: weeks worth of work rides on a thumbs up or thumbs down from a few key people; money, egos, time, and people's futures are all at stake. Walters ran the commercial through, and when Margaret Wheeler delivered her final line, "Anytime, Jimbo, " Chairman Hogg looked pleased. It was the perfect line for the spot to end on: the timing was just right; it was both funny and unexpected; only the world's biggest sourpuss could fail to smile. And since this zinger of a line came at the commercial's end, it meant viewers would be wearing smiles when the MasterCard logo flashed on the screen. In short, Chairman Hogg and the MasterCard people loved it and they asked for no changes. "Same Card/Coburn" was exactly what they wanted. Client approval granted.

REFINING THE PRINT

Now that the agency and client had agreed on which version of the commercial to use, Bob DeRise would refine it into what is known as an "optical negative." This results from rephotographing the original camera negative of the selected scenes to incorporate such optical effects as dissolves, fades, titles, and other artwork as well as the correct colors. After that is done, DeRise goes to a tape session to put the spot on one-inch tape, required by all the networks now. Once again, each scene has to be color corrected.

And that's it. "Same Card/Coburn" was now finished, ready to go to the agency traffic people, to be reproduced and then distributed to the various television stations and networks around the country, inserted into its appropriate spot in the various programs it would run with, and appear on the screens of all those millions of Americans who where about to discover that they could use the same credit card as James Coburn . . . MasterCard!

Peter Cooper
Commercial Director

 There is an aura of the heroic that surrounds the occupation of film director. One thinks of Cecil B. De Mille moving armies of extras. Or John Ford making cowboys into myths. Or Woody Allen dreaming up newer and newer forms of urban angst. Commercial film directors are heroes in a different arena, but heroic nonetheless. Though their epics last only sixty or thirty seconds (or, more and more frequently, fifteen seconds), they regularly play before audiences in the millions. Vast sums of money pass through the hands of commercial directors in producing these minifilms, and exceedingly impressive amounts of it remain in their hands as their reward. They are the ones who hold the real power of translating the stick figures on an art director's storyboard into moving, living, filmed action.

Peter Cooper is one of these heroes. He is a big man in every way—tall, expansive in speech and gesture, generous with his time and with himself on the set, large in his knowledge of both the emotional and technical aspects of his trade. Cooper is a "film person"—it's a medium that comes naturally to him and he's been at it a long time. He started at the very bottom of the field—driving a truck for a film company—and through many, many years and many jobs, but mostly through his instinct, his talent, and his endurance, he rose to his current position of solid success. The scores of commercials he has directed include spots for Sears Financial Network with Hal Holbrook, spots for Jell-O (one of which featured Louise Lasser), for American Bell, for Oreo cookies with Dinah Shore and Alex Karas, Post cereal, Kool-Aid, Purina, Crest toothpaste. Cooper has his own production company, Cooper & Co. with offices in a wonderful loft in Manhattan's Flatiron District and a West Coast office in Los Angeles; he has a small but dedicated staff of a producer, a person who does estimates of production costs as well as research and coordinating, a receptionist, and a bookkeeper. And, as the icing on the cake, Cooper has recently realized every commercial director's dream: he directed a feature film (the forthcoming "Ordinary Heroes," a remake of the 1940s film "Pride of the Marines" starring John Garfield).

The story of how Cooper got from truck driver to director, while curious, may not be terribly illuminating for aspiring commercial directors. The moral of Cooper's story—as of so many of his colleagues'—might be: directors are born, not made. It's not the kind of job you can decide you want and work your way up to. Rather, if you've got what it takes and you know it and you can convince others of it *and* you're lucky—then things might happen for you. Cooper had all of these things going for him, and one more besides: he got in when the business was still young, hence more fluid and less competitive. After driving the truck, Cooper (who never attended college) worked for a while as an editorial apprentice, then assistant film editor and a stint as an animation cameraman. He seemed to have a feel for filmmaking from the very start. At the age of nineteen he went up to the Gaspe region of Canada with some friends and made a film about the people there, a documentary which he edited himself. "It was twenty-four minutes long and very, very boring," he recalls, "but I learned a great deal." He ran an animation studio for a commercial production company and he also wrote commercials. This turned out to be one of the springboards that got him into directing. As Cooper tells it, "I wrote these witty commercials, which the client loved, and they would send them out to a television director and they'd come back dull and lifeless. So finally I said I wanted to direct them myself. It was a time in the business when a director did not have to show a sample reel. It was enough for my boss to go in to his client and say, 'Here is Peter Cooper and he's your director' and they bought me. It was a little bit like learning how to swim by being shoved off the end of a pier." Cooper stayed up all night before the day of the shoot, figuring out what he was going to do on the set—but when the moment came and he hit the open water under the pier, he swam wonderfully. Cooper himself might have been going through agonies over the job, but it was clear to professionals who saw the footage that he had a career as a director in front of him. "Actually," says Cooper now, "it never occurred to me that it would get less painful."

He next did a stint as head of the radio and TV department of a good-sized ad agency. "That was enormously valuable because I learned there that I was not in the motion picture business, but that I was in the advertising business." Two years later he went back to directing and he's been at it ever since. In 1966–67 he started up his own production company, then called Peter H. Cooper, Inc. The company has had a number of twists and turns, different names, different partners, but the one constant has been Peter Cooper himself. Success has not blunted Cooper's inherent modesty. Looking back on his progress, he comments: "I thought I was a truck driver who had somehow fallen into this good thing."

Though it's difficult to pigeon-hole work as varied as his, one thread that seems to run through Cooper's commercials is their human warmth. "I'm very good with actors," he says of his work, "and I get the kinds of performances out of actors that make people praise my casting. Mostly what I get to do are *people* commercials, dialogue commercials, and humor. For me, the juiciest part of the job is getting performances out of actors. I also get a lot of pleasure out of framing pictures that are interesting compositionally." It's easy to see how these elements would suit him perfectly for working on the larger canvas of feature films.

In Chapter Six, we took a close look at the making of a "typical" thirty-second spot from the agency's point of view. Cooper shows us the process from the *director's* point of view: "A storyboard is sent to my producer, who shows it to me. Since she knows my style and pace of work, she can tell as well as—and in some cases better than—I can how long it will take me to shoot. She'll look at it and say, 'This is two days, this is one day, etc.' We'll talk about sets versus location, though very often that comes from the agency. My producer does an estimate and this goes to the agency producer and then the agency makes a recommendation to their client.

"Once the job is awarded, then meetings get set up—usually a preliminary meeting with the agency producer, writer, and art director in which I get all the history of the work—and we start setting up the rest of the process, which is casting, location scouting or set designing, wardrobe. We plan for a full-dress meeting with their client. If the agency has its own casting facility, they'll hold casting sessions and put people on videotape, then I get to look at the tape, along with the people from the agency, and we'll call back those we like the best. I run the callback session in which we all make a decision jointly about who is going to do what parts. I hire a set designer to do set sketches or locations are found by location scouts that I hire. In that case the agency and I will go to look at a location, and occasionally the client goes along too. There are a certain number of obligatory meetings even before the preproduction meeting. These meetings are such an important part of the business: a lot of battles are lost and won, a lot of impressions are made in those meetings."

The director's role at the actual shoot is, of course, all-important. Cooper offered this broadstrokes description of how he works: "The director sets the tone—for the crew, for the actors, and for the relationship between the clients and the job they have come to participate in. The director's function is to create an atmosphere in which everybody feels free—and in fact encouraged—to do the best that they possibly can with their skills and talents. Including the agency. It is counterproductive to have the agency fighting amongst themselves, fighting with the director or with actors. I think it's important to have everyone agree on a unified goal, though our perceptions might be different about *how* to achieve it, or *when* it's been achieved.

"More specifically, I set the camera. I talk to the actors—pretty much no one else talks to actors. The client watches what is being filmed on a monitor. When I get performances I think are really going somewhere, I will excuse myself for a moment and go to talk to the client about what they feel. Sometimes we just know that we have it. The only time friction arises is when I feel someone from the agency is wrong and being rigid about it.

"In terms of the crew, though it's a free-lance business, it's rare that I get someone whom I've not met before. I do such a large volume of work that I usually work with people I know and with whom I have ongoing relationships.

"How long a shoot takes—and how long a day I work—varies enormously. I have days that start at 8:30 and end at 3:30 and then there are twelve- to fourteen-hour days. Some are one day shoots, six or seven days is probably the maximum. The more successful a director becomes, the less time he has between shoots. There's the greed factor. I may be shooting the day after, so there really isn't much time for me to get involved in the editing."

As one might expect, the job of directing commercials can involve tremendous pressures, though Cooper said that he feels the most pressure not from too much work but from too little: "When there's a lull in business I begin to feel like I have enormous holes in my pockets. The lulls still happen. I think it's only me, but when I go asking people I find it's been happening to others as well."

When the work comes in, however, as it has been for Cooper (with those brief lulls) for twenty-some-odd years, the money is very, very good. "It's one reason that so many agency people want to be directors: there is an inordinate amount of money to be made in directing commercials. The highest paid creative person at an agency doesn't make anywhere near what commercial directors make. A successful director makes from $500,000 a year and up. Of course," he adds with a smile, "we're all experts at spending it."

There's the money. There's the power, the power of being the person with the ultimate responsibility to take vast sums of the clients' money (Cooper estimates a day's shooting costs around $65,000) and transform it into winning, selling film. There's the success element of having risen very high in an intensely difficult field. And yet even with all this, Peter Cooper retains a kind of innocence and wonder about what he does: "I don't jade," is how he put it. "I carry around a sense of awe, so that I'm always intrigued by meeting stars and fascinated by working on big Hollywood sound stages and working with sports heroes. I've been doing it for so many years now, but I never tire of it. None of it becomes commonplace."

The story of how Peter Cooper went from driving a truck to directing big-budget commercials for major clients almost sounds like an old-fashioned Hollywood movie. Unfortunately, it doesn't usually work that way anymore. "My route is closed," Cooper told me. "People who want to get into commercial directing today would probably do best to establish themselves on the agency side first. It's very hard to become a director today unless you have a sample reel and a certain chic. Some people start as freelance production assistants and scrounge a living that way for two to three years. From that you would become a coordinator for whom others work, but that's also very hard, and it still doesn't lead to directing. Some cameramen are making the leap into directing. But really, there's no set route. Wanting it badly enough is a big part of it."

MEDIA:

AS CRUCIAL

AS THE MESSAGE

No matter how great the copy lines, the visuals, or the campaign concept, if the ad or commercial runs in the wrong medium it's just not going to work. Anyone can tell you that beer ads will have greater impact if shown on televised sports events than during soap operas. But let's say you're advertising blue jeans, milk, *Business Week* magazine, root beer, Jaguar cars, vacations in Ireland. Do you want thirty-second network spots during prime time? color spreads in Sunday magazines? billboards? radio? In which markets should you run the ads? How often? How do you get the best discount rates from the networks? What about local programming and cable? Getting the answers to these questions is part of the job of agency media people.

Back in the days when the media were newspapers, illustrated magazines, billboards, placards, and handbills, there really wasn't much need for media specialists. But today, with ever more specialized cable networks, syndicated programming opportunities, satellite broadcasting, and a growing number of special interest magazines joining the already existing broadcast, print, and outdoor media—it's another story entirely. Advertisers are beginning to recognize that knowing and using the media effectively (which means creatively and flexibly) can make all the difference in the success of a campaign. And as a result, the media function has become an increasingly crucial part of the advertising process. Media, in short, has come in from the cold.

"Media used to be thought of as a 'green eyeshade' kind of function," one associate media director told me. "The image was people sitting there crunching numbers. But that's no longer true, as the large agencies, the account people, and the creatives realize more and more that they have to get media people involved early on. As the media become more complex, media people are going to be more necessary." Mike Hedge, associate media director at BBDO in New York, entirely agrees: "Since I've been in media, it's become so much more important within an agency. When I started [in

Mike Hedge, vice president associate media director, BBDO/New York: "Media is definitely a career path to upper level management."

1976], there were very few top executives in an agency who came up through media; but now almost all major agencies have an executive vice president or representative on the board of directors with a media background. It's definitely a career path to upper-level management."

As media people become more necessary and more important, media opportunities are going to expand. Those who really understand the media are going to play a bigger and bigger role in planning advertising and running ad agencies. Media is on a roll—and now might be just the time to jump on board.

What is the media function at an advertising agency all about? Joel Kushins, senior vice president and media director at Bozell & Jacobs in New York, answered this way: "A media person, as best he or she can, gets to understand the character of a medium—what its product is, who it appeals to, where it's distributed, how well it's accepted, and finally what its pricing is. Once you've gone about doing that for a particular medium, you then want to get to know all of its competitors. And then you want to classify them in codifications that will be acceptable to your particular needs and your clients' needs. Then you take that pile and put it on the left side of the desk. On the right side of the desk you pick on everything that your marketing and account teams have culled together from working with the client on who it is they're looking to reach: when? where? how? and essentially with what selling proposition? Then you put that in the center of the desk. Then you go off and meet with the creatives, and if you do it well, you get a sense of what they're thinking and they get a sense of what you're thinking, and through some collective bargaining that goes on, you pull it all together."

The first function Kushins describes—understanding and classifying media—remains the most fundamental responsibility of media staff people. At nearly all agencies, this responsibility is divided between the two main media groups: planners and buyers. In the most general terms, media planners take the client's budget and their advertising objectives and translate them into a highly detailed schedule of dates, times, regions, and frequencies in which the advertising will appear in the various media—print, broadcast and out-of-home (which includes billboards, bus shelters, subway posters, and sky-writing). The media buyers implement these plans, bargaining with the sales forces of networks, radio stations, and magazines for the best possible discounts on time and the most advantageous space, keeping abreast of which publications or which shows would suit the advertising best, playing the media market shrewdly. Both planners and buyers rely heavily on media research, and as part of their basic training they learn how to use secondary source material. At some agencies, there are a few people who specialize in media research.

Planning and buying attract very different sorts of people at the entry level. Joyce Fritz, associate media director at the Bloom Agency in Dallas, puts it this way: "If you love wheeling and dealing and if there's no greater high for you than negotiating, then go into buying. Planning is more theoretical. Buying and planning require different skills, but one is not necessarily better. Ultimately, whatever side you start on, you must understand both if you're going to advance."

This is the consensus: given the growing role of media people in agency planning and key decision-making, the leaders are more and more going to be those with expertise in both planning and buying. Mike Hedge points out that at BBDO "we're trying to get people to cross over and learn the other discipline, because we feel that in the future the leaders of the media departments will be the generalists who understand both sides." And Mal Gordon, senior vice president and director of media and marketing services at the mid-sized (and fast growing) Chicago agency Grant/Jacoby, says he takes his new people through all the media areas—first print and broadcast buying and then planning.

That's not to say there won't be room for the specialists—people like John Mattimore, a vice president and network supervisor at McCann-Erickson, who has chosen to stay in the buying area because its exactness and its pace appeal to him—and because he's good at it. But even Mattimore admits that some opportunities may have been closed to him because of his preference to remain specialized. The management track belongs to the generalists with the broadest backgrounds: people who know not only planning and buying, but who are familiar with the ins and outs of advertising many different products in all the media.

Which is more prestigious, and which will get you to the top faster? Planners would say planning and buyers would say buying. So where you start is perhaps most a matter of temperament and circumstance. Some feel that planning gives you the wider focus, more contact with other departments in the agency and with the client. "You really get to see what's going on with the product," one associate media director said. And another felt that it would be easier for a planning person to learn buying than a buying person to learn planning. However, a top network buyer can command top dollar in media departments. Client are beginning to appreciate just how crucial this function is and how much money a first-rate buyer can save them; and what clients appreciate, the agencies reward.

One talent all media people need to have is a facility with numbers. Whether you're in planning or buying to start with, you'll be dealing with numbers routinely as part of your job, so you have to be comfortable with them. It needn't mean majoring in math or being a statistical whiz kid; but, as Joel Kushins phrased it, "You must have a creative feel for numbers. It's an intuitive facility for blending numbers together to make them jump off a page."

Let's take a look in more detail at the key functions within the media department.

MEDIA PLANNING

The core responsibility of the media planner is to research, create, document, analyze, explain, present, and revise the media plan Here's a highly simplified model of how it works: The media and account groups meet with the client at a preplanning meeting to discuss in basic terms what they're trying to do with the brand—who they're trying to reach, when and where it would be best to reach them, who the competition is, and how best to win market share away from them. The client will also set a media budget. Then you go to work. After the client meeting, there will probably be an internal media department meeting with assistant planners, planners, supervisors, and associate media director (see below for descriptions of each of these jobs) to hash out ideas, objectives, and strategies. This "idea session" may last an entire day. Then comes research: for television, planners will consult Nielsen and Arbitron, the two major services; for magazines, there are syndicated research materials such as Simmons and MRI. With these tools you can get a good picture of who is using the product, how often they use it, what magazines they read, how often, etc. You draw on all this material in putting together the media plan.

DIET SOFT-DRINK
1985 MEDIA FLOW CHART   11/19/84

1985

(WEEK BEGINNING MONDAY)	$(000)
PRIME NETWORK TV	6,558.4
DAY NETWORK TV	2,263.6
EARLY FRINGE SPOT TV — TOP 10 DMA's; 31.1% U.S. TV HH's	1,603.2
SPOT RADIO (:60's) — 15 MARKETS; 33.5% U.S. TV HH's (see attached list for markets)	760.0
MAGAZINES - P4CB	
COSMOPOLITAN	132.6
GLAMOUR	122.1
MADEMOISELLE	80.4
SELF	77.5
WORKING WOMAN	53.1
	$11,650.9

KEY: W18-34 GRP's/wk / # WEEKS

Mock-up of sample media flow chart for imaginary diet soft drink.

The plan itself is a flow chart (see illustration): it lays out the times that the ads will run, what media vehicles will be used and, for television, at what weight levels. Nancy Schneider, vice president and associate media director with HBM/Creamer New York whose accounts include A&W Root Beer, Sweet 'n Low Sugar Substitute, Palm Beach and Evan Picone fashions, and San Giorgio pasta, explains the process of devising a plan this way:

"In television, we don't buy number of spots, we buy GRPs or gross rating points. A GRP is a percent of a target audience. For example, our product is pasta and our target audience is women eighteen to forty-nine. We may plan seventy-five GRPs in one week, which means we will reach 75% of women eighteen to forty-nine in that week. Now, it does not mean we will reach all of them at one time. Because of viewing

Nancy Schneider, vice president associate media director, HBM/Creamer, New York.

habits, you may be reaching only 25% of the target audience with each of them begin exposed an average of three times.

"There are curves we refer to to figure out duplication of viewing between dayparts and/or media. For example, if you think you'll reach 20% on "Dynasty" and 20% on Johnny Carson, you don't have 40% because some women watch both. You have to figure for the overlap. The same is true for magazines.

"For us, the end tool is the percent of unduplicated reach. That will give us our reach and also the average frequency, which is the average number of times each person will be exposed to the ad. We know what percent of our target audience we want to reach at a certain time, and we will try to work backwards to see what combination of dayparts and/or media will accommodate that *within our budget*. There is always that budget limitation.

"Often we will recommend one media plan and have two or three others that would be good alternatives, all based on the same marketing strategy. First you take the recommendations to the account person, and then, if he or she agrees, you present it to the client. Sometimes you really are selling your ideas."

Media plans have become more complicated as the media, and particularly television, grow ever more specialized. Cable and syndicated programming (shows like "Entertainment Tonight" and "Solid Gold" that local stations around the country buy on an individual basis from syndicators and that will appear in different markets at different times) are two particularly fast-growing areas in television. These changes, Mike Hedge feels, "make the planner's job a lot more challenging, but they can also provide a lot more opportunities." Market segments can be pinpointed a lot more precisely through cable or certain syndicated shows, but it's tricky. Media planning is becoming more and more of an art requiring flexibility, imagination, and intuition.

For the purposes of media planning and buying, television is divided into two types: network and spot. The networks—ABC, CBS, and NBC—are nationwide: when you buy network airtime, your commercial will run across the country on the same night in the same time slot. With spot TV, you're going into individual markets and buying airtime from the local stations for local airing. If, for example, your client is an airline and you're planning commercials for winter getaway vacations to sunny climates, you'd probably want to concentrate on cold northern markets (New York, Chicago, Boston) so you'd buy spot. On the other hand, if you're advertising a nationally distributed cola drink in July, when it's hot everywhere, chances are you'd go network. The media plan will show on a week-by-week basis the GRPs you want to get in spot TV and network TV. When you look at an actual media plan, you'll see how the advertising falls into patterns; given the parameters of budget, reach, and frequency, the planner may, for example, come up with a plan in which the commercials appear at two week intervals—two weeks on, two weeks off. These patterns are called "flighting patterns"; the specific period of time is called a "flight."

Planners will make up separate plans for all the different media: radio (spot and network), print (trade and consumer), out-of-home, etc. In most cases, though, for any given product, it's common to use one or two media at most. McDonald's, for example, is one of the heaviest broadcast advertisers, but you just don't see a lot of McDonald's ads in *Time*, *Newsweek*, or even *Family Circle*.

When it's presented to the account people and the client, the media plan is surrounded by lots of backup material: explanations of why the plan was designed the way it was; analyses of goals and strategies, including the rationale for media selections; summaries of key features of the plan; comparison of previous plans or alternative plans; charts showing reach and frequency. For a major plan, the whole report may be quite a fat booklet.

Preparing the plan and writing up the backup material is only part of the planning function. Even after a media plan is approved, it must be frequently updated if it is not to be implemented at once. The media, and especially broadcast, change quickly and media planners have to stay on top of these changes and how they might affect the client's advertising. "It never leaves my desk," says Nancy Schneider. "There are always changes, revisions, updates, evaluations. Even after the approved plan is given to the buyers, I will have to make sure that they have bought all the markets and that everything is fairly smooth. With broadcast, there is also what we call a post-analysis. An evaluation is done to see what you really did get in terms of planned weight (GRPs).

In spot TV you do this on a market-by-market basis, and then you present it to the client, showing him what he paid for and what he actually received."

So media planning is not a matter of making up a plan and then forgetting all about it; it's an ongoing process that requires scrupulous attention to details and following through.

MEDIA BUYING

Media buying requires equal precision in details and thoroughness in following through. While the buyer does have some input in the planning stage because he or she provides the planner with the basic costs, the real work in this job takes off once the plan is approved. John Mattimore, of McCann-Erickson, explained to me how the buying function works at his agency. McCann, a huge agency, divides broadcast buying into network and spot; so Mattimore, on the network side, deals with the three networks along with cable and syndication, while an entirely separate department handles the spot buying. Television is broken down into segments called dayparts: daytime, when the soap operas and game shows dominate the air; early fringe, from 4:30 to 7:30 in New York; then the period when the news programs run; then prime time, that crucial stretch from 8 to 11 P.M. when Americans are most plugged into their televisions and television is plugging the most important products; then late news and finally late fringe. At some large agencies, buyers are divided by daypart: one person will buy fringe for all the clients, another daytime, another prime time, etc. At McCann, however, a network buyer like Mattimore deals with all dayparts and all networks, but he only handles four or so clients.

Once the media plan has been approved, Mattimore takes a look at all of the individual brand requirements, puts them together, and comes up with a total client need: the buys are made by client not by brand. Then he figures out which type of buy he should make—upfront, scatter, or opportunistic. "Upfront," Mattimore explains, "is the long-term commitment. The buys are usually made in the spring and summer for the fall and through the next year. You're not buying individual shows, but a package by account that the networks put together. You give them your preferences in programming, flighting, efficiency, and they put the package together. Upfront is bigger in dollar commitments and it gives you a large mix of programs. The benefits of it are that you get audience guarantees, you have your preferred flighting because the networks still have the avails [unit of time for commercials available for purchase], you have options for cancellation in second and third quarter if you want to get out, and you just have a better relationship with the networks."

But there are some drawbacks for upfront buying. Since the buys are made so far in advance, you can never be sure what the brands will be doing by the time the airdate comes up. A brand in test market may have been canceled, and you're stuck with fourth quarter inventory. Or there may be pockets in a given quarter when you might be able to get a better price than upfront. With a scatter buy you avoid these problems, because you're buying short-term: if you want second quarter time, you'll buy it right at the start of the second quarter. The media marketplace has a lot in common with the stock market: prices go up and down depending on market conditions, supply and demand, time of year, ratings. A smart buyer stays on top of the market and makes predictions as far as a year ahead. His decison to buy upfront or scatter will depend on his reading of market conditions.

An opportunistic buy takes place the day or week of the show. "Opportunistic," Mattimore points out, "is the cheapest way you can possibly buy. You get your best prices, but there might not be inventory available or you might be buying less than desirable programming." When would you want to buy in this way? "Let's say there's a new campaign that your clients want to break in a big way. Even though they have their long-term buys, they'll say, 'Let's heavy up in these two weeks and really make the needle move.' In an opportunistic situation, you usually take everything that's out there if you have a big budget and there are only minimal avails. You just try to beat the networks down as low as you can."

The actual negotiating requires both shrewdness and a close working relationship with the network salespeople. Mattimore disclosed one fairly common tactic:

"Let's say the approved specs for the year give us $20 million for prime time and we want to spend 90% of that upfront. So you're talking $18 million for an upfront buy. What you want to do is to get the networks to bid against each other. The easiest and most frequently used way is to split your budget in half and make the three networks compete against each other, knowing that one is going to get shut out. You tell them what your demographic [audience composition broken down by age, sex, income, occupation, etc.] is going to be and you also have programming preferences. For example, one of my clients likes what they call 'silk-blouse programming'—'Dynasty,'

'Dallas,' 'Knots Landing,' the fantasy/glamour world—and they will pay a premium for that. So you give all that information to the networks and they submit a plan to you that has shows, dates, and times. The networks have account executives, who are sales-people by daypart, and they also have planners who produce plans for the salesmen to present to the agencies.

"We get the plan, and if it's major, we'll run it through our computer. Then we go back to the networks and discuss with them what it would take to go lower—whether it's moving a flight by a week or throwing out a very popular show with a high premium. Then you ask for a second submission, possibly a third and fourth until everything is lined up the way you want it and you feel that you've gotten the best efficiencies [a measurement of advertising effectiveness based on the cost in advertising dollars to reach 1,000 viewers]."

Then Mattimore will really start to play the networks off each other. He might go to NBC and tell them that CBS and ABC have perfect programming for his client, so if they want a piece of the business they're going to have to be cheaper by X. Finally he gives each network a last shot, and then makes a recommendation to the client.

Once a buy is made, however, the easy part of Mattimore's job is over. Now he has to allocate the package by brand, making sure each brand gets its requirement, that it's on budget and has its proper flight. He works with the account group to figure out which commercial goes in which spot, the legal department has to clear it, and he has to produce billing estimates broken down by brand, month and daypart, network, unit, and spot. Meanwhile, there are screening services that screen all the prime-time pro-grams to make sure the content does not clash with or undercut the commercial (for example, if it's a murder mystery and the victim died by drinking poisoned wine, you don't want a commercial for Paul Masson table wines to appear in that show).

Two days after the shows run, there are national overnights, which are the numbers off the Nielsen meters indicating the audience. Every two weeks Nielsen publishes a "pocket piece" which gives the household viewer numbers by show, by date, and by demographic. This allows the buyer to do an interim post-analysis and see how the schedule is doing. Based on these numbers, you might want to adjust your allocations or complain to the networks that you're not getting the proper weight. As Mattimore says, "You really steward and shepherd your account, by brand and by network, so you know exactly what you're getting. You stay on top of it."

When the quarter is over, the buyer prepares a post-analysis report showing how well the total account did and then showing how each brand did on each network.

The peak season for network buyers often begins in early May, when the networks introduce their prime-time schedules, and extends through the end of July or August, when upfront buys are locked in. This means that buyers don't often take vacations in the summer. Naturally, the buyer must be familiar with the content and appeal of all the shows and keep abreast of all the new shows and pilots that the networks launch each season. Like media planners, buyers must have a good aptitude with numbers as well as a feel for the nuances of the media they work with. On top of that, the buyer must be organized, detail-oriented, and conscientious about following through.

While broadcast buying is the more complex and high-powered area because the variables are greater and the money is bigger, print buying involves its own special kind of expertise. A print buyer must stay on top of the ever-changing magazine and newspaper scene, determining whether new publications would be suitable vehicles for the client's advertising and monitoring existing publications for changes in editorial policy, any special editions that would offer good advertising opportunities, shifts in readership. Since rates for the cost of space in a given publication are set (based on circulation), print buying does not involve the wheeling and dealing of broadcast buying. But the job does entail establishing good working relationships with print salespeople and mastering the nuances of the various print vehicles.

POSITIONS AND PAY

ASSISTANT PLANNER

At many agencies the entry-level job in media planning is assistant planner. Like many entry-level advertising jobs, it involves lots of numbers-crunching and grunt work. You're pulling together the statistics that the planners will use in making media plans. You're becoming familiar with the basic tools of media research—the sources that list the ratings, the readership of magazines, information about product usage broken down by demographics, region, etc. As Mike Hedge of BBDO said, "When you start out in media, one of the first things you have to do is learn a new language, because there is a terminology that is specific to this business. It takes a long time just to get your feet on the ground." An assistant planner learns by gathering the research that will document the planners' recommendations, and with time he or she gets a feel for the larger patterns and relationships. Concepts begin to emerge through the haze of statistics, and soon the assistant planner will begin tumbling the numbers according to his or her own ideas.

Some agencies have a job one step below assistant planner called *media estimator*. This person looks up rates and cost information for the various media personnel, orders space in magazines, executes a lot of the clerical paperwork of the media department, and generally becomes familiar with how the whole operation works.

The pay range for assistant planner is $11,000 to $15,000.

JUNIOR BUYER

This is the entry-level position on the buying side, also called coordinator or assistant buyer at some agencies. It is, like assistant planner, a grunt work job involving lots of running numbers through the computer, maintenance of schedules, departmental paperwork, and, of course, learning the ropes. Though as a junior buyer your day-to-day tasks may be less than inspiring, you're being immersed in the media world and you're being groomed to advance. It's a necessary training period and in most cases doesn't last that long.

Junior buyers command salaries similar to assistant planners.

MEDIA PLANNER

The media planner is crucially responsible for coming up with the media plan. Using numbers and research gathered by the estimator and assistant planner, this person will devise multiple plans for the various accounts he or she handles, keep in close touch with the account people on the business, and present the work to the client. A planner may work on a piece of a really large account or may have responsibility for several smaller accounts. Nearly all planners have a year or two experience working in a media department.

The pay for a media planner can range from $18,000 all the way up to $40,000 at some large agencies.

MEDIA BUYER

At most agencies, the media buyers will specialize in either network or spot buying (and some agencies further divide their buyers up by daypart). Through contacts at the networks or at the local stations, the buyer negotiates the smaller buys and he or she will sit in on some of the larger buys to gain familiarity with how it's done. The buyer is also in charge of maintenance of long- and short-term buys, keeping track of market conditions, budgets, and schedules. And of course, he or she stays on top of the numbers that are used to document buys and follow up the results in post-analysis reports.

Pay range for a media buyer can range from $17,500 up to $40,000, depending on experience and track record.

MEDIA SUPERVISOR

In most cases the media supervisor will have come up through the ranks as assistant planner and then planner and so will have an intimate knowledge of the jobs of the people under him or her. The media supervisor's job, as the title indicates, involves a good deal of coordinating and guiding other people in the department. He or she oversees the planners and assistants and checks over the plans they devise to make sure they optimally serve the client's needs. The supervisor, for example, may attend meetings with the planner and then afterwards discuss objectives with the planner to make sure he or she is on the right track. Presenting work to the account group and client is also an important part of the supervisor's role.

Pay for supervisors is $30,000 and up, depending on the agency and experience.

BROADCAST SUPERVISOR

The broadcast supervisor will head up the buying operations in either network or spot, depending on which area he or she specializes in. He or she will negotiate the major buys and will have good working relationships with a wide range of salespeople at the networks or local stations. Keeping abreast of broadcast market conditions and new developments in programming are second nature to broadcast supervisors. He or she will also oversee the buyers and junior buyers, make sure the broadcast department is running smoothly, and see to it that the necessary reports and post-analyses are being carried out.

ASSOCIATE MEDIA DIRECTOR

Joyce Fritz, who holds this position with the Bloom Agency in Dallas, defines her responsibilities this way: "I head a planning group so I'm responsible for [overseeing] quality control of the media product for my assigned accounts, training my group, and explaining media recommendations to the client. Of course, I also still do some planning. When it's crazy, we all do everything, from crunching numbers to client presentations." Mike Hedge, another associate media director, described the job this way: "My primary responsibility is making sure the client is happy with the quality of service he's getting on his account and that the service is the most professional we can perform. At the associate level, you start to get more involved with departmental policy and administration—there's a bigger scope and more long-range concerns as opposed to focusing only on the specific accounts."

The associate media director works closely with other media department people as well as with the client and account group. People in this position very often have the title of vice president.

Associate media directors at large agencies make $40,000 and up.

DIRECTOR OF NATIONAL BROADCAST

At some, especially very large, agencies, there may be a person in a management position who oversees the broadcast department. Among the responsibilities of this person are the smooth functioning of broadcast buyers and supervisors, coordination with other agency department heads, staffing, training, and new business.

MEDIA DIRECTOR

As head of the media department, the media director sets the tone and pace for his or her staff, ensures that the planning and buying functions are working properly and profitably, coordinates media efforts with the other major agency functions, keeps abreast of media innovations and new opportunities, and develops new business. Joel Kushins, media director of Bozell & Jacobs in New York, sums it up this way: "As with any manager, the media director plays 'what if?' with his people, makes sure that his department is properly staffed, trained, oiled, greased, and well-met within the agency. He or she attempts to put forth a look, color, and feel for his or her department and for the agency before the public and in the press."

Chances are the media director will be an executive or senior vice president, sit on the management committee of the agency, and thus play a key role in guiding agency policy.

Media directors command salaries ranging from $50,000 all the way up to $100,000.

BREAKING IN

As long as you have a facility with numbers and a good basic business sense, you won't need any special preparation or education to break into an agency media department. An MBA is *not* an advantage, and in fact one media person I spoke to was advised to leave this credential off his resume when he was applying for entry-level media jobs. Even a college degree is not absolutely essential, although without one you'll probably have to shine a little brighter to prove you've got what it takes to succeed in media. Clerical can be a route in: intelligent, ambitious and organized secretaries who have shown an interest in media have been taken in, trained and promoted.

Media director Joel Kushins says he likes to look for people who have taken some marketing courses in school and who have done some extracurricular activity that shows a real interest in media, whether it's involvement on a newspaper or in advertising industry competitions. Kushins also stresses the importance of "interviewing back": "I find that the person who is most intent on telling you about themselves, without sitting back and asking you questions is not the person I want. I think that it's every bit as important for me to be given the opportunity to tell job candidates about what I represent and what my people represent and to feel that they're making a decision as well as I am."

Mal Gordon, senior vice president and director of media and marketing services at the Chicago agency of Grant/Jacoby, agrees that interviewing effectively is crucial. He adds that smart candidates will be prepared to tell just what makes them different from the rest and how these differences would benefit the agency. All too many job hunters come in with practically identical resumes. Gordon says that Chicago is an excellent place to break into media today, with plenty of opportunities at all levels.

Tom Coughlin, vice president and associate media director at Ogilvy & Mather/Los Angeles, offers this advice to job seekers: "We like someone who is *focused*, who knows what media is, who is well acquainted with how the agency works, and who has specific career goals. This is a person who is assertive but not abrasive. It's also wise to know the agency and know the accounts." Coughlin adds that the advertising industry is expanding in Los Angeles and that media job opportunities, while fewer than in New York, definitely exist at all levels. If you're good, he says, you'll be snapped up.

John Mattimore, a network supervisor, stresses that people interested in coming in on the buying side should be organized and detail-oriented, ambitious and level-headed. And confident: "I want somebody with a cocky attitude who says, 'You're making a mistake if you don't hire me.' "

Candidates for media jobs should apply either through personnel or directly to the media director. Of course, if you know someone in an agency, go through your contact first. Joyce Fritz told me that the Bloom Agency in Dallas pays its employees a "finder's fee" if they bring in new talent. As a result, she says, "we're all willing to look at any resume that comes along."

And Nancy Schneider has this tip to share: if you are calling the media director, look for ways of getting past the secretary. Many media directors start work early and/or stay late; most secretaries work 9 to 5. So plan your calls accordingly. Be polite, but try not to take no for an answer.

A word of caution: if you're intending to use media as a steppingstone into account work, you'll have to play your cards very carefully. Media people are all onto this ploy (many have tried it themselves) and it's a topic that may very well come up at the interview. Unfortunately, there is no way to predict how a particular interviewer will react to the truth. Some are willing to hire good people on the theory that media is an excellent discipline to learn and that once these people move from media to account work they'll be "allies" of the media department and thus easier to work with. Others, like Tom Coughlin, say flatly that they hire only media professionals who intend to remain media professionals. John Mattimore takes an even stronger position: "If you come in here looking to spring into account work, you'll get buried. Media used to be a steppingstone, but we no longer want to be a breeding ground for account people. You don't want to train people and lose them. Personally, if I find out my assistant wants to move to account management, he better move fast."

There is, in short, no easy answer and no single way of handling this tricky situation. The best general advice seems to be: for whatever reason you're applying for a media job, go in with the attitude that you'll give it a fair try and learn as much as you can. You just might find, as so many media people have, that the "steppingstone" turns out to be the place you really want to be.

JOEL KUSHINS,
Senior Vice President, Media Director
Bozell & Jacobs, New York

"My first job was pushing a mail cart," recalls Joel Kushins, looking back on his long and successful media career. "That was a summer job after high school, back in 1960. I was torn between advertising and becoming a doctor—but decided to find out what advertising might bring me." What it brought him was a top executive position at the New York headquarters of a large national agency, clients that include Lee Jeans, Jaguar cars, *Business Week* magazine, *The New York Times*, *Seventeen* magazine, Nabisco, Lifesavers candy brands, and

Jockey men's underwear, and the chance to be a leader of media at a time when the media function was burgeoning. All this and a fabulous office high up in a midtown tower overlooking practically the entire east side of Manhattan.

Kushins, like many advertising people, has done his share of moving around. Starting as an assistant buyer at Richard K. Manoff (now Geers Gross), he has also worked at Grey Advertising, where he rose to the level of assistant media director, and Norman, Craig and Kummel, where he came aboard as associate media director. After rising quite high up in media, Kushins had a sudden change of heart and decided that maybe he was missing out on all the fun, so he became an account executive. Though this proved to be something of a detour in his media career, Kushins feels it was a tremendous learning experience. Ultimately, he realized he was more of a specialist, "an artisan of a particular craft as opposed to a collator of events that an account executive is," and he returned to the media fold. "I took what I learned and it made me better when I went back to media." Norman, Craig and Kummel agreed; they made him media director, the position he held before moving over to Bozell & Jacobs in 1980. Naturally, Kushins's stint in the account services area has made him more sympathetic than many of his colleagues to job seekers who wish to use media as a springboard into account work. On the other hand, his experience and success may convince many that media offers all the opportunities for success and fulfillment one could wish for in an advertising career.

Q: Tell me how you first got interested in media.
A: I knew about media because I had developed an interest in the advertising business, I read the trade press, and to some extent through my education, which involved advertising and broadcast production. Also, pushing a mail cart in an agency was a big help because I got to network myself around and find out where all the bodies were buried. Media seemed to turn me on because it brought together a number of things that interested me: a general interest in marketing, the ability to demonstrate logical thinking, mathematics—all of those good things.

Q: Did you enter as a buyer or a planner?
A: I started as an assistant buyer—but in the mid-sixties, "buyer" was a euphemism for "do everything." First, you went about creating a media plan and then you bought it. The distinction between planner and buyer had not yet gelled. That happened in the late sixties as a consequence of buying services. The concept of buying services forced

agency mangement to become a heck of a lot sharper at specializing their skills. Suddenly, everybody had to choose between planning and buying, and you had to choose mighty fast and move.

Q: For someone who aspires to become a media director today, would you recommend starting as a planner or a buyer?
A: Ultimately, you have to do both. I still feel that planning probably gives a more all-encompassing perspective, recognizing that if at some point you don't become involved in buying I think you've missed a good deal of the boat.

Q: Is it crucial to choose the right agency to start with?
A: I think that the smart track is to seek an agency—and it need not be a huge agency. In fact, it could even be a smaller agency where there is a diversity of businesses so that you can get to pretty much understand all facets of media. It's important that you're picking and choosing not only the *company* but the *people* you're working for. The background of the people you're working for is every bit as important as the company itself. I find that very often, when somebody comes into an interview intent only on telling you about him or herself—without interviewing back—that is not the person I want. The best entry-level candidate is one who is truly looking for that well-rounded spot that is going to give them not only the opportunity, but the people who will provide that opportunity.

Q: Can you describe what the "perfect" media department would be like?
A: The perfect department is one that has a good balance of the intelligent, well-rounded, culture-enriched individual—who also has street smarts, who is attuned to what is happening out there. It's a person who is aware, introspective, but outgoing and capable of drinking in an endless amount of information. And who has the sense of what it takes to make an advertising message meet a prospect.

Q: Can you describe how the position of the media department within the agency has changed in the past few years?
A: I think that there is more of an opportunity for the department specialist—whether it be media, creative, research—to take a lead position, to become a star, to really be part of the process as a contributor. It wasn't so long ago that service department personnel were merely considered to be manufacturers of information not unlike assem-

blers on a production line. Now, we media people almost always find ourselves playing a significant role in key meetings with clients and with new business prospects. All of this attention to media has grown tremendously in the past decade, and it makes me feel good that I chose this area.

Q: How about the role of the media—what changes and trends do you see on the horizon?
A: I think that the tendency toward media specialization that has been growing for years in magazines and has now grown in television will persist. I think that marketing at less than national or less than full segment is going to continue to be the order of the day. Market segmentation is unquestionably the key that unlocks the door for many media decisions.

Q: Does that make you job more difficult?
A: Sure. But that's one of the things that makes a media career interesting.

Q: How do you feel about hiring someone who plans to jump over into account work?
A: If I sense that someone is harboring a desire to get into account work, I like to know what's behind it and whether there's really an interest in devoting some years to media. I'm willing to take a person on for a couple of years, though there are a lot of media people who are not. I find no problem in training a person for a year and a half or two years, because I'm gaining benefit from that person within a couple of months of employment. If they then want to go into account work, I will not only allow it, I'll support it if I think it's right. We'll try to find something within the agency—and I now have an ally in the account group. It's somebody we've trained and who can talk our language. It can be a benefit, but I wouldn't want to overencourage it.

Q: What's your favorite aspect of the job?
A: Teaching and sitting back and appreciating the process of watching people grow. I find this forever a joy.

RESEARCH:

INSIDE THE MIND

OF THE CONSUMER

They were supposed to be stubborn, egghead statisticians, the ones who shuffled grayly into meetings with forbiddingly fat reports tabulating toothpaste tube squeezability curves, the ones who threw their cold numbers all over the creatives' creativity, who never took their noses out of printouts and reports, who never ventured out of their ivory towers. That, anyway, was the myth of the advertising researcher.

Now listen to the rather startling reality as described by real-life researchers: "We researchers are the representatives of the consumer within the agency. When you look at the definition of research, it actually has very little to do with numbers. Yes, you must know about statistics, but you bring to it an element of humanity. If we are really and truly to represent the consumer, we have to have a knowledge of what people are all about and why they are motivated to do certain things." "Our philosophy is that we really want to understand people, so that we incorporate all of these one-to-one, qualitative, ethnographic approaches. Yes, we take advantage of the computerization and data availability, but at the same time we bring insight to it, so that we don't get too far removed from people and what they really feel and how they react to things." "We deal with facts—but the facts are always presented in terms of a story. They bring a person alive."

Understanding people. Representing the consumer. In-depth, psychological portraits. One-on-one interviews. Insight. Intuition. Attitudes. Behavior. These are the crucial terms in research today. Psychographics—understanding the psychology, motivation, secret wishes, and fears of the consumer—has supplanted demographics (breakdowns of populations by age, region, occupation). The question researchers persistently ask has become: What is this prospective buyer like? If I want him to buy our brand of beer, I should know not only how much he drinks but why he drinks and with whom; not only how he likes the taste but how he reacts to the brand's image. Does he drink because he's thirsty or because picking up a six-pack somehow reassures him, confirms some aspect of his identity?

Researchers have added art and heart to their science, and smart creatives and account people are responding. The ads reflect the change in research focus too. More and more, the best ads, to borrow AT&T's tag line, reach out and touch you. The guy wearing worn and comfortable boots, sitting in front of his cabin with his dog seems to epitomize a lifestyle and certain values. The subtext of Geraldine Ferraro advertising Diet Pepsi says: Look, all you successful and would-be successful women, look, all you aware and openminded men, it's okay to drink Diet Pepsi. (The commercial was okay for her too: her fee was reported to be over $500,000.) The unstated message of the Charlie Chaplin figure advertising IBM personal computers is: Hey, you're a little person with a big job to do; you have a sense of humor; you're smart—smart enough to make the best computer choice without being clobbered over the head.

It's not that researchers provided the formulas for all of these campaigns, and then creatives simply plugged in words and images to fit the psychographics. Rather, the creatives and the researchers are collaborating more closely than before, the researchers providing information leading to profiles of consumers, the creatives translating this information into advertising, the researchers testing the resulting ads on consumers and reporting back the reactions, the creatives revising the ads, and so on. It's a flow, an ongoing process. Bill Wells, executive vice president and director of marketing services at Needham Harper Worldwide in Chicago, explained to me how researchers work with representatives of the other major agency departments in task forces. "It's a collegial rather than a hierarchical arrangement," he said. "Researchers here are not just order takers, as they are in some agencies." It's this team structure, as much as new trends in studying behavior and attitudes, that has changed the face of research so dramatically in the past decade.

In the simplest sense, research provides the link between the marketer, the creative, and the consumer. Studying trends, behavior, and attitudes, researchers come up with ways for the clients to increase their business. Bill Wells gave me the clearest definition: "If you consider the agency's products as being advertising, marketing plans, media plans and media purchases, then the agency's products are made of information. Research supplies an important part of that information."

An executive research director at a good-sized New York shop put it slightly differently:

"Let's take a simplistic definition of advertising: Advertising delivers a message about a product/service to someone. We then have a basic equation made up of three variables—the message, the product/service, the someone—which cannot be solved until we determine the value for each variable. We do this by answering a series of questions for each one. About the someone: Who do we want to talk to? What are they like demographically? psychographically? behaviorally? About the product: What do we know about the product category, in general, and our product, in particular? How is it similar to/different from competition? About the message: What is important to the consumer in this product category? What needs are and are not being satisfied?

"It is the job of the researcher to help answer these questions. Once that has been done, a strategy can be developed, which will clearly state what it is that we want the advertising to do. Our job as researchers is then to help determine if, in fact, the advertising is doing what it was intended to do."

Though researchers were traditionally divided into specialties—market research, copy testing, consumer studies, media research—more and more research departments are made up of generalists who follow through all of these areas of research on specific accounts. For example, at Wells, Rich, Greene, some of whose major accounts include Procter & Gamble (Pringles, Prell); Ralston Purina (Tender Vittles, Chex); Philip Morris (Benson & Hedges, Players), there are five small research groups, each of which handles just a few accounts. Specialization in this way allows the researchers to become intimately involved in the needs of the account and it insures continuity. Researchers immerse themselves in the product just as creatives would, working closely with clients, seeing each project through from beginning to end, and seeing how the various research studies overlap and interrelate.

Advertising research relies on two basic kinds of sources: original and secondary. Secondary research can be any material that sheds light, no matter how obliquely, on consumer trends and behaviors. As one research directory says, it's everything from *The Culture of Narcissism* to *The Pursuit of Excellence*, from magazine articles about teenage movie stars to studies of product usage and sales prepared by various corporations. For original research, the agency and the client decide together on the type of information they need. Agency researchers then design questionnaires, hire outside research suppliers to recruit consumers who fit various demographics or to conduct interviews with people at shopping malls, and analyze the information through computer programs they have devised. Once the original research material is analyzed, researchers will present the results to the account group and the client. Big clients very often require major research studies; however, they usually have their own research

Edith Gilson, senior vice president in charge of the Consumer Behavior Group at J. Walter Thompson/New York: "The people I hire are uniquely committed to living."

departments that pursue these studies in collaboration with the agency.

Edith Gilson, senior vice president in charge of the Consumer Behavior Group at J. Walter Thompson/New York (her department used to be called the Research and Planning Department, and the change of name reflects the new thrust of advertising research), gave me a good example of how research works at a huge agency with a huge client—in this case, Kodak. Kodak is a longstanding client of J. Walter Thompson, so when Kodak decided to introduce their Disc camera not long ago, J. Walter Thompson was working hand-in-hand with them on positioning the new product, deciding on the target audience, and generally testing the waters of public reaction to this breakthrough in picture-taking technology. Gilson and her staff got involved very early on, though she points out that the initial research was restricted to some extent by the need to maintain secrecy. "The way we always start," she says, "is to look at the current needs of the marketplace, to understand the picture takers in the U.S., and to find out how the new product would fit those needs, which change constantly. At the time we introduced the Disc, it was really a very revolutionary new product, because it was the only one that used the disc film." From ongoing research gathered over the years of Kodak's relationship with J. Walter, Gilson and staff knew that the source of business for this product was a group they called "snapshooters"—not the people interested in the picture quality and technical precision you can get with a 35-mm camera, but people interested in taking "fun" pictures in rapid succession: the kinds of pictures people take at parties, or of children playing or pets romping. This was the great selling point of the Disc camera: you could just keep snapping away without worrying about advancing the film, adjusting the light setting, or getting an extra flash.

So they knew their product; they knew the needs of the consumers they had identified and how the product would suit those needs. But even so, they made a crucial mistake in the early advertising. Gilson explains: "Because it was a new technology, we, as marketers, felt we had to communicate this new technology to the consumer, and in the beginning we actually went overboard. Our audience was really very picture-oriented and not tool-oriented. We gave them too much technology, and they said, 'This is not for me—this is more like for a 35-mm person.'" Initial sales were disappointing, and the research department set out to learn why and to discover how the advertising should be changed. A research firm was hired to recruit people in the market for a camera, then J. Walter staffers conducted in-depth, one-on-one, exploratory interviews with these people. The results of these interviews helped the staff develop hypotheses about issues that they would then want to quantify through polling a wider sample. For this they arranged for 500 "typical" consumers (again, recruited by research suppliers) to answer a long and structured questionnaire. The two studies were put together in a report, which was presented first to the account and creative groups to get their input and then to the client.

Based on this extensive study, the Disc camera advertising was changed dramatically. The new ads tone down the technological advances of the product and play up the ease of handling. The picture taker in the new ads is now a person the target consumer can relate to and associate with; in fact, the people in the ads are really composites of the target consumers. And the photos framed in the commercials are photos that these consumers want to be able to take: kids and teens having a good time at the beach, for example. The underlying message is: Have a good time with your Disc camera, a message that the J. Walter researchers helped discover was what consumers wanted to hear. Sales reflect the success of this new approach.

Another research director explained to me how research contributes to the overall advertising process at his agency by focusing on the launch of a new (hypothetical) brand, Happy Face Lip Gloss, a spin-off from the successful Happy Face cosmetics line, best known for Happy Face Lipstick. Back in the sixties, Happy Face made a big splash with sexy, funny, somehow real-feeling commercials for its youth-oriented lipstick, but by the early eighties, Happy Face was losing market share as women abandoned it for brands they perceived as healthier and somehow better for your lips. In thinking about how to market the new lip gloss, the agency research director, his research staff, and the Happy Face researchers first wanted to identify the target audience. For this they took several approaches: first demographic, making use of the

Simmons syndicated service (Simmons provides information on magazine readership, television viewing, and product usage) as well as attitude and usage studies that Happy Face had done in the past. Next they looked at the target audience psychographically, and for this they applied the VALS categories, the latest tool (some would say fad) in advertising research. VALS, which stands for Values and Lifestyles, is a system of categorizing the American consuming public into psychological types that was devised by SRI (formerly known as the Stanford Research Institute). There are four VALS categories: "Need Drivens," who are people so limited in resources (especially financial resources) that their lives are driven more by need than by choice; "Outer-Directeds" whose consumption, activities, and attitudes are all guided by what they think others will think; "Inner-Directeds," who conduct their lives primarily in accord with inner values rather than in accord with values oriented to externals; "Integrateds," individuals fully mature in a psychological sense who meld the power of outer-direction with the sensitivity of inner-direction. Determining which category your target audience falls into can be extremely useful in devising advertising. Even more useful in fleshing out an image of the typical consumer are in-depth, one-to-one interviews which researchers, account executives, product managers, and creatives observe behind a one-way mirror. The interviewees are aware that they're being observed during the interview.

From all of these sources, the agency and Happy Face researchers learned that Happy Face users were overwhelmingly female, better-educated, urban; the VALS category they would fall into was "Emulators," a subcategory of "Outer-Directeds" (ambitious, upwardly mobile, status-conscious); in addition to Happy Face they tended to purchase designer jeans, Perrier, and Grey Poupon; and from the interviews they learned that these women aspire to the lifestyle the brand represents (chic and monied) and view the distinctive package itself (a big selling point for Happy Face) as a symbol of their desires.

Next, the researchers turned to the content of the ads. Happy Face already had a clearly defined image of sophistication and youthful elegance, and this was something they wanted to retain in the advertising for the new lip gloss. Having learned that many lip gloss users were not entirely satisfied with the limited color choices of other brands, they felt that by introducing a lip gloss into this category that had more colors as well as special weather-sensitive formulas that changed with the seasons, they could win both sophistication-conscious *and* health-conscious users. The researchers also got the reaction of consumers to the advertising for High Gloss, the leader in this category, and learned that many felt it was flat and clinical, not something they could relate to. So, based on all of this, they had some good clues about the direction to take in their own advertising and packaging.

This information was translated into a basic strategy statement as follows: to convince women to buy Happy Face Lip Gloss instead of any other lip gloss because it is a sophisticated *and* healthy gloss that can best represent how you feel about yourself.

The creatives would use this strategy in devising the initial ads for the campaign, and once the ads were prepared, the researchers would get involved in copy testing. The two questions they wanted to answer here were: What do consumers take away and remember from the advertising?, and How do they feel about it? In this case, a series of in-depth one-to-ones and a portfolio test were used. For the portfolio test, the Happy Face ad was put in a book with other ads, sample consumers looked through it and were then questioned about which ads they remembered. The Happy Face ads did quite well—there was high recall, strong "playback" of both the classy and healthy aspects of the message, and many expressed an interest in trying the brand.

Now they were ready to go into market simulation testing. In test situations of this sort respondents are shown the advertising, then they're given seed money and taken to something that looks like a store and told to go and shop. From this you can determine how many people "buy" the product. Often there is a follow-up, in which the consumers are called a few weeks later and asked whether the product lived up to their expectations. Based on this test, you can get an estimate of trial and repeat purchase and decide whether it's really worth taking the new product into the market.

Happy Face Lip Gloss did exceptionally well in simulated testing and the brand was launched. Research, however, does not cease. Once the advertising starts, you want to know how successful it was, and for this researchers carry out tracking studies, contacting consumers and asking such things as what they remember about the ads, how they would rate the brand vis-à-vis other similar brands in the category, what image they have formed of the brand. This type of study is concerned more with attitudes and awareness than actual usage: it tracks the reactions of consumers to the campaign. Then of course there is the all-important bottom line: How is the brand selling? The research team will evaluate the sales figures on the brand, look at repurchase statistics, usage frequency, when the brand is used, and whether it's the only one used. In addition, studies are made comparing the advertising expenditure and sales results of competition to see how the brand measures up.

The results of all these studies were excellent. The tracking study showed that there was high brand and advertising awareness and the sales were phenomenal. In a short time, Happy Face became the leading lip gloss, and sales of Happy Face Lipstick also climbed. The researchers, of course, cannot take full credit for this impressive success story, but they were there at every stage of the new product launch, working as part of the agency team.

Researchers, like creatives and account managers, work long and hard hours, but unlike other advertising executives, they tend to spend a lot of their time working alone. They don't go on shoots or travel. They don't brainstorm in teams as much. They simply spend more time sitting alone in an office and thinking. The loneliness can be hard to take, particularly in such a people-oriented environment. Some researchers also complain of a certain hostility from other departments within the agency. "We're not always the most welcome member of the team," one research director told me, "because sometimes the team might have very strong preconceived notions and the reality is quite different." The others may not want to hear about the facts that research has uncovered.

Researchers are the philosophers of the advertising industry, philosophers who must always keep their eyes on the bottom line. They are the ones who push the cutting edge that much further into the future. One of the newest cutting edges is Behavior-Scan, a computerized, single-source data system that provides information about purchasing behavior and exposure to advertising from a single household. For each market that BehaviorScan covers, a researcher can monitor all sales of nearly all items as well as track every purchase that designated households make; and, since the BehaviorScan system includes a way of cutting in test commercials on cable TV, the researcher can use this system to evaluate the impact of the advertising that he or she has helped to develop. More sophisticated computer technology allows researchers to perform such experiments with a precision not possible even a few years back. Bill Wells of Needham in Chicago feels that BehaviorScan and similar systems will become more influential as they proliferate. And George S. Fabian, a group senior vice president at Backer & Spielvogel, was quoted in *The New York Times* as saying that these "single-source date suppliers" now constitute a "power base in the industry." Such systems are "having an incredible impact on marketing and advertising, and . . . take us closer to measuring the effectiveness of advertising [than] we have ever been, in a realistic time and with realistic budgets."

Like all demanding and rewarding jobs, research can consume your personal time and energy. "You cannot succeed if you come in at 9 and go home at 5 and then forget about it," according to a research director. "It's pretty much with you all the time."

Positions and Pay

Research departments tend to be quite small in comparison with other major agency departments. J. Walter Thompson/New York, a large shop, has a total of twenty-seven professionals in its research department, and at the small shops there may only be a handful of researchers or perhaps one or two people who farm out most of the work to research suppliers or independent market research operations. There are many more research jobs available inside large corporations and with research suppliers than there are at advertising agencies. The levels of research positions listed below are likely to exist only in fully staffed departments of large agencies, and, as with most advertising jobs, the titles and exact responsibilities will vary greatly from shop to shop. The salary figures quoted below reflect the pay scales of large agencies in major cities.

PROJECT DIRECTOR

Junior project director is the entry-level position at many agencies (though some big shops have research trainees who rotate through training programs that expose them to all areas of agency work) and the level above that is senior project director, a job usually open to those with four or more years of research experience. The project director, whether junior or senior, is primarily involved in gathering background information: you amass facts but don't yet analyze them. A big part of the job is organizing data in such a way that more senior researchers can utilize it more readily. For example, you would read through a report on buying trends and write a synopsis of it. For the less complicated research studies, the project directors would write the questionnaires and conduct the group sessions and in-depth interviews that have become such a key part of advertising research today.

Pay for project directors ranges from $15,000 to $26,000.

RESEARCH SUPERVISOR

Next step up is the research supervisor (sometimes known as research account executive). Because the research supervisor is more involved with planning and designing research studies for specific accounts, he or she will have more contact with the client. This is really an intermediate job—part executional, part supervisory. Other responsibilities of the research supervisor include writing research proposals and questionnaires, overseeing the field work and tabulation of research studies, and assigning work to and checking up on project directors.

Pay for research supervisors is in the $25,000 to $35,000 range.

ASSOCIATE RESEARCH DIRECTOR

A level above is the associate research director, and this job is usually held by people with a minimum of ten years of experience. One director of research described the people in this position as "the most visible researchers" because they work very closely with the client, with the creatives, and with the account group. They attend agency-wide meetings, get ideas into circulation, do presentations and see to the daily research needs of the accounts they work on. The associate research director will supervise both the junior people on the research staff and the outside research suppliers that the agency uses for various studies.

Pay for associate research directors ranges from $40,000 to $60,000.

RESEARCH DIRECTOR

The senior people in large research departments hold the position of research director, a job that usually requires fifteen or more years of experience. A research director very often has developed a particular area of expertise, such as finance, copy research, or consumer motivation, and will be the agency specialist in this area, consulting with other directors as the need arises. He or she not only represents the agency to the client, but to the research community at conferences and symposia. A research director will assign work to the research staff and maintain quality control over the work produced for his or her accounts. This person in effect heads up a research group. A research director may also become involved in new business pitches.

Pay for research directors ranges from $60,000 to $100,000.

EXECUTIVE RESEARCH DIRECTOR

At the head of an agency research department is an executive research director. One person who holds this position with a major New York agency describes his job as "overseeing the work of the department, working closely with the three research directors, establishing philosophies for the department, working very hard in an administrative capacity to make sure the department gets what it deserves and stays where it should stay. I'm also very involved with new business and I'll present the research work and the philosophy of the department to a prospective new client." The executive research director is usually a member of the agency management committee, the group of top executives who run the agency, and he or she reports directly to the agency's CEO.

Although a good part of this job is supervisory, many executive research directors insist on remaining involved with the actual carrying out of research studies, working right alongside their staff on important projects. As Edith Gilson, of J. Walter Thompson, told me: "I believe only in hands on, so I will get involved in guiding through the nitty-gritty of a report. We just did a highly publicized work on the impact of fifteen-second commercials together with ABC. When we worked on that study, the juniors were here all weekend and so was I. We did the same work together."

Executive research directors earn salaries in the $100,000 to $150,000 range.

BREAKING IN

Edith Gilson, who came to this country from Germany twenty years ago, got her first research job by walking into the offices of Cunningham & Walsh and saying, "I need a job." She had worked previously as an au pair in Scarsdale, New York, and a photographer's assistant in New York City, and her English was still not perfect, but Cunningham & Walsh was willing to take a chance on her. Gilson recalls: "I tried to convince them that I was really logical, good in mathematics, and that I needed a break. And, lo and behold, Cunningham & Walsh gave it to me. They said, 'You have six weeks in research to prove yourself.' I stayed there four years." From there she moved to Grey and then to J. Walter Thompson, where she now heads the Consumer Behavior Group.

Hardly a typical break-in story in research but it's possible, even today. Gilson herself insists that she would be more likely to hire someone "off the street who really seemed *alive* than someone with a Ph.D. in psychology and statistics who was a total deadbeat. I'm also very careful that the people I hire are uniquely committed to living, if you will, or curious about living, that they are excited about something. So, if I were to interview you and you said you're a hot air balloonist, I would say, 'Oh, that's interesting . . .' I ask people what book they have read that they really like, what movie they have seen, whether there's an issue that they read a lot about. These are the people that turn me on and these are the people I'm going to hire."

Bill Wells, of Needham Harper Worldwide, took a more traditional approach: "We look favorably on people with Ph.D.-level training in one of the social sciences—political science, psychology, statistics." Though Wells also mentioned that a few people recently hired into the department had such nontraditional backgrounds as graduate training in aeronautics, Asian languages, and divinity studies.

Because of her own background, Gilson may be unusual, but she is not unique in her preference for people "curious about living." With research itself geared more and more to understanding the consumer, researchers are getting away from the ivory tower types who surround themselves with numbers but can't deal with people. "My objective," one research executive told me, "is to get as far away from the egghead image as possible." The point is, there is no single requisite background—aside from a sophisticated understanding of the useful forms of statistics. Ideally, you should be able to demonstrate that you can apply whatever background you have to the day-to-day tasks of explaining the mind of the consumer to the agency and the client. One research director calls it "a holistic approach."

Because research departments are usually quite small, there is often no position open to someone with no previous work experience. However, such experience can include working on research studies at a research institute, which is part of the training in many Ph.D. programs. Any work in the field, any hands-on experience, counts for more than classroom training alone. Another place to get this kind of hands-on research experience would be in research jobs outside of advertising agencies. One good place to break in is through a research supplier—an independent company that the agencies hire to recruit consumers for interviews and to conduct surveys. Your first job may be screening hundreds of people a day through telephone calls or quantifying results of surveys; hardly an inspiring prospect, but it's a start, it's good experience, and it may prove useful in getting your foot in the door of an agency. After all, David Ogilvy worked as a researcher forecasting movie audiences and the box office appeal of movie stars for George Gallup before he became a star himself as a copywriter and founder of Ogilvy & Mather.

Perhaps most useful of all is a genuine enthusiasm for research and a desire to work in it. This area of advertising is undergoing great changes at the moment, and there is a certain fluidity in the structure of departments and in the requirements for job candidates. More and more, it's the people with imagination, new ideas, and the ability to make people listen who are taking the lead in research. The future of advertising research belongs to the innovators; those who show the capacity for new thinking are going to be the ones who land the research jobs.

PRINT PRODUCTION AND TRAFFIC: MAKING IT RIGHT

Let's say you're advertising a car in a magazine. The art director and copywriter come up with a terrific concept: "Wheels Into the Future" is the headline; the art shows the car sort of going into orbit, with its rear wheels touching earth and its front end whizzing out into the stars. Under the headline there'll be a couple of paragraphs of copy set in white on a black background explaining how this is the automobile of the twenty-first century. The client loves it but wants to know how much it's going to cost to produce. *Somebody has to find out.* The media planner fiddles with his reach and frequency and decides it would have the widest impact in *Time, Newsweek,* and *The New Yorker.* How big are the pages in each of these magazines? When do they need to receive the ad in order to start running it the first week of August? What kind of printing processes do they use? How will these processes affect the look of the art? *Somebody has to be up on all this information.* The client approves the ad and the creatives are ready to go ahead. They're going to have to photograph the car, but the art director thinks that they might be able to get hold of existing artwork for the earth-and-stars background. Where can they get it? Will they have to commission it, or can they buy it from some stock house? How much are they going to have to pay for it? How will it reproduce? What's the best way to put the two pieces of art together? *Somebody has to attend to each detail.* Then there's the question of type for the headline and body copy. The color separation. The print run. Proofreading the copy. Sending the right ad out to the right magazine at the right time and checking the magazine to make sure it ran in the right place and in the right size. *More work for somebody.*

The somebody who has to take care of all of these essential details of advertising is actually a department of somebodies—the print production and traffic people. Though print production and traffic are often grouped together in one department and overseen by one director, they involve very different functions and responsibilities. Dick

Madigan, vice president and production manager of print production with McCann-Erickson, summed up the role of production people in this way: "We are responsible for trying to get the art to reproduce in magazines and newspapers as close as possible to the art director's original intentions. We really have to feel what the art directors feel. Of course, we want to keep the art directors contented, and we hope in keeping them satisfied that the client's wishes are fulfilled. We work with typographers, engravers, and printers, all of whom are outside vendors. In a way, we're the mediator between the magazines, newspapers, and art directors."

Traffic, on the other hand, is more a matter of coordinating, keeping track of all the pieces, making sure that approvals are obtained at each stage of the print ad, that deadlines are met, and that everything is in the right place at the right time. The term "traffic director" was originally adopted by freight companies for the person who kept track of where any given shipment was at any given time. In advertising, the traffic people keep tabs not on freight shipments but on all the elements and phases of print ads. A more accurate, if less colorful, title would be "internal control coordinator." In essence, traffic people are a bit like account managers: they don't actually do anything, but they help everybody else do what they should when they should. They direct the flow of work into and out of the agency and also between the various agency departments. Traffic, like account management, is positioned right in the middle of things; because of this shared perspective, traffic work is one fairly common route into account management.

A typical print production and traffic department may be structured like this:

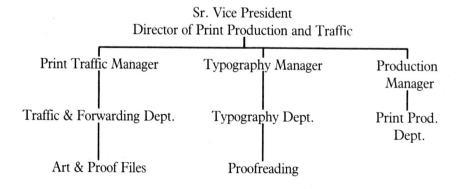

The production manager will have a staff of production supervisors or buyers who divide up the agency work by account. In the example used to open this chapter, the production supervisor in charge of the automobile account would talk over the technical aspects of the ad with an art director at a very early stage (before the shoot) and spot any problems that could come up. He'd know how the printing process would affect the color of the car and what process would make the car stand out most clearly against the background. He knows whether some of the original sharpness could be restored through retouching and how much compensation must be made for the printing processes of the magazines involved. The best print ads usually result from a collaboration between the production person and the art director. In a way, the production person must look at an ad with the eyes of both an artist and a technical expert in printing.

The engraving process affects not only the look of the art, but the cost of producing it, which is something else the production supervisor must always keep in mind. Basically, the processes in use today are offset, rotogravure (printing is done from an incised copper cylinder), and the new process of halftone gravure, kind of a compromise between offset and the more expensive rotogravure, which is just now becoming commonly accepted in the industry. The production supervisor sends the job out for bids, usually to three photoplate makers who have done good work on similar ads, chooses the best bid, and sees the contract through. Being a good production person means keeping up on the latest technical advances. "There is always new equipment and a new process coming into use," one production manager told me. These days, most production people are generalists: they must know about all phases of production—four-color printing, black-and-white printing, color separation, etc. Though at some shops, a different person will specialize in each of these areas, this setup is increasingly rare. So the more you know, the more in demand you'll be. Production people develop a feel for the artwork ("You get to know whether the reds are too red," is how one put it) along with the technical proficiency to handle whatever kinds of special problems are thrown their way.

Another branch of production is the art-buying group. Let's say the art director wants to use existing art for the earth-and-stars backdrop for the automobile ad. The art buyer will contact artists, photo supply houses (or whatever source there might exist for the particular art needed), and negotiate a contract to use the work. They know how much money they have at their disposal for the art and what the going rates are for various types of artwork; they also regiment the spending of the art directors. Sometimes the art buyer will also handle things like retouching.

Typesetting is taken care of by yet another branch within the department—the typography manager and his staff. The type director, like the production supervisor, will work with the art director on the technical aspect of the ad; in this case, the type style and size. Once typefaces are decided on for headline, body copy, and photo caption, the type director contacts an outside typographer, gets the type set to the correct specifications, and assigns a proofreader who will read the set type against the copywriter's copy.

Dick Madigan points out that it's crucial for production supervisors and type directors to maintain good working relationships with the various photoplate makers, printers, and type houses that they use and with the agency people with whom they come in contact. Having a good rapport with outside vendors can make all the difference in getting out of a tight squeeze, say, if a deadline or budget problem arises. "In fact," one production manager told me, "having a good relationship with the vendor is more important than the actual job. There's *always* a way of working around something." Diplomacy is also the name of the game with some art directors inside the agency. "You want art directors to feel good about you and themselves," says Madigan, "and you don't want to destroy their creativity. You have to be tactful: telling someone that their art simply won't work can be very difficult. Diplomacy is thus a huge part of the job."

The studio bullpen is yet another section of the production department. The people working here are mechanical artists responsible for making exact mechanicals of the layout that represents the ad that will run in magazines or newspapers. Using stat machines, ruler, dividers, and calipers, they lay down the type where it's supposed to go along with the photograph, artwork, or photostats of these. Their specifications must be accurate to 1/32, so the job demands a lot of precision and concentration. It can also involve a certain amount of tedium. This is not a creative opportunity, in the way that an art director's job is, nor does it usually lead into the art department. Bullpen artists are considered mechanical artists, and their function is to render the art director's ideas as precisely as possible on the page—not to come up with ideas of their own.

The traffic people are in there at every stage of the production process, keeping the flow flowing. Bill Harris, a veteran of sixteen years' service with BBDO/New York and currently the print traffic manager there, explained the basics of how traffic works inside a large agency:

"There are currently sixteen of us in the print traffic department here, and we coordinate internally all print advertising that goes out of the New York office. We receive our assignments from the account groups and, in turn, we help the creative department in doing layouts for the different publications. What we'll do is look up the sizes of the proposed publications for them so they can plan the layouts. The account people obtain the client approvals, then we get the copy and layout back. The next step is estimating how much it's going to cost to produce the ad. I'll go to the art directors and obtain their costs for photography, retouching, models, props, in fact, anything to do with the actual shoot. Then I'll go to the typography department and obtain the cost of the type for the ad, then to the production department and obtain the cost of engraving the ad, which means creating the printing material that the publications need. Once we get a print production estimate, the account group takes it to the client, gets it approved, and then the creative department may go ahead with the shoot.

"The next step is setting the type. The type people will bring us the typeset copy and the proofreaders will read the typeset copy against a manuscript that a copywriter wrote to make sure that everything is there. Then we deliver the type to an art director, and if there are any corrections to be made, the art director will go directly to the type department. Once the type can be put down on a board, along with a photostat of the photograph in the form of a mechanical, we take that mechanical and route it around by first having it proofread against the type that was set, and then showing it back again to the art director who had it prepared and to the copywriter who will read it to make sure that all his words are in the right place. Then we take this mechanical to the account group and they take it to the legal department for its approval; then it's ready to be taken to the client by the account group. The client signs off on it, the account group brings it back to us, and we, in turn, give it to the production department and it goes into production."

The print traffic people also generate the insertion orders, which are the binding contracts between the agency and a particular publication that authorizes the publication in the name of the client to insert an ad of a certain size on a certain date in a certain position. Keeping track of these and making sure that the right ads go to the right publications is an important part of the job.

Foul-ups may occur, but they are rare at big, professionally run shops like BBDO because of a system of what Harris calls "checks and balances." There's always someone to check up on the work of another person, so nothing falls between the cracks. "Deadlines," Harris adds, "are a crucial part of the job. You take a publication like *Time* or *Sports Illustrated*, they have a closing date of maybe five weeks prior to publication and they'd like to have their printing material at that time. If [the closing date] is tight, we in the print traffic department are the ones who coordinate with that particular publication and get an extension. Some publications will give you just a couple days, others may give as much as a week."

Deadlines and details keep print traffic people on their toes. It's not a job for just anyone. "You have to have a certain temperament," says Harris, "and you have to be able to work under pressure. You can't let it rattle you. I like to hire someone who gets to work on time and isn't looking to run out at 5, because there are times when you have to stay late—it can be an hour, or it can be three hours. In the course of my experience here at BBDO, I've stayed until midnight some nights, just coordinating particular jobs."

Print traffic is basically the same all over, according to Harris, though the details may vary a bit from agency to agency. As a result, print traffic people have a lot of options open to them in moving around from agency to agency or in moving into traffic work for publications or publishing companies. In fact, people with agency experience are often looked upon favorably by magazines and book publishers because the pace and variety of agency work provides a thorough grounding in all areas of traffic and production.

POSITIONS AND PAY

TRAFFIC ASSISTANT/PRINT PRODUCTION ASSISTANT

For the most part you enter print production and traffic departments as an assistant. Chances are you'll be assigned to several production supervisors or print traffic coordinators and you'll be in charge of keeping track of department paperwork, staying on top of deadlines, and looking after the many details that this type of work generates.

Though in some cases you may enter production departments with no previous work experience, more and more production and traffic managers prefer people who know what they're doing from day one and who will commit themselves to the department rather than pass through it quickly. As Dick Madigan put it: "There really isn't room for gradual development today. When we hire into this department, we are looking for someone with the technical knowledge needed for the job." Preparation through technical courses at school can help, though work experience is invariably preferred. A college degree in and of itself is no advantage in breaking into production or traffic work.

Salaries for assistants start at around $12,000 to $13,000.

TRAFFIC COORDINATOR

The next step up in traffic is the traffic coordinator, the key person who actually carries out the work of coordinating and control. People in this job keep in daily contact with the creative groups, the account group, and the accounting department, and they act as liaison with the various publications. Some of them will deal directly with clients. As a job makes its rounds through the various departments of the agency, the traffic coordinator (or supervisor) shepherds it through.

Pay for someone in this position is in the $15,000 to $25,000 range, depending on experience.

PRODUCTION SUPERVISOR

At the same level as the traffic coordinator is the production supervisor (or buyer), the person who actually deals with the photoplate makers and printers on each particular print ad. At a large agency there will be a group of perhaps ten people in this position, and they divide up the accounts of the agency among them. Similarly, there is a type director who handles the agency work with matters related to buying, setting, and designing type and who deals with the outside type houses.

Pay for production supervisor and type director is at about the same level as traffic coordinator.

PRODUCTION MANAGER/TRAFFIC MANAGER

These are the positions held by the overseers of the production and traffic departments. These people see that the work is being executed at a professional standard; they assign work to their staffs and deal with the heads of the agency departments on matters relating to all phases of print advertising. Budgets, schedules, quality control, hiring, and firing all come under the jurisdiction of the production and traffic managers. As one production manager summed up: "My job is to get the best possible price on each job and to try to keep control." In many cases, a traffic manager will coordinate all the work on a new account to get things started and then, when the account is running smoothly, turn it over to one of the traffic supervisors. Production managers will keep in contact with clients and may have to travel at times to consult with an out-of-town client or to check a press run.

Managers earn anywhere from $25,000 to $40,000, depending on experience.

Very often there will be one person who heads up all of the various branches of traffic and production including art buying, studio bullpen, and typography and to whom all production supervisors and traffic coordinators report. Dick Madigan, who holds this position with McCann-Erickson in New York, has been with the agency for thirty-five years. During this time he moved up from checking regional newspapers to see if the ads were appearing correctly to the top position in the print production department—an indication that print production and traffic offer fine opportunities to those with the dedication to take advantage of them.

THE VIEW FROM THE TOP:
AGENCY CHIEF EXECUTIVES

When you're out there on the street trying to hustle your first advertising job, it can be consoling to consider that all those bigshots, those seeming deities who preside over their global advertising agencies, started in exactly the same place you're in now. Tom Clark, president and chief operating officer of BBDO, once had $75 to his name and was desperate for work. Bill Phillips, chairman of the Ogilvy Group and of Ogilvy & Mather Worldwide, once sold magazines door to door. They too had to worry about things like whether the account supervisor would return their phone calls and whether their checks would start bouncing before their first paycheck arrived. They started pretty much at the bottom and rose pretty much to the top—and they did it themselves. That's the great, and also the somewhat scary thing about advertising: you do it yourself. Connections, money, family, or school ties may get you in the door, but you rise or sink based on your own abilities. And anyway, lots of other things, such as talent, perseverance, or a good portfolio, also get you in the door.

The four chief executives interviewed in this chapter head up agencies that rank in the nation's top 12 (I hit numbers 1, 2, 6, and 12). The one thing these presidents and chairmen have in common (aside from all being men) is that not one of them had any plans (or even dreams) of going into advertising. It just sort of happened. Tom Clark wanted to work for Edward R. Murrow at CBS. Alex Kroll, president and chief executive officer of Young & Rubicam, seemed destined for a career in professional football. Bill Phillips had a fine career going at Procter & Gamble. None had any special sense of destiny, none had visions that he would sit at the head of the table and hold the reins of power in his hands. The success of these men was not just luck, circumstance, leadership, force of personality, or sheer talent and brainpower, though all of these elements played a part. The crucial factor can perhaps be compared to the bond that makes a happy marriage. There was passion, love, suitability, dedication, and lots and lots of hard work to make it work. Though the choice of advertising was accidental, it was in all cases ultimately the right choice. It fit.

In advertising, it's possible to rise to the top through any of the major functions. Of the six chief executives I interviewed (four for this chapter, two for Chapter Four), one had been an art director, two were writers, two came up through account management, and one had done just about everything an agency offers. There are also chief executive officers from the ranks of media and research. As Alex Kroll has said, "Leaders are chosen because they're outstanding leaders, not because they represent a particular craft or cult." There are, however, trends in advertising leadership as there are trends in advertising everything else. Today's trend is a return to creative leadership after a period of domination by businessmen (account people, researchers, and financial types) in the seventies. *Return*, because many of the great and most celebrated agency leaders of yesteryear were writers and artists—Leo Burnett, Fairfax Cone, Bill Bernbach, David Ogilvy, Mary Wells Lawrence, to name some of the better known. Of this group, Mary Wells Lawrence is the only one still officially at the helm of her agency Wells, Rich, Greene (and the only woman chief executive of a major agency—some things haven't yet changed, even in advertising). But of the top six shops today, three of them—Y&R, J. Walter Thompson, and BBDO—have creatives at the top. This trend, says Burt Manning, former copywriter and now chairman/CEO of JWT/USA, indicates that "we're getting back to our heritage, acknowledging the primacy of the product of our business" (quoted in *New York* magazine, October 15, 1984).

So what is life at the top like? What does the job of chairman, president, chief executive entail? Bill Phillips, of Ogilvy & Mather, described it this way: "It is a job that is by definition impossible. I take organizational responsibility for the alignment of our forces throughout the world. I try to make sure the organization is putting our primary emphasis on our creative work and our service to our clients. We seek to pursue excellence in all aspects of our work. I watch the finances of the company, and that's made somewhat more complicated by the fact that we're a public company. I spend a lot of time in community and civic affairs. I travel a great deal—130,000 miles a year. Staffing is also a part of the job in the sense of filling key mangement positions, encouraging our training programs, hiring the best people, firing the worst."

Alex Kroll took a slightly more abstract approach in identifying the core of his job as president and CEO of Young & Rubicam: "I believe that our fundamental business is to help build our clients' businesses by being the best at creating marketing and communications ideas. Ideas are the centerpiece of Y&R and they always have been in the sixty-two years that the company has been in existence. I think of my job as starting with a mission. What do I do to help that come true? The first thing is clients: helping our clients build their businesses. That means understanding those businesses and then understanding how we can help and then providing a framework where ideas can productively assist in that process. The first thing in the morning, before I open my briefcase, before I look at any phone messages or begin to organize the business part of my day, I try to participate in this process. I take one client and think about his business and think of something new. That's what I want all of our people to do. That is where it begins."

Kroll went on to explain how this translates into specific functions that he performs: "A goodly percentage of my time is interaction with clients and our people; because this is not a business that you can capture from cold reports. I spend a considerable amount of time involved with the ideas of our business, particularly the creative ideas at the conceptual stage. There also is a part of me that is a planner, because we must do a good, disciplined job of long-range planning. There is a part of the job that has to do with finances worldwide. So you'll find me at the intersection of those streets on any given day." That is, on the days when he isn't traveling—which he ordinarily does forty to forty-five percent of his time.

Barry Loughrane, president and chief executive officer of the Doyle Dane Bernbach Group, insisted that "there's no such thing as an average day or an average week. Of course that's one of the reasons I love this business so much. You have to be prepared for anything. The phone can ring and any one of fifty clients can be there asking a specific question, and you have to be up to speed with the answers. There's the knowledge base, the time management problem, the keeping up and being flexible enough to go from one client's business to another or one facet of the advertising business to another, back and forth rapidly. That is probably the most difficult part of the job."

Bill Phillips said his "typical day" starts at quarter to six: "I wake up then, do probably an hour and a half of paperwork at home, because that's about the only time I have clear. Then I send my briefcase to the office and maybe I'll meet someone for breakfast. Then I'll come to the agency, meet with various people, and go to lunch with a client. In the afternoon I might go and visit a client, look at some creative work, go to a board meeting of a volunteer group, go home, put on a black tie, go to some dinner at the Waldorf or whatever. Or, a typical twenty-four-hour day is sometimes to get on an airplane at 6 o'clock at night, fly to London, get there, change my clothes, do business that day, take the Concorde back the next evening." Phillips adds that "physical energy, stamina, and the ability to sleep on airplanes are absolute requirements for the job."

Tom Clark, president and chief operating officer of BBDO, emphasized that managing people is one of the keys to the job: "This is a people business; that's the primary resource you have and you must be able to recognize and nurture people. The president of an agency in large measure is really in charge of human resources. He is the personnel man first and foremost."

Taken all together, the responsibilities of the chief executive can seem awesome. How could one person do all this? The answer is, seldom is there only one person at the top. Most large agencies have a group of chief executives—operating officer, chief financial officer, executive creative director—who run the company, as well as an executive committee that meets periodically to advise, guide, and report. At Ogilvy & Mather, for example, there is an executive committee made up of Phillips; Ken Roman, president of Ogilvy & Mather Worldwide; Michael Ball, vice chairman of O&M; James Benson, vice chairman of the non-Ogilvy agencies; John Gill, secretary-treasurer; and David Ogilvy, who remains very active in agency affairs from Touffou, his medieval French chateau. In addition, there is a board of directors of twenty key people from the Ogilvy offices around the world.

Things work a little differently at BBDO, where there are three key figures in charge; Allen Rosenshine, chairman, chief executive officer; Phil Dusenberry, vice chairman and executive creative director; and Tom Clark, president and chief operating officer. Clark describes the CEO as the "the court of last resort, the arbiter who makes or reverses the final decisions." The CEO is in charge of all of the company's operations—overseeing the largest pieces of business; managing the senior account people; and running public relations, personnel, research, and media, all of which report directly to him. Dusenberry's domain is the entire creative output of the agency (he's the man behind those fabulous Michael Jackson and Lionel Richie Pepsi commercials). The three top honchos "counsel together usually once a week or so," says Clark. While each has his area of responsibility, Clark points out that there are no clear dividing lines in the decision-making: "Rarely is there an instance where you say to yourself, well, that's my decision to make or Phil's to make or Allen's to make. It's just a natural order of things." In addition to the leadership provided by these three, there is an account management committee that Clark formed two years ago. Its members include senior account managers, the heads of research and media, and a senior creative. Dusenberry and Rosenshine are ex officio members, but they usually don't attend. The committee meets once a month outside the agency at a dinner and more frequently when difficult issues arise.

Clark says the committee is "a great sounding board for me to exchange information and attitudes on what may be important issues, on certain pieces of business, or evolving questions about policy or procedures in the agency. We try as much as possible to leave the titles outside the door."

Though each agency operates differently, the pattern of chief executives and executive committee holds true for many large shops. At small agencies, one or two people—the founding partners, say, or a business person and a creative—may run the show all by themselves.

One question you can't help wondering about when you encounter an agency head is: How do you do it? How did you get from the bottom to the top? This question was at the top of my list when I got Tom Clark, Alex Kroll, Barry Loughrane, and Bill Phillips to talk candidly about the ups and downs (mostly ups) of their careers. I also asked them about their greatest accomplishments, their philosophies of advertising, and their advice for people trying to break in to the business.

(One question I didn't ask was how much money they earn. You can be sure, however, that they're all making out quite well. *Advertising Age* reports that the 1984 average salary range for agency presidents was $250,000 to $400,00 with $75,000 bonus. So put these four, heads of *un*average agencies, above the $500,000-a-year mark.)

Here, then, are profiles on these four advertising success stories.

TOM CLARK
President and Chief Operating Officer
BBDO

Here's an advertising success story with all the elements: small town boy comes to the big city without much cash but with a lot of ambition, stumbles into advertising (starting in the mailroom), and works his way, over a period of thirty years, to the top of one of America's strongest and largest agencies. It's the story of Tom Clark and he tells it best in his own words:

"I had no idea when I was a young man in college that I wanted to get into advertising or marketing at all. I was born and raised in a little town in Maryland, I studied journalism, and my bet was to be in broadcasting. As a matter of fact, until I went to an advertising agency the first time, which was in 1955, I didn't know what an advertising agency was and had no idea what it did. I had been a student of broadcasting and held the celebrities of broadcasting somewhat in awe. I was a huge fan of Edward R. Murrow. So I decided that the best thing for me to do if I was going to realize my ambition would be to go to New York, the center of broadcasting.

"Through my father I arranged an interview with a man who owned an advertising agency in New York and who was an ex-officer of CBS. His name was Paul Gaynor. The name of his agency in those days was Gaynor and Company; later it became Gaynor and Ducas. That's the first agency I was ever in and the only reason that I was there was so that Gaynor could see me and find out whether or not I had two heads and if I did not, as the case turned out, he would arrange interviews for me at CBS, ABC, and NBC. I tried to get an interview with Ed Murrow, but I was interviewed instead by his secretary.

"I think I came to New York with about $75 in my pocket, and after a week of interviews it became crystal clear that in spite of my absolutely 'incredible' talent, I was not going to be offered a job as a broadcaster and I was running out of money. But, of course, I couldn't go back home, because how could one admit failure at such an early age? Anyway, I hung on through the following Monday and Paul Gaynor took pity upon my sad and sullen countenance and offered me a job in the agency. This is almost a dinosaur's tale now, but then the only entry place was the mailroom. The day I started, which was the following day, he paid me the astronomical sum of $45 a week. The next day, CBS called and offered me a job as a page at $42 a week and I said no, because at that time $3 meant a lot to me.

"That is how I got into the agency business. I worked through every department of the advertising agency business over a period of what has come to be thirty years, starting at the mailroom and then going into the traffic department and the production department. I went into the billing department. I did accounts payable. I did some copywriting. I gravitated into account work because I wasn't talented enough to write, and I certainly didn't have the talent to be an art director and I didn't have the patience for numbers in accounting. I like people—so I went into account work.

"I was at Gaynor and Company for seven years, got to be an account executive, then after a stint on the client side, which was one of the worst mistakes I ever made, I went back to Maryland near my home and sold some advertising space for the Baltimore *Sun* papers in the New York market. I got back in the agency business with a company called The Kudner Agency, which is now Tatham-Laird & Kudner. I got to be an account supervisor, then the business I was on, which was General Telephone and Sylvania, went to Doyle Dane Bernbach and I was asked to go along with the business, which I did. I was at Doyle Dane for a year and a half. Then one of the people I knew at Tatham had joined BBDO in San Francisco and I was offered a job by that gentleman in the San Francisco office of BBDO—that was about eighteen years ago. I took it and I've been with the company ever since."

Clark joined BBDO as an account supervisor in San Francisco, moved to Cleveland as management supervisor ("that was traumatic," he recalls), returned briefly to New York, and then moved to BBDO/Detroit as assistant office manager, from which he was soon promoted to general manager of the Detroit office on the Chrysler business. Then it was back to New York as executive vice president and, about three years ago, he stepped into the office of president.

Clark draws two morals from this incredibly varied experience: the first is the importance of maintaining relationships—genuine relationships—with people "whether you're on the way up or on the way down"; the second is the value of working in different parts of the country. "The time I spent in San Francisco, Cleveland, Detroit, and New York has given me a much broader perspective on communications in terms of the people you really have to reach. The country isn't just 42nd Street. So much of what is prepared in advertising today is written for New York and it simply doesn't play in Peoria."

Clark does not limit his relationships to people at the higher levels: "I try and see as many young people as I can. Interview them. Try and give them advice. We have a sensational training program in the agency now for entry-level people. We bring young people in, and I'm pleased to say that there are about sixty-five to seventy percent women in the ranks of the account management trainees."

Q: Can you pinpoint your accomplishments that you think have been most crucial to your success?
A: Well, that's hard. That's hard because so much of what an account manager does, he does in tandem with other people. It is hard to say that I did this as opposed to the creative guy who can show you a film and say "I did that campaign." Broadly speaking, I'd say the one thing that I think I have done well is I have recognized talent when I've seen it, managed talent well, which is always a sensitive task, particularly with the creative people, and nurtured it. This is a people business: that's the resource you have

and you have to be able to recognize and nurture people. The president of an agency in large measure is really in charge of human resources. He is a personnel man first and foremost.

I personally am involved in every decision for every promotion or switch of account people in the agency. It's important for me to address that because I can watch people's career paths, and it's important for the people in the agency to understand that the president is paying attention to that. Nothing is more important than having the right people in the right job in the right business.

Q: What is it about advertising or working in an agency that has kept you all these years?

A: The creative process. It's the application of marketing strategy to the creative process. I absolutely love being involved in the creative process, and by that I mean contributing thoughts; watching a campaign evolve; being involved in its development, its strategic direction; selling it to the client; watching it come to fruition as it's produced; and then watching the results when it works. I couldn't find that on the client side because even though I was working with an advertising agency, I was still removed, removed by being the client. Some people just aren't built to be outside of the agency business, and I guess even though I accidentally got into it, once I got into it and realized what it was I said, "Gee, what a lucky guy I am. I fell into something I really love."

Q: I'd like to talk a little bit about BBDO. This agency used to have a rather staid reputation . . .

A: The gray grandmother of advertising.

Q: Right. But now, all of a sudden it's *Ad Age*'s Agency of the Year and it's being written up as a super hot creative shop . . .

A: This is the place.

Q: What happened? Has there really been a change—or is this just something the press is creating as a new image?

A: There's been a change. Some of it very intentional and some of it luck. Intentional in that in the 1970s, ten years ago, we were, shall we say, uneven in our creative products. We weren't doing knock-your-socks-off creative. We'd gotten a little conservative, a little comfortable. We got a little stultified and we hadn't brought in new, young, fresh talent. Then Bruce Crawford, who had my job then, set about to do that. He put

Allen Rosenshine in charge and told Allen to go out and start hiring some terrific people, and Allen did. He brought in people like Phil Dusenberry, and Phil brought in people like Ted Sann and Charlie Miesmer, and those people are superstars, and that's why we've got the work we do today. It's sensational stuff.

Q: In addition to its new-found reputation for creative brilliance, BBDO has a long-standing reputation for top-rate management. What does that mean? What are some of the qualities that make a good management good?

A: Judgment, experience, training, attitude. Judgment in the context of grace under pressure. Don't panic. Experience in the context of every time you think something is new, you have people in the agency who have seen it before and experienced it before and have been through it on another product in another category—that kind of thing. It's a combination of all those things rolled up into people who fit in an environment which is largely unstructured. This is a very unstructured agency. We don't have strategy review boards, we delegate to people who we believe have the judgment and the talent to do the job, and we let them do it and we reward them for it.

Q: Where do you see the agency headed?

A: Well, I think we'll continue to grow. I think the creative product will stay at the level it is, maybe get a little better, although that's going to be hard to do. I think we have to get a little smarter in terms of strategic sense. I think we will probably become more internationally cohesive through networking; that we must do to compete in multinational marketing. But I hope we don't change the persona of the company, because it's a good place to work, it's got good people.

Q: Could you characterize the persona?

A: BBDO is an agency that takes the business seriously but doesn't take itself too seriously. *[For more about BBDO, see a profile of the agency in Chapter Three.]*

Q: Where are the future leaders of advertising now?

A: I don't know where they are; hopefully, some of them are here. People come to this business from a variety of avenues. I think the MBA route is overstated. People will come to us from all sorts of places. Some people back into this business, like me. Some people absolutely say to themselves, "I want to be in marketing, and I want to study marketing, and I want to get into the agency business, and I want to work on packaged goods accounts, and"—even—"I want to work on Procter & Gamble or

General Foods." Some people really focus like that. Most people who will succeed at the upper levels, though, will be generalists rather than specialists. Being a generalist requires a broader range of talents and a broader range of experiences, and that's what makes it.

Q: What sort of people do you want to attract to BBDO?
A: People who really like this business, who aren't cynical about the business, who understand that the role of advertising is an important one, but also understand that it isn't the most important thing in the world. They've got a set of values.

Q: Do you have any advice for people who are trying to break in?
A: Well, first of all, make sure that you understand that the advertising agency business is a service business. That you are an agent. Very few people remember the fact that they are an agent representing a client and using the client's money. If you're not prepared to be in the *service* business, with all that implies, then you shouldn't be in this business. Having made that decision, you should learn as much about the business in as many different areas as you can and keep your options open from the standpoint of whether to choose marketing or research or media or creative or whatever. Before deciding, wait until you've seen firsthand all of those functions work in an agency.

ALEXANDER KROLL
President and Chief Executive Officer
Young & Rubicam

In Chapter One, Alex Kroll told about how he got into advertising and why he chose copywriting over football. Let's pick up Kroll's career where we left off and then listen to what he has to say about creative leadership, about his own commitment to advertising, about the people who work at Y&R, and about how to join their ranks.

Kroll has only been at one agency his entire advertising career. But saying that Kroll has been at Y&R is like saying that Bruce Springsteen has been on a few records. Kroll has helped to *make* Y&R what it is today—the largest advertising agency in the world. A *New York* magazine profile of Kroll stated that Kroll's "leadership, tenacity and grit" brought in over $400 million worth of new business between 1977 and 1982. The article declared flatly that this is "the best new-business record in advertising history."

Kroll started at the agency as a research trainee back in 1962; he didn't like research much and moved into copywriting in 1965. Things clicked, and his advertising career—his Y&R career—was off and running. By 1969, Kroll was senior vice president and associate creative director. In 1970, when Ed Ney took control of the agency in a dramatic "palace coup," Kroll became executive vice president and creative director of the agency; at thirty-three, he was the youngest man in the agency's history to hold this position. Six years later, he was made president of Y&R/USA. His title changed to chief operating officer in 1982, and in 1985 Ed Ney announced that Kroll would take over as president and chief executive officer. (Ney himself retains the position of chairman.)

Alex Kroll starts his day at 5:15. Catching a train about half an hour from his home in rural Connecticut, he gets to the Y&R New York headquaters a little after 7 A.M. and starts wading through reports and memos. Kroll has already put in a couple good hours before the daily round of meetings gets underway. Interaction with his staff is, he notes, crucial to his job, and a good deal of this interaction is still devoted to the creative process. Getting people excited, stimulating creative ideas, leading, and inspiring— that's what it's all about for Alex Kroll.

Q: When you began to write advertising copy here at Y&R, did you have any sense of where you were headed, of how your career was going to unfold?
A: No. I stayed because I liked it. I think that's the wonderful thing about writing copy—the satisfactions are immediate and tactile. You get the feedback from the page. I thought of writing as a craft, as an end in itself rather than as a steppingstone to becoming a supervisor or creative director.

Q: What has kept you in advertising all these years?
A: The experiences of being in advertising. After playing football, I took a pay cut of about $13,000 a year for the honor and privilege of doing this. This was hard. I had a nice apartment, my wife was pregnant, and I had a Mercedes in the parking lot. I had to support all of them. So I started taking extra jobs. I ghost-wrote books. I broadcast football games. I remember I got an offer to broadcast sports on WCBS in the afternoon. It was a possible alternative to advertising. It was quite a lot of money. But I chose not to do that because sports was a field that I had really done. I had immersed

myself in it for all of my youth and a lot of my young adulthood. I just didn't see enormous personal growth in that. Whereas advertising was still immense, open spaces, frontiers beyond frontiers, places you couldn't anticipate going. I was learning all the time.

Q: What kept you at Y&R all these years?
A: The same thing. Y&R kept providing the kinds of experiences and stretches and challenges that seemed to be necessary for me. It had a cordial, civilized environment. An environment of men and women who really do practice civilized behavior, maybe my own perception of what Renaissance people are supposed to be like. People of great, broad interests beyond just the business day. People with high expectations of themselves, both personally and in business.

As far as new experiences, one came in 1968 when I went overseas for the first time. That fall I went over to work in Germany and in London, and it was the first time I ever gathered a team of people from different countries. The experience of trying to *organize* creativity rather than doing it myself was a stretch. In 1970 I became creative director of the whole agency. This was another kind of stretch—to try to bring some philosophical uniformity to the creative process for an agency which was highly decentralized.

Q: Can you define that philosophy in some way?
A: Part of it is that we developed an intelligent discipline for thinking through problems. We devised tools for thinking, a system that people around the world could use to think through issues. It arose from our experiences on thousands and thousands of brands, services, products, corporations. At the same time we demanded that the finished advertising itself deal with what we call the *human truth* of the product, which required us to drive away from talking about the attributes of products toward dramatizing the human values that the product would deliver. Our advertising has a wonderful dialectic to it, a tension between a highly disciplined process which gets you to a strategy and an extremely emotional presentation of that strategy. (Some recent examples of this include campaigns Y&R has prepared for Kodak, Irish Spring, Johnson & Johnson, and Jell-O.)

Q: What are some of your accomplishments that you think contributed most to your success?
A: I think the most important is that I have a good ability to help other people create

YOUNG & RUBICAM NEW YORK

CLIENT: DR PEPPER
PRODUCT: DR PEPPER
TITLE: "SPACE COWBOY"

LENGTH: 90 SECONDS
COMM. NO.: DPYT-4579
DATE: 3/18/85

(SFX: SPACESHIP LANDING)

(SFX: JUKEBOX MUSIC, OTHER-WORLD VOICES AND CROWD SOUNDS THROUGHOUT)

SPACE COWBOY: Gimme the unusual.

I said, gimme the unusual.

I *said* the unusual

CHORUS: HOLD OUT . . . HOLD OUT . . .

FOR THE OUT OF THE ORDINARY . . .

HOLD OUT FOR DR PEPPER.

DON'T BE SOLD OUT, HOLD OUT . . .

IT'S A TASTE THAT'S EXTRAORDINARY

NO DOUBT IT'S DR PEPPER. DR PEPPER . . .

Young & Rubicam president Alex Kroll's philosophy—to dramatize the human values of a product, be it Dr Pepper or Mercury cars (see next page).

better. I believe that all people are more creative than they think they are, and under certain circumstances with the right guidance they can accomplish a good deal more than they thought. If you can communicate that to people, if you can get them to understand the game, understand the field of play, what the goals are, understand what it takes to win, and then excite them—you know, those little exciter lights that come on when there is enough electrical energy—if you can do all that, they will undoubtedly come back with a solution far better and far more idiosyncratic than I would. I found out by accident many years ago that I could do this with groups of people. They could get the sense of the game, the target, what it took to win, and leave more energized than before. Nine times out of ten those people returned with better solutions than I would have been able to deliver if I had sat down to solve all those problems myself. That was an interesting thing to find out about myself, so I began to put myself more and more into those kinds of situations where I could be the person who stimulated the exciter bulb. If you think that through, that ability has something to do with management. Thus, it became possible for me to make a bridge from creating to managing.

Q: Is there some lesson from sports that you have found particularly helpful in your advertising career?
A: Keep getting up. Run "north and south," meaning toward the goal. The fact is that the problems arise when you go sideways. Most people find it easier to run sideways, why not? There is no particular resistance, nobody tries to stop you. It's easy to avoid the hard course.

Q: Do you still play sports?
A: Oh yes. More than ever. I hate to think of stopping. I play tennis. I cross-country ski. And then, just as basic conditioning, I run. I ride a stationary bicycle with those heavy-hands weights. And a moving bicycle on the weekends. I love sports. I've always loved sports. I just like to play.

Q: One executive I interviewed told me that he loved the advertising business but would never want his kids to go into it. It's just too brutal. How do you feel about that?
A: I'm not sure that, even as we speak, my oldest son isn't moving into the advertising business. He works for a radio station in Westchester County and he seems to have some facility with doing commercials. I didn't tell him to play football. I didn't tell him to stop playing football. He did both those things. And I'm not going to tell him to channel his creative energy into one particular field. Brutal? I don't agree with that. At heart this is a creative enterprise, where the exceptional people can make quite a mark and actualize their potential almost faster than in any other business and deal with such a multitude of issues and problems on a worldwide basis. We have terrific jobs—dealing with the most changeable things on earth, *human beings*—not human nature, but human beings and their interrelations. So I don't agree with this "brutal" business at all.

Q: Can you put your finger on the personality, background, education, or character traits that separate someone who strikes you as *right* for Young & Rubicam from someone who strikes you as *wrong*?
A: Yes. Almost none of them ever study advertising. They are usually the kids with the broadest range of interests who have tried the most things, who are also intellectually honest, who call good, good and bad, bad. And the spinoff of that, interestingly enough, is a sense of humor. There is some relationship between the ability to create and see things in new relationships and the ability to respond to humor and to be hu-

morous. The kids we take into our training programs and who succeed have one over-whelming common factor—raw intelligence. They're smarter than hell and they're honest. They don't delude themselves. At the heart of creativity (and I think almost everybody who is successful in this business is creative) is the necessity for intellectual integrity. If you don't have that, nothing else really works.

BARRY LOUGHRANE
President and Chief Executive Officer
Doyle Dane Bernbach Group

Doyle Dane Bernbach has had its ups and downs since it opened its doors in 1949. In the late fifties and early sixties, Bill Bernbach's small, iconoclastic shop practically invented the creative revolution all by itself. Volkswagen, Avis, Levy's Jewish Rye Bread, Ohrbach's—campaigns for these compa-nies were the banners of the revolution and they had all been hoisted by the same amazing agency. But then, as the econo-my shrank and the fires of revolution burnt out, DDB seemed to lose its way. There were reports and rumors of nasty inter-nal battles, disorganization, creative tyranny over business sense, out-of-control egos, and disgruntled clients. Some major accounts departed. The advertising stopped win-ning raves. When Bill Bernbach died in 1982, DDB was in serious disarray. Now, suddenly, in the last year or two, the little bastion of zany creativity that grew into an international giant (ranking twelfth in the nation) seems to be back on its feet, and a lot of the credit for it goes to Barry Loughrane, president and chief executive officer of the Doyle Dane Bernbach Group, the holding company for all of the DDB agencies around the world.

There couldn't have been a more logical choice of leader to put DDB back on course. Loughrane had worked at the agency during its first flush of creative break-throughs. He was brought on board by Joe Daly (now DDB chairman) to work in account management in 1959, and he had risen to group head in charge of fourteen accounts with responsibility for the Detroit office. Loughrane reminisces about those days: "It was such an honored place and such a curious place—and I guess it was a little nutty since we were all kind of revolutionaries. It was wild, it was growing, it was excit-ing, but underneath it all there was a certain wisdom that this is a better way to handle a given product because it's a better way to communicate with people. We had cheap, little, ugly offices at West 43rd Street; there were no fancy conference rooms, we had no big marketing/merchandising department, no new business department. We were a maverick sort of group. But it was a lot of fun to work there."

In 1972, Loughrane moved to St. Louis to manage Gardner Advertising, which Wells, Rich, Greene had just acquired. He returned to DDB in 1978 when Joe Daly asked him to run the West Coast offices. He agreed, and it turned out to be a fantastic opportunity. As Loughrane tells it: "I'd always been interested in the West Coast, but it used to be thought of as a place to drop out—send someone out there and he sits under a palm tree and everything is very laid-back with no professionalism. But 1978 was just about the time it was really changing. All of a sudden, there was so much activity out there, in packaged goods, agriculture, financial services, and all the Japanese products coming in to the U.S. So I thought the time was terrific to go out." It was terrific and so was Loughrane: in his five and a half years on the West Coast, the DDB operation grew from one office billing $30 million to four offices billing $170 million.

When he returned to New York in 1982 to take charge of all DDB domestic operations, he'd been with the agency nearly twenty years, so he knew the company very well, he knew the people and the mentality, but, as he puts it, "I was not here in New York while a lot of the turmoil of the seventies was going on, and so I was not involved with the squabbling on a firsthand basis. When I came back here, I think a lot of people said, 'Well, good. We've got somebody we know and this guy knows us, and he knows the company, he knows our heritage.' It's for that reason that the spirit of cooperation has been very good."

Since Loughrane has taken command, the company has done some reorganizing, some weeding out of personnel, some restructuring, especially in the way creatives work with account people—and it has also produced some exceptional advertising (see illustrations). Under Loughrane, the agency shows every sign of surging back to advertising's forefront again.

Loughrane himself had an unusual entree into the business. Back in high school, he was tapped to write an essay about advertising for an essay contest sponsored by the Advertising Federation of America. "My essay was pretty negative," he recalls, "and the fact that I won was very surprising to me and to my school and to everybody else." But the fact that he won got him a summer internship at Dancer Fitzgerald. When that ended he thought that was it on his advertising career—but it wasn't, by a long shot. In 1951, Loughrane went to work in the one-man radio/television department of a tiny,

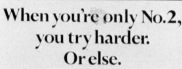

Doyle Dane then…

...And Doyle Dane now.

fledgling agency called Hewitt, Ogilvy, Benson & Mather, but, since there wasn't yet much action in TV, he moved into account work as an account executive on the Sun Oil account. The fledgling agency was, of course, destined to become the giant Ogilvy & Mather, and Loughrane himself, after a stint on the client side with Hathaway Shirts, was destined for DDB.

Q: What was it like to be at Doyle Dane Bernbach when you first started here?
A: I came to Doyle Dane Bernbach in 1959 and I was very fortunate, because I came here at a time when this agency was becoming very well known and growing very fast. Whenever you're in a high-growth situation it obviously presents many more opportunities. The agency was revolutionary in the sense that Bill Bernbach brought a new style to the advertising business and a new way of working. Certainly not new now, since practically everybody does it, but in those days advertising was pretty dull until Bernbach came along. The way advertising was done was that a writer would write a piece of copy, he would send it down the hall to an illustrator who would go out and get some photographs, and they'd build an ad. The whole concept of copy and graphics working together was really an art form that did not exist, so Doyle Dane Bernbach presented, if you will, a kind of new horizon. The idea was to use advertising in a certain sense of verbal and visual reality, as if you were talking to your neighbor over the back fence, and that was really Bernbach's approach to this business. We grew very fast, we were successful, we were talked about, there were some very good people. We were all kind of working together as one happy, little, single band.

Q: What would you say is the toughest job you've ever had?
A: Well, I think that the jobs only get tougher as they go along, simply because there's more responsibility and because decisions that you have to make are sometimes not only difficult, but can have a rather large impact emotionally, financially, or otherwise. I think the job has become more difficult as we've gotten larger and as the business got more complicated. It's a much more complicated business today than it was several years ago. It seems to me that the most difficult thing is not any one individual issue, not any one particular client problem or people problem or recruitment problem or anything like that. They all kind of have a life of their own, but I don't think they are that difficult. The difficulty is in trying to keep up with all of it. I got back on Sunday night from a week in Europe at pan-European meetings. My calendar this week is filled with all sorts of varied things including a one-day trip to Canada for some meetings.

There are acquisition meetings; there are financial meetings; there are client meetings; there are new business meetings; there is merchandising, promotion, marketing—and all of these things are telescoped into a week. So there's no such thing as an average day or an average week. Of course, that's one of the reasons I love this business so much, because it's not dull. You have to be prepared for anything. But this is also the thing that makes it difficult, because it is very hard to be expert in so many different things.

Q: Is there one area of your work that you get the most pleasure out of?
A: There's an awful lot of work in this business that is unseen, that Hollywood has never glamorized, novelists have never written about—there's a lot of hard work. Ninety percent of it is learning your job, learning the business. It's all the hard sweat to get to a position where you know what to do with the advertising problem. But, of course, the real fun is the end result. This is a problem-solution business. The fun is being able to solve the problem and do it in an artistic and creative way that people are going to recognize.

Q: So that the creative side really never stops being the central thing, even to your job?
A: Well, that's the product. In the final analysis, that's what they come here for. The marketing, the merchandising, public relations, media, research testing, new product development—all of these things are part of it and they're all very necessary, and we do them all. But the fact of the matter is when I meet people for dinner or I go to a cocktail party, people can't wait to say, "I saw your campaign for so-and-so." That is the visible element that makes you known, that makes you respected; that's the thing that drives everything else.

Q: *Business Week* magazine described you as a tough manager. How are you tough and to whom are you tough?
A: Well, first of all, I don't know that I agree with that. I think there are different definitions of the word "tough." I am pretty much to the point and I am fairly blunt and I have a point of view and people can say that is tough. On the other hand, most of the clients I like are like that. I think the toughest thing in this business is being wishy-washy, not being able to make a decision, not being able to give direction; trying to play the kind of political games where you really do not have a point of view and you think you're trying to please somebody else. So if I am tough, I'm tough in the sense

that I tell everybody kind of what I expect of them. I try to provide clarity and direction.

Q: A lot of the credit for DDB's recent turn-around goes to you. What is the role you saw yourself playing in this process? How did you do it?

A: There are several aspects of that, and I think the first is strictly internal. If you have problems, the first place to start to solve those problems is internally. You are not going to change external perceptions unless/until you've changed the internal attitudes. People will bitch about it, but I think, particularly when times are a little tough, people want a leader, people want somebody to tell them where we're going and what we should be doing. So the first thing in any kind of turnaround situation has to be one where you reshape the attitudes and the desires. Along with that there are other things like organization and financial planning. But fundamentally you have to settle things down. People have to have a sense of purpose, people have to be on the same wavelength. When you start reorganizing and reshaping around that, then people feel both comfortable and more energetic all at the same time.

Q: In some ways, DDB seems to be a paradigm of advertising in the past twenty-five years: it started off as a small, creative maverick; then it got very successful and very big; now it's in a period of regrouping. What do you see in the future? Where are DDB and agencies like it headed?

A: I think we will continue to grow. I think all the large agencies will continue to grow just like the larger companies are continuing to grow. I think that's just a natural phenomenon of the times we're in. I think growth is a wonderful thing. So, given that growth is necessary for business vitality, does that mean to say it's stifling to creativity? I think the answer has to be no. I think that's a crutch. There's no reason you can't be every bit as vital a little bit larger, and, anyway, what the hell's the difference if you're a billion five or a billion seven?

Q: What kind of people do you want to attract to Doyle Dane at the entry level?

A: At the entry level I look for a variety of talents. I am not a great believer in having a short list of criteria—let's say MBAs, eastern schools, so on and so forth. If we have an army of those people then we really do have a gray-suit kind of mentality. Also, while they may fit certain kinds of clients or situations, they will actually not fit others. So I look for a mixture of people. I look for people who want to work here. I think desire is a very good thing. I look for people who are basically bright and not only bright in an intellectual sense, but bright in a kind of curiosity sense. A kind of willingness to explore new things, to travel and learn, to read and see theatre and see arts so that they can learn from many other different media, not necessarily commercial media, what goes on in this world and what human behavior is all about and what turns them on and what turns them off. That is essentially what makes this business go.

WILLIAM PHILLIPS
Chairman
The Ogilvy Group and Ogilvy & Mather Worldwide

 Considering he holds the position of chairman of one of the largest agencies in the world, Bill Phillips is a surprisingly modest, quiet-spoken man. He has the deliberate, collected air of someone who never has to shout to get what he wants. Though he describes himself as "about as undiplomatic as people come," Phillips is also clearly about as unflappable and untyrannical. In fact, he seems ideally suited to lead the agency built by David Ogilvy, who himself has a reputation for acerbic wit, creative flair, and uncommonly keen business sense. Sophisticated, worldly, and civilized, Ogilvy and Phillips are the kinds of ad men who are giving advertising a good name.

Like many of his colleagues at the top, Phillips had no great master plan to launch a career in advertising that would take him to the chairmanship of a major agency. "I started by selling magazines door-to-door when I was just a kid in Chicago," he told me. *"Women's Home Companion, The American Magazine*—you used to sell them for a few cents a copy. I had a myriad of jobs when I was young, selling jobs as well as manual labor. At Cornell, I was Advertising Manager of *The Cornell Daily Sun* and on the football team. After I finished three and a half years in the Navy as a deck and operations officer in 1954, I went back to school at the Graduate School of Commerce at Northwestern, where I got an MBA in eleven months. After sales training, I started at Procter & Gamble in 1955 in Cincinnati, working in the newly formed Food Advertising Department."

So what happened? What prompted the move from P&G to an agency?

"I was doing well at Procter, but I concluded that I didn't want to work for a big company like P&G in what seemed like a too narrow town like Cincinnati, but I was in no hurry to get out. Then I was offered a job for about fifty percent more money than I was making. It was in New York for a small, budding agency called Ogilvy, Benson & Mather. The train was in the station and I decided I would take advantage of the opportunity."

Phillips was hired as an account executive on Maxwell House Coffee, a new assignment that General Foods had just given the agency. At that time, Ogilvy, Benson & Mather was a small agency billing abut $17 million a year with about 170 employees in one office. Phillips rose as the agency expanded. His specialty was packaged goods marketing, the classic route for account people to follow. In 1969, Phillips's career took a crucial turn when Ogilvy & Mather gave him the job of setting up the agency partnerships in Latin America, which he did while also running his GF accounts in New York. In 1975, Phillips stepped into the job of president of the U.S. company, which then included offices in New York, Houston, and Los Angeles. In 1976 he spearheaded the Big Apple campaign for New York City. In 1978, when Andrew Kershaw died, Phillips became chairman and president of the U.S. company. In 1981 he got the title chief executive of the worldwide company and in 1982 chairman of the parent company.

Q: When you first started out as an account executive, did you have your sights set on the top?
A: No, when I started here as an account executive, I thought I'd be in the agency business three years and then probably leave and become a client again.

Q: What happened?
A: Well, this agency has done very well, and it's continued to grow, and that growth has afforded the people here a lot of opportunity for personal growth and expansion and diversity. We now operate in forty-one countries, 220 offices, so it's been a changing scenario. While I've been at one place, it's changed enormously in terms of size, scope, and the things I've been responsible for. And I guess to some extent I was having some impact on that growth. So that while the company was expanding, I was growing in terms of my relative importance.

Q: What accomplishments of yours do you think contributed most to your success within Ogilvy & Mather?
A: I have a good marketing sense, I think I have good people sense, I'm very objective

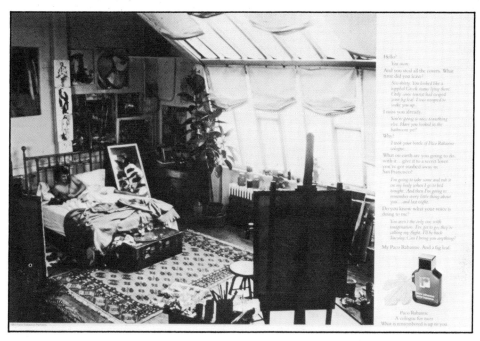

The sweet smell of success: This print ad created something of a sensation for Ogilvy & Mather.

and nonpolitical about things. I think I'm very straightforward. I've had my share of creative ideas. I work very hard. And I've been lucky.

Q: What would you say your favorite part of the job is?
A: I think my favorite part of the job is seeing a great piece of advertising we've done, hearing about something terrific we've done for a client, seeing some young person I've taken interest in move up in the company, or seeing our earnings go up—all of those things.

Q: Does Ogilvy & Mather still reflect the creative philosophy of David Ogilvy?
A: I think that the philosophy that David espoused has continued to be practiced. "Look before you leap." I think there is probably an old testament and a new testament. I would say that the new testament has tended to give more emphasis to emotion

in advertising and has tended to give the execution and *how* something is said as much importance as *what* is said, and I think we now create advertising that is somewhat more attractive and likable by consumers, but that reflects the change in consumer behavior and changes in the perceptions of consumers.

Q: Does Ogilvy remain active in the company?
A: Yes, he's very active. He lives in Europe and doesn't travel outside of Europe too much, but he is actively involved in all the key issues of the agency and is very much a force in the agency.

Q: Aside from the tremendous growth, how has the agency changed since you joined the company back in the late fifties?
A: Because we've grown, we've become somewhat less of a personal company, just because of our size; but I think we're more professional today, more creative, and, in a sense, we've maintained our atmosphere of being a good place to work, being a civilized place to work. We've maintained and built our ethos, our culture, if you will, through management's involvement with all of our agencies, through David's continued presence, so that we've had a good preservation of spirit of the company.

Q: What sort of young people do you hope to attract to O&M?
A: We hire a lot of people with different backgrounds: we hire people who are obviously bright and interested in advertising, a little unorthodox, willing to work hard, willing to pay the price; who can write well and speak well, who have a wide band of interests.

Q: One person I interviewed said, "Generals rise to the top of corporations, while diplomats rise to the top of agencies." Do you think that's a fair assessment?
A: I'm about as undiplomatic as people come, so I would dispute that. There are some agencies where diplomats have done well, but what it takes is leadership and it usually takes the form of a fairly forthright sense of purpose and direction. I do think, however, that agency people tend to be less structured than people in client businesses. You have to win by intellect and charm a little more. Agencies also tend to be much less hierarchical and fit different talents together in a complementary fashion.

Q: Do you think we're in a period of creative resurgence in advertising?
A: Yes.

Q: What would you attribute that to?

A: Consumers. I think that as people have gotten more accustomed to television and more knowledgeable about products, they take advertising for pretty much what it is, and thus there is a need for more creativity, less blandness. To the extent that so many consumer fields have been so well cultivated in terms of product improvements, product differences are somewhat smaller, and for that reason the advertising has to be in proportion to the product—it can't take itself so seriously. You can't talk in a deep stentorian voice about another product breakthrough in cornflakes, because people will laugh at you—or about a new Coke, for that matter. They really object.

Q: So that people who make advertising are responding to a change of awareness in consumers?

A: Yes. A change of awareness and, more importantly, a change of sophistication. Also because of the plethora of advertising, it's required that advertising stand out, and that's becoming more and more difficult.

Q: What are some of the major trends that are changing advertising now?

A: There have been a number of trends. The advent of technology in broadcast has brought about a break-up of the concentration of the broadcast share of the audiences by the three networks, and that's probably going to continue with the advent of cable and more software from different sources. I think the magazine business is moving from mass to class and that magazines are either "special interest" or upper income demographically or psychographically. Newspapers have changed their make-up and become more localized. Radio has fit into a rapidly paced lifestyle. With all of those changes in media, selling products has changed. People's lives are different now, more women work, more people travel, they have different needs, and the advertising business reflects all of that and is being changed by all of those changes. We have a less predictable society, and as a result of that the agency business has had to continue to be restructured. Agencies are getting very large, of course, and the trick is how to run a big agency, which is a tough job. The perfect agency to run is one that is about 200 employees—that's the perfect size. That way you know the first name of everyone who gets on the elevator. When you start getting bigger you can have people problems. How you manage that becomes a real challenge.

Q: How *do* you manage that?

A: With great difficulty. But we do a lot of things around here to keep this a good place to work. We have a staff meeting every December, daily issues of the *Flagbearer* and a lot of things. We put out a magazine called *Viewpoint* every quarter. We've tended to keep to ourselves, with a point of view and a sense of principle. We have kept a sense of pride by being the best.

Q: What advice would you offer to people trying to break into advertising?
A: The first advice is, if you think you want to go into the agency business, get a job. I'm not being facetious—get a job as a secretary or in the mailroom or in some department, and you can usually wiggle your way on up if you are good, because agencies tend to be unstructured and people who solve problems and do a good job get ahead very quickly. One of the big mistakes is that ninety percent of the people going into the agency business want to be in an account management training program. But remember, agencies hire a wide spectrum of people. As David said in his first book [*Confessions of an Advertising Man*], people should have a specialty that they really know—and that means marketing or pricing or media or research. Be an expert before you become a generalist.

AND DON'T FORGET
ABOUT THOSE OTHER JOBS

Creative, account management, media, research, top management, production, and traffic—what more do you need to run an agency? You'd be surprised. How about a legal staff (or outside counsel), for starters, to review the ads and make sure they comply with federal regulations, network and magazine regulations, industry and agency regulations; an accounting department to make sure money flows in and out the way it is supposed to; personnel and benefits office; mailroom and messengers; receptionists and secretaries.

These are just the basic support people who make the wheels of agency business turn. There are also a host of other jobs available in various specialized branches of advertising and advertising-related functions—direct marketing, public relations, sales promotion, new business acquisition. At some large agencies, there may be a direct marketing division or a public relations department with a full staff of people taking care of this business for the agency's clients; or an entire agency, either independent or a subsidiary of another agency, may devote itself exclusively to direct marketing. Similarly, there are public relations departments at a few agencies as well as independent and subsidiary p.r. outfits that perform this function for companies and/or for advertising agencies. And then there are freelancers of various stripes, usually writers and artists employed by agencies on a project-by-project basis.

The list goes on and on. One of the wonderful things about advertising is that it's such a multi-faceted industry—it brushes up against show business, business business, art, journalism, broadcast, high finance, law—and each facet opens up different career opportunities. There is no way to cover *every* advertising job or even to determine what counts as a "genuine" advertising job and what doesn't. But here is a sampling of some of the "other" career opportunities available in agencies and independent companies that work with agencies.

DIRECT MARKETING

Direct marketing is the world of selling things (and services) direct to the consumer without going through any kind of retail outlet, sales office, or middleman. When L.L. Bean sends you a catalogue and you order a new pair of hiking boots from it, that's direct marketing. Advertising for direct marketing can thus use any media—TV commercials, print ads in newspapers and magazines (fill out this coupon and send it in with your check to receive . . .), radio, telephone solicitation—but by far the largest channel is through the mails. All those offers you're constantly receiving to join a book club, get a new credit card, subscribe to a new magazine, buy your mother a fruit-cake—it's all direct marketing.

People used to be a bit snobby and snide about direct marketing. They dismissed it as junk mail, schlock advertising used by vaguely disreputable companies and produced by the "polyester" crowd of advertising. No longer. Direct marketing is now hot—and direct marketing ad people are getting more and more respect and clout. David Ogilvy, a great advocate of direct marketing (he calls it his "first love and secret weapon"), attributes its current "explosion" to computers: "Computers make it possible to select names fom mailing lists by every imaginable demographic classification, by frequency of purchase and by amount of purchase." The great thing about this form of advertising, he adds, is the way it lends itself to *testing*: "You can test every variable in your mailing and determine *exactly* its effect on your sales." Pinpointing markets with precision and instantly testing results: these are two of the most prized and elusive elements in advertising. No wonder direct marketing is booming.

As direct marketing booms, more and more consumer agencies want to get in on the action so they can offer clients direct marketing as part of their "full service." Some agencies, for example, Ogilvy & Mather, have started their own direct marketing divisions (Ogilvy's is called Ogilvy & Mather Direct Response); others such as Young & Rubicam and McCann-Erickson, have bought previously existing independent direct marketing operations. Y&R has three: Wunderman Ricotta & Kline in New York, the nation's largest direct response agency, Stone & Adler in Chicago, and Chapman Direct Marketing; and McCann has March Direct Marketing. Direct marketing agencies and subsidiaries are set up pretty much like consumer agencies, with creatives, account executives, researchers, production people, etc., but, of course, the work does differ in certain fundamentals. Since the mail remains the predominant direct marketing medium, there is less focus on the types of issues that TV commercials raise—budgeting the production, gross rating points of various shows, networks versus spot. As one direct response account supervisor explained it, "It's a question of what mailings are most appropriate, what time of year to mail, how often, when or whether to remail." Nonetheless, account managers are still shuttling back and forth between agency and client side, creatives are writing and designing the most effective and appealing art and copy, researchers are prying into the mind of the target audience, and so on.

Direct marketing offers a terrific way to break into the advertising business, particularly for copywriters. Because of the ever-increasing volume of direct response advertising, there's lots of work for writers and less competition to get this work than there is in the general consumer area. Direct response is a field in which many writers work on a freelance basis and do quite well.

PUBLIC RELATIONS

Many different kinds of jobs in many different kinds of organizations fall under the rubric "public relations," and for this reason many people don't have a clear focus on what the term means. It's actually pretty simple. The basic thing about PR is that you don't *pay* one of the media to run your messages—you may spend a lot of money devising and producing the message, but you don't spread it through purchased time and space. One of the essential PR techniques is *publicity*, wherein you convince a magazine, newspaper, or television show to feature whatever you're publicizing as part of the *content* of the article or program. Turning a product, service, company, or personality into news is the heart of publicity. For example, when Shirley MacLaine goes on a talk show and, in the course of talking about her diet, her views on the world beyond, and her famous friends, drops the name and publisher of her new book, it's *publicity*. When the publisher buys a full-page ad in the *Times Book Review* announcing the publication of this book, it's *advertising*. Similarly, articles in travel magazines about new ports of call of the *Queen Elizabeth II* are publicity. Articles in local newspapers about the gala opening of a new department store branch are publicity.

Publicity, while crucial and highly visible, is just one of many public relations methods. Others include speeches made by company executives; community events sponsored by the company; lobbying in Washington for favorable legislation; funding scholarships; sponsoring public television shows, concerts, or sports events. Occasionally, PR *will* involve paid advertising as a way of building the *image* or *identity* of the company or of getting behind a cause. For example, when a national distiller runs a magazine ad featuring a bottle of Scotch dressed in red for Christmas—that's consumer advertising. But then that same distiller runs an ad soberly advising caution in drinking and driving over the holidays, that's public relations. The immediate intent is not to sell more scotch but to convince people that the company is concerned about their well-being. (Of course, the long-term hope is that people will want to buy more Scotch from such a humane, friendly, and caring distiller.)

The public relations work described above is usually handled by PR firms, either independent organizations or subsidiaries of advertising agencies. There is yet another area of PR within large companies that is often described as corporate communications. This may involve press relations (establishing good understandings with editors and writers in order to get good publicity and to avoid bad press) as well as many purely in-house functions, such as putting out the company newsletter or magazine, working on annual reports, writing speeches for company officers, aiding other members of the company in preparing written material, and perhaps handling liaison with outside PR firms.

Some advertising agencies have public relations departments included with the other major agency functions, but the trend these days is for PR to be broken off as separate subsidiaries of the agencies. For example, J. Walter Thompson owns Hill & Knowlton, Young & Rubicam has Burson-Marsteller, Grey Advertising has Grey-Com, Ogilvy & Mather has Ogilvy & Mather Public Relations, and so on. These companies or divisions will service the clients of the parent agency. Then there is a slew of independent public relations outfits, large medium, and small—they have no agency affiliation and they acquire clients on their own, whereas the agency-owned firms generally perform the PR service for agency clients. For a good listing of PR operations, see *O'Dwyer's Directory of Public Relations Firms*.

Public relations offers a range of job positions including account executive who, like the ad agency counterpart, develops strategy; maintains contact between clients and the other members of the team; cultivates people in the magazine, newspaper, and broadcast worlds; and hires and supervises freelancers. Public relations writers write and edit press releases and press kits, put out in-house organs, newsletters, and annual reports, and may get involved in writing speeches, reports, and various sorts of business proposals both for clients and for the firm itself. They may have the additional responsibility of convincing newspapers and magazines to feature the stories and press releases they have written. At a large firm, there may be researchers who supply background material and analyses of special needs and issues for the client. Assistants are hired at the entry-level to help out the account executives or writers in organization, clerical work, and contacts. At the head of a PR department of an agency or of a PR division will be a director who runs the show, goes after top-level new business, hires the best possible staff, and works with top agency officers on coordinating objectives, budgets, and strategy. Even agencies that don't have a public relations department (or that rely on a subsidiary) may employ a few people to handle *agency* public relations— in other words, as one such person put it, they're running a PR operation and the agency is their sole client. This staff will see that the agency is getting good press, will produce in-house communications and publications, and will work with writers on articles and books (including this one) to see that the agency and its client are well represented.

In addition to the major advertising centers covered in Chapter Three, Washington D.C., has a lot of public relations outfits and jobs because of the importance of lobbying in that city. In addition, PR, like direct marketing, is a field open to freelancers, who may work as writers, spokespeople, or coordinators of special events on a project-by-project basis.

SALES PROMOTION

This is another advertising-related field in which job opportunities exist both in the agency and on the client side, as well as in independent firms specializing in this area. Sales promotion is a rather loosely defined area that falls somewhere in between advertising and publicity. Like advertising, it consists of material that is produced, printed, and placed by the advertiser or its agency—promotional material includes point-of-purchase displays such as posters, special racks, labels, stickers, matchbooks, coupons, brochures, give-aways, sweepstakes, booths at fairs and conventions. As in publicity, there is no payment made to the media for running promotional material, in fact, the media are rarely involved. Often, promotion and publicity work together in a kind of two-pronged attack. For example, a company might take out a booth at a trade fair and distribute pamphlets and samples as part of its promotional efforts while placing stories in the local newspapers about the products as part of the publicity campaign.

Within an advertising agency, the work of sales promotion may be handled by a "design group" consisting of account managers, art director, copywriters, and production people. (Often the posters, brochures, logos, and point-of-purchase devices produced by a design group are termed "collateral" material, and the design group may be known as the collateral group.) One design group account supervisor explained that her department handled all sales promotion planning and production for the agency's clients and took on clients of its own for which it did *only* sales promotion. In this case, direct mail and in-store promotion for a large department store client also came under the banner of "collateral." "We want to help our clients *be* somebody," is how she defined the essence of sales promotion, "and we create a real look for them, whether it's in product brochures, posters, or the selling space of a store."

Sales promotion jobs on the client side may involve all of these same functions—planning, designing, and producing collateral material—or they may be devoted to guiding and coordinating the agency's sales promotion efforts.

In this age of specialization, it was inevitable that companies would arise that specialized in various types of sales promotions; for example, such "below-the-line" vehicles as couponing, sweepstakes, special offers, and massive giveaway campaigns. When an advertiser decides it needs one or more of these special promotional methods, it may direct the agency to hire the company and coordinate its efforts or it may do this job itself. In either case, there are jobs to be had—jobs with the promotional specialists as well as agency or client jobs hiring and guiding these outfits, assigning them objectives, and approving their work. The *Advertising and Communication Yellow Pages* is one good source of listings of such firms.

FINANCE AND ACCOUNTING

As one controller for a medium-sized agency told me, "Advertising is a very creative field, but without the money you can't do anything." The main function of people in the finance and accounting departments of advertising agencies is to make sure the money comes in on time and goes out in the proper amounts. When you stop and think about all the steps and stages involved in even the simplest print ad, from engraving the plate to setting the type to placing the ad in various newspapers and magazines, and the bills that each one of these steps entails, you begin to realize just how complex advertising agency finances can be. The situation is further complicated by the fact that agencies receive their bills from media often *before* they have the money in hand from the client. If they don't pay up within a specified period of time, they lose the agency discount. Cash flow crises can arise in a flash if a major client drags its heels. Promptness really is the name of the game in agency finance.

Another point to consider is that the big ad agencies have become major corporations, with the same financial pressures, needs, and issues that any major corporation faces. Decisions about investment, long-range financial planning, stock issues or buy backs, mergers and acquisitions will be made by top agency management—but the finance department will get involved in all the nuts and bolts aspects of all these crucial corporate areas.

At many agencies of a substantial size, the accounting department is divided into two distinct areas—media and production. The media billers (and staff) charge the clients for the cost of advertising space and time and see that the various media are paid promptly enough to retain the 15% agency discount. Usually the way it works is that the agency bills the client the full (gross) amount and the media bills the agency the net (discounted 15%) amount. It is on this 15% that advertising agencies have survived since the system got going in the nineteenth century.

Production billing works a little differently. In a typical setup, each job would be assigned a job number at the outset and the people in accounting would record all expenses for a given job number as they came up. When the job is finished, the production biller puts all the various expenses together, prepares the bill, and gives it to the account person involved to review and approve. Here it's a question of keeping track of a huge number of detailed items, sometimes keeping after the production people to see that they submit their bills and expenses on time, and, if the job went over budget, accounting for all the extra costs. In the case of really big jobs, such as big-budget TV commercials, the production biller would do a partial billing, perhaps in two or three stages as the job progressed.

For the most part, production billing and media billing are kept separate—once you get into an area, you're likely to stay with it. There are cases of people jumping from finance and accounting jobs into account work or some other agency department, but they had to hustle to make this move. It's not that common a career path. At many larger agencies, the media billers will be attached to the media department and the production billers to the production department instead of being grouped with the financial staff. When this is the case, movement into media or production tends to be easier.

Other jobs in this area include controller, the person who runs the day-to-day affairs of the department, including supervision of personnel, troubleshooting, and payroll for agency staff, and reports major departmental matters to the agency president or chief financial officer; bookkeepers, who keep track of all financial records; accountants, often assigned to various areas such as print, media, broadcast media, production, and accounts payable; and assistants of various sorts.

PERSONNEL

Though personnel is the department that job-seekers often have the most contact with, few think of it as a place to work. But it's worth considering. Personnel (sometimes known as human resources) staff members do more than keep your resume on file, schedule interviews, and issue polite rejection letters along with enthusiastic job-offers, though these functions are certainly part of the job. The personnel department also keeps track of employee health plans, benefits of various sorts, sick or maternity leaves, vacations, and pensions. If and when you leave the company, they may conduct a "termination interview" and keep track of you. These days more personnel departments are taking an active role in training new staff members and making sure all workers are functioning well and happily within the agency. The whole field of corporate psychology is attracting more attention, and personnel is the most likely department to implement changes and improvements in the working environment based on advances in this field.

NEW BUSINESS

New business is the lifeblood of advertising agencies, and so quite naturally it is a top priority, usually attended to by top executives. Occasionally a very large agency will have a new business department with a small staff assigned the mission to find and woo new clients. This group would assess the advertising needs of various companies, determine which accounts to pitch, and work with the various agency "teams" on developing new business pitches and presentations. Since attracting and winning new business depends largely on contacts and the ability to demonstrate a superb track record, the people who specialize in new business tend to be ad executives with a lot of experience. There are, however, some opportunities at the lower levels for ambitious juniors to do a lot of the leg work. You work hard, you move in the highest circles (though at the fringes of them), and breathe the heady air of corporate power and competition at its most intense. It is, as one might expect, a superb way to learn the business.

LEGAL SERVICES

As business has grown bigger and more complicated, lawyers have become increasingly important in providing guidance, interpreting federal, state, and local rules and regulations, and figuring out new ways to get around them. The advertising business is no exception. The most obvious task of advertising lawyers is to review all advertising produced by an agency or company to make sure it complies with the tangle of official and unofficial laws, regulations, rules, customs that control the industry. "This is the meat and potatoes of what we do," one lawyer for a large agency told me. "It's the most visible and it's what people think of most often when they think of agency lawyers. We clear every piece of advertising that comes out of this agency at several stages—concept, rough, and final. We must be satisfied that what we're saying is legitimate, and we frequently ask for written substantiation of any claims made in the copy."

This, however, is only part of an advertising lawyer's job. The other part concerns the same types of responsibilities that any corporate lawyer would handle—everything from contracts to real estate, personnel matters, and equipment and office space leasing; any litigation that may arise from employee-related issues or breach of contract from a supplier or outside vendor or client; the occasional copyright infringement; and dealing with various government agencies. When a giant New York-based agency buys a smaller affiliate agency in Cleveland or Calcutta, the lawyers get involved. When the creative team decides to put a tap dance act in a soft drink commercial, the lawyers write the contract (or farm out the work to an entertainment specialist). Lawyers review the public statements made by employees of the agency, including many of the interviews that appear in this book. For major deals or really complicated projects, the agency lawyers may hire an outside counsel to assist, and their responsibility will then be largely a matter of liaison.

Though lawyers are crucial to the workings of contemporary advertising, there are very few of them doing the work. Only a handful of the largest agencies even have legal departments as part of the agency staff; these include N W Ayer, Ted Bates, BBDO, Campbell-Ewald, Leo Burnett, Dancer Fitzgerald, the Interpublic Group, Ogilvy & Mather, J. Walter Thompson, and Ketchum Communications. The majority of agencies rely on outside counsel to handle their legal affairs, and there are a few law firms that specialize in advertising law. The legal department at a mega-agency may total six people, so jobs of this sort really are scarce. Demand for these jobs is, as one might expect, intense. One in-house attorney told me he gets three to five calls each week from young lawyers eager to get into advertising because they think it would be more fun and more glamorous than whatever else they're doing. They might be right, but they have to be lucky and probably patient in order to get one of these jobs. Also helpful is related experience—say working in entertainment or communications law.

The list goes on and on. Advertising offers loads of jobs that are not usually considered careers but that can lead to a career if you want it badly enough. The mailroom and messenger center used to be the standard way of starting at an agency, and you still hear of eager, ambitious college grads who begin there and push their way into creative or account management jobs. Likewise secretaries and receptionists can position themselves for advancement in career path jobs if they show an interest and an aptitude. Even temps have been known to fill in for a few weeks at an agency, find a niche for themselves, and work their way into the media, research, or production department.

Then there are all the jobs on the other side—working in the advertising or marketing department of a client organization or for one of the media companies that run the ads, selling TV or radio time or space in magazines. If you're thinking about one of these areas or want to find out what it's all about, turn the page. This is what the next section is devoted to.

PART THREE

ADVERTISING JOBS ON THE OTHER SIDE: THE ADVERTISERS AND THE MEDIA

ADVERTISING JOBS IN COMPANIES THAT ADVERTISE

There is probably no single word that commands more respect within an advertising agency than CLIENT. When the client speaks, the agency jumps—as high and as far as it can. Of course, this makes perfect sense. Without clients there would be no agencies—no business, no ads to create and place, no marketing plans to devise, no bills to bill. What you sometimes forget when you're considering advertising from the agency side is that the client is not one awesome entity but a lot of people (some awesome, some not) doing a lot of jobs. Someone has to hire the agency in the first place; provide input about the company's advertising and marketing needs; review and approve the creative work, the media plans, the research suggestions, the overall agency performance; pay the agency and, in some cases, fire the agency. These someones frequently have a lot of responsibilities that do not involve advertising—but advertising is one of the key functions, often the most visible, and in many cases the most challenging and absorbing.

Just how much someone on the client side will be involved in advertising varies enormously from company to company. In some cases, the people in the client's advertising department are really just administrators: they review the work and pay the bills. Other companies have in-house agencies—autonomous divisions that perform all the work of an agency, from creating to placing advertising—though this mode seems to be dying out because it's not that economical. Some corporations have advertising departments that mirror the departments in agencies: there are creatives, media people, researchers, and marketing directors who work with and guide their opposite number at the agency and sometimes do the work themselves. The work may be divided up; for example, the agency may handle all the consumer advertising while the in-house people do all the trade advertising and the promotional work. Large department stores and other retail organizations may dispense with agencies altogether (or use them only for "image building" or national campaigns); instead, they'll staff full-service advertising departments to handle all advertising and promotion.

In this chapter, we'll take a look at some of the typical setups of advertising/marketing departments on the client side and discuss the job possibilities they offer. But first, let's consider some of the basic differences between working for an ad agency and a large corporation.

AGENCY VERSUS CLIENT: STYLE AND SUBSTANCE

Who works harder? Who has more fun? Who makes more money? Who has more flexibility—agency people or client people? If you're trying to decide which side to pitch for, you might want to think about some of the basic differences in style and substance between the two sides.

In terms of style, the thing you'll hear most frequently is that life on the agency side is looser. Since the primary product of an ad agency is advertising, everything is done to foster the creation of advertising, and if this means art directors have punk haircuts and come to work dressed in leather, so be it. Of course, no one in an agency is going to be quite as funky as the creatives, but even the account people tend to be less buttoned-down—less purely numbers-oriented—than their equivalents at corporations. One advertising director who has worked on both sides put it this way: "The agency side is much more exciting; the client side is much more conservative. I would say that on the agency side, one out of every three people is a character. On the client side, it's one out of every three hundred. On the agency side, people talk about sports, art, politics, gossip; on the client side they talk about lawn drainage and business."

In a word, corporations are more corporate. You're all but required to have an MBA just to get in the door. There is more hierarchy, more rigidity—you progress through levels that can sometimes seem to go on forever and you progress in an orderly fashion; you report to someone who reports to someone who reports to someone . . . And the work you're doing, even if your title is manager of advertising, is likely to be much more heavily administrative. Budgets, fiscal reports, sales projections, market surveys, updates to senior management: these are the dominant themes of life on the client side.

There are, however, some pretty enticing compensations for work in a corporation, the two most enticing of all being more money and more power. At a rough estimate, people who work in the marketing/advertising departments of large corporations make about twenty percent more than people in agency account management departments. The power can be equally stimulating. "I was frustrated on the agency side," said this same advertising director quoted above who had come from a large agency, "because there was not much control. At an agency, you're once removed from the decision-making that the client has. It was very frustrating to know a business well and not to be able to *do* something. You'd have to hope the client would do something that you had recommended." A product manager I interviewed put it this way: "On the client side you have all the fun of advertising without all the work. Power is ultimately in the client's hands. He makes the decisions, and his input into the development of the ads may be fifty percent." Another summed up: "Clients have more controlling personalities. They want to control their destinies and their business." The client is not the one who is sweating it out over the tenth copy revision —he's the one putting his thumb up or down on the work. In an ad agency, you're living with the anxiety built in to a service business. You may think the client is an absolute fool who is wrecking his business, but it's *his* business and he calls the shots. And he pays your salary. To some extent, this fundamental difference between agency and client side tends to attract different personality types, characterized by one client side executive as the difference between diplomats (agency people) and generals (client side). But see page 000 for what agency head William Phillips has to say about this.

If you want to succeed on either side, you're going to be working very, very hard. The difference is that on the agency side the work tends to come in peaks and valleys, whereas on the client side there is more of a "diurnal grind," as one person put it, a grind that may easily last twelve to fourteen hours every day.

Aside from the money and the power and the fun, maybe the basic thing you should consider is how closely you want to be involved with *advertising*. For the most part, the longer you stay at a major corporation, the further away from advertising you get. Advertising directors are usually middle management; to rise, you must broaden yourself by taking on marketing responsibilities or new product development. At many companies, the advertising people are off on the sidelines—it's simply not where the action is. Whereas at an agency, no matter how high you rise, your basic business is always going to be advertising. Even chairmen of major agencies spend a part of their time reviewing campaigns and keeping in touch with the agency's creative energy. Advertising is a business like no other. And if advertising is your passion, you'll probably be better off on the agency side. On the client side, ultimately, you're a business person—

advertising will take its place as one discipline among many.

The other thing to keep in mind is that you can move from one side to the other. People do it all the time, and sometimes even move back again. These days the strong current seems to be flowing from agency to client side, probably because of the money. But lots of people go the other way. If you can't make up your mind, don't. Go where the jobs are and see how you like it.

PRODUCT MANAGEMENT

Procter & Gamble, the giant packaged goods company that is among the nation's largest advertisers, inaugurated the product management system back in the 1930s, and it has since spread to many of the nation's major packaged goods and food corporations. Essentially, this is a way of organizing the marketing and sales within a company by product rather than by department. Instead of having a group in an advertising department that handles marketing for all of the company's products, there is one person assigned to an individual product (or group of products) who takes care of all of the major duties relating to the effective marketing of this product.

Dana Gioia, who rose up through the ranks of product management at the General Foods Corporation in White Plains, New York, to his present position as manager of new business development, defined the product manager's job for me in broad strokes: "What it comes down to is that, within the context of a major corporation, you're running a business for someone else. You have responsibility for every last detail. You will be spending the majority of your time managing business systems, checking up on inventory control, studying costs versus profits. But, since you're running a business you don't own, you also have to answer to the company's general management. In this sense, you're also managing management—keeping them constantly posted on developments and on the financial status of your product, while they're constantly pressuring you about profits." Working on advertising and media may occupy only twenty percent of a product manager's time. However, it's a crucial twenty percent. "You can ruin your brand if you don't do a good job on the advertising," Gioia points out.

Gioia, who ran General Foods' vastly successful Kool-Aid line in the Beverage Division, in some ways epitomizes the successful product manager—young, aggressive, sharp, and very hardworking (twelve-hour days are the norm, he told me). But there's another Dana Gioia as well, one known to readers of *The New Yorker*, the *Hudson Review*, and other literary magazines as poet and essayist. Gioia kept his "other" life more or less a secret from colleagues at General Foods and the advertising agencies they used ("Agency people don't want the client to be too creative," he joked), but his cover was blown when *Esquire* magazine featured him in its December 1984 issue as one of "The Best of the New Generation" of 272 men and women under forty who are "changing America." Gioia may be one of the few established poets to have come through the ranks of brand management, but he is by no means the only resourceful, imaginative person in this end of business. Creativity and energy are just as valuable to the product manager as they are to the account executive.

A brand manager will work closely not only with agency account people, but with creatives as well on developing campaigns. The agency people learn as much as they can about objectives and strategies from the product manager, and they will use all of this information in coming up with the original concepts for a campaign. According to Gioia, the most important meeting of a new campaign is the agency's initial presentation of rough concepts. "You have a give-and-take here and you must tell people what you honestly feel—tear their ideas apart, if necessary, and talk about all the implications of them. It can be an emotionally trying situation—the account executives are trying to sell the work, the creatives have their egos all tied up in it—but this session is the client's best opportunity to give the agency direction. The best refinements on a campaign's ideas come from the client but they are best done early in the creative process." One technique Gioia has used successfully is showing storyboards to focus groups of consumers and analyzing their reactions before agreeing with the agency on changes. "It makes the copy development process less political," he says.

Gioia himself clearly enjoyed the advertising aspect of his job—from copy development to commercial shoots to the final edit—but not all people on the client side have this knack. And furthermore, they don't really need it. "What it takes to succeed in product management at one of the country's large companies," Gioia told me, "frequently has little to do with a person's ability to develop and judge advertising. What it takes is to be a good businessman." A product manager, to repeat, is really running a business, and advertising is only one phase of this. As a group product manager with Nabisco told me, "I'm responsible for setting strategic directions, business goals in terms of volume, market share, profitability, for really managing the business. Part of my compensation ties in with ability to deliver. In addition, the quality of my marketing plans is a major factor that I'm evaluated on, and this includes advertising, promotion, sales issues, pricing, packaging. There is also a lot of time involved in operations—research and development on new products or product improvements, new package size or type, distribution—and a lot of time spent with sales and manufacturing people. It's both strategy and execution." Product management is millions of details—*business* details. However, if you have a flair for advertising and promotion, you can have fun with it and really take your product far. Gioia, during his time in the Beverage Division, opened up the advertising and promotion of Kool-Aid in new directions, including movie tie-ins, toy licensing, comic books, and personality appearances. A product manager is in the perfect spot to initiate this kind of expansion in the advertising of a particular brand. He's the leader and the agency will be following his cues.

HOW THE SYSTEM WORKS AT GENERAL FOODS

The exact structure of product management systems varies from company to company, but the basic idea is pretty much the same everywhere. Here's how it works at General Foods, the giant food company (and one of the nation's largest advertisers) that makes over 400 individual items sold under thirty brand names including Jell-O, Crystal Light, Maxwell House, Sanka, Post Cereal, Kool-Aid, Log Cabin, and Tang.

The lowest ranking position is *marketing assistant*, essentially a trainee spot that the company is still experimenting with. Marketing assistants, who are recruited right out of the top colleges, assist the people above them in developing plans for a particular product, in testing markets, and in analyzing data. The job offers an excellent way of getting to know how a large corporation works and of becoming familiar with marketing. GF currently has only about five marketing assistants, with a mid-range salary of over $25,000.

A much more common way to enter the company is as an *assistant product manager*, a position for which you must have an MBA, preferably from one of the top business schools (Harvard, Stanford, Wharton, or Columbia). This year, approximately twenty-five people were hired for the job from a pool of 500 to 600 applicants. The competition is stiff, but it's worth it—assistant product managers started at an average of over $30,000 (compare this with the $15,000 to $20,000 a year that an assistant account executive can expect to get from a large agency). Assistant product managers, like marketing assistants, devote a good deal of their energy to learning. They will assist in the marketing plans for a given brand, participate in sales promotion and research, make sure marketing plans are on line and meeting their objectives. Their exposure, both within and outside the company, is not yet very great, although they may have contact with the assistant account executive over on the agency side. Essentially, people in this position are being groomed. There are around fifty of them working at GF now.

After putting in a good fifteen months to two years as an assistant product manager, you have a crack at a promotion to *associate product manager*. The average salary jumps to over $40,000 (these are mid-range statistics), but the number of people at this level shrinks a bit. The associate will have more responsibility in all areas than the assistant and his or her reporting level will be higher. He or she will have more impact on the business and will be making more decisions, but there is still an important step to take before you have full responsibility over running the daily business on a brand. It may take around two years to win that promotion to the position of product manager.

A *product manager* at GF will have responsibility over the profitability of one product made by the company—it might be Jell-O gelatin or Maxwell House coffee or Post Fruit and Fibre cereal. This person will direct all marketing efforts including promotion; research in developing new recipes or improvements in the existing product; advertising campaigns, which means working with the advertising agencies (GF retains a number of agencies for various products, including Young & Rubicam, Ted Bates, Benton & Bowles, Grey, and Ogilvy & Mather); consultations with the financial departments in determining market share and budgets, and check ups with the company's sales force to make sure in-store promotions are working and that the product is being displayed effectively. A product manager sets objectives for his or her product and makes sure these objectives are being met. The job involves a certain amount of travel—to the marketplace to check up on outlets and interview consumers in focus groups, sometimes to the manufacturing facility, to commercial shoots. A product manager may work closely with the account executive and account supervisor within one of the agencies on developing packaging, pricing, and sales forecasts. Agency creative work, media plans, and research projects will also pass across the product manager's desk for review and approval. He or she becomes involved in every stage of a commercial shoot—from choosing the director to preproduction meetings to the actual shoot to editing. An advertising campaign is a complex process involving many people and many inputs, but the product manager's input is perhaps the most crucial. After all, it's his or her brand that is being advertised.

The mid-range pay for product managers at GF is over $50,000 a year.

The company also has a rank called *senior product manager*, which is essentially a promotion in place to recognize star-quality product managers and let them know they're doing great work. The mid-range pay for this position is about $60,000.

Now comes the great divide. Up to this point, your career is more or less predictable: you put in your time and work hard, and you'll get promoted. But some never rise higher than senior product manager. Those who make it to the next grade—*product group manager* (at some companies this rank is known as marketing director)—have really made it. This is where the big bucks and the power start to roll in. "You're now a member of the club," one such member told me. "It's like being a junior partner at a law firm." Product group managers are also eligible for annual performance awards. As the title implies, a product group manager oversees the marketing of a number of related products. For example, a group might consist of all the Jell-O brands—puddings, gelatins, pudding pops, gelatin pops. The product managers working on these individual brands would report to the product group manager, who would supervise marketing plans and stategies while not getting involved in all the daily details. "A large amount of my time is spent directing the activities of others," one product group manager told me. "And a lot of my day is spent in meetings. Interpersonal involvement is great and it's vital to getting the job done." On the agency side, the product group manager would be in touch with the account supervisor and the management supervisor.

The average salary is over $70,000 plus eligibility for a target bonus opportunity of up to 18% based on performance. Five to eight years of experience are required for this job.

Climbing still higher up the GF corporate ladder, we get to the *category manager*. A category manager will have responsibility for a number of related product groups—for example, dessert enhancers and ingredients, which would include Bakers chocolate and coconut, baking powder, chocolate chips. The number of people holding this position at GF diminishes even further. These key employees earn salaries of $80,000 on average with target bonus eligibility of 26% of base pay.

At the top of the brand management pyramid are *marketing managers* who have total responsibility for marketing plans for the divisions they head up. For example, there would be a marketing manager in charge of all GF coffee products, another in charge of all packaged grocery products, and so on. These top individuals report directly to the *general manager* of the division they work in. Mid-range salary level is over $90,000 with a target bonus eligibility of 26%.

BREAKING IN

The best way to break into product management at a company like GF is to get an MBA from a top business school. There are a few marketing assistants hired right out of college, but opportunities are extremely limited. The traditional entry is as an assistant product manager, and for this an MBA is all but required unless you have some highly impressive previous work experience. GF likes to promote from within the ranks, so if you start your career there and you like it, you can do well by staying and advancing.

Large corporations, as we have said, tend to be more conventional and buttoned down than advertising agencies, and it's crucial when applying for a job to look and act like one of the insiders. Project a professional image, which means business attire, confident attitude, and, above all, familiarity with the company's products, history, top personnel, and any news that it has made recently.

Women, by the way, are being recruited heavily at the entry levels and are doing well in these positions. The GF upper management, however, is an almost exclusively male domain and seems likely to remain this way for the near future.

T HE ADVERTISING DEPARTMENT

Product management follows the same ground rules in most large organizations that use it, but once you start looking at companies that don't use it, you'll find a tremendous diversity in the way advertising is handled. At an automobile company, for example, decisions about advertising are usually made by directors of sales and marketing— it's one facet of a job that also involves promotion, research, and a lot of administrative liaison work. Until you're pretty high up, you're pretty far away from anything to do with the actual content or placement of the ads. A large service corporation, such as an airline, may have a marketing/advertising department set up as a kind of shadow of the advertising agency: the marketing people will deal with account managers and creatives, media people will review the work of the agency media department, corporate research will work with agency research, etc. The company will rely most heavily on the agency for creative output, which no one can do as well as the creative staff of a top ad agency. As a rule, company advertising departments are made to suit the specific requirements of the type of product that the company makes and sells. Thus no two departments will look alike. Another example: paperback book publishers that put out as many as thirty new titles each month may retain the services of an ad agency for the lead titles that get radio and (rarely) TV advertising, but an in-house advertising and promotion staff may prepare ads and promotional pieces for the lesser titles or for ads that will appear only in trade journals. The advertising manager will meet with agency account and creative people and supervise their work as well as the work of his or her own staff. A publishing company may even have its own art and production departments that execute work done in-house. Large retailers and department stores use fully staffed advertising departments that handle almost all the work (see below).

By and large, the more the company relies on an advertising agency for its work, the more administrative the company advertising jobs will be. When the agency is creating and placing the ads, you, on the client side, are reviewing and approving the work, writing internal memos, and keeping track of the advertising money. Corporations can generate a fantastic amount of paperwork, studies, files, charts, and forms to circulate. One advertising director told me that on the agency side, the work is two-thirds advertising and one-third administrative, while on the client side the ratio is reversed. If advertising is your real love, you could get frustrated inside a large corporation.

THE ADVERTISING DEPARTMENT AT AMERICAN EXPRESS

Glen Gilbert, who holds the position of director of advertising, card marketing at American Express Company, took me through the basic functions that he and his staff perform. Gilbert broke into advertising in a way that used to be fairly common but now seems almost old-fashioned and romantic: he started in the messenger room—in his case, the agency was Young & Rubicam, the world's largest. Gilbert was all set to go to law school when a college professor convinced him he had some talent for advertising and helped him get his foot in the door at Y&R. His days as a messenger did not last

Glen Gilbert, director of advertising, card marketing at American Express, started in the messenger room and now heads up the "Do you know me?" campaign.

long. From running errands, Gilbert jumped into traffic and from there he ascended to Y&R's executive floor to work as "a lackey to the gods" helping on new business. ("I was twenty-four and I was right in the thick of things," he recalls. "I worked weekends, nights, but I loved it.") Eventually, he became an account executive, and then he made the move over to the client side. Experience on both the agency and client sides puts Gilbert in an ideal spot to compare the kinds of work that each entails.

American Express, Gilbert explained, does not use the traditional brand management system, but rather has an advertising staff that is roughly divided by the kinds of advertising the company runs. Gilbert himself heads up acquisition advertising, which is designed to get new cardmembers and which pours its major resources into the now-famous, "Do You Know Me?" campaign. Over the last ten years, personalities ranging from Pavarotti to Tom Landry to Itzhak Perlman to Jim Davis (creator of Garfield the cat, see illustration in Chapter One) have all plugged the American Express card with TV spots that open with the question, "Do you know me?" and close with the motto, "The American Express card. Don't leave home without it." This campaign, created by Ogilvy & Mather, has the most money behind it of any American Express campaign and the most presence: it drives not only the American Express card but creates an image for the entire company. Other branches of advertising within American Express include retention advertising, designed to keep current card members; ads done cooperatively with hotels, restaurants, and airlines, designed to increase usage; and the "take one" ads, which may appear as posters in trains to which a little pouch of applications is affixed—you're supposed to take one, fill it in, and mail it back to American Express.

Unlike a brand manager, Gilbert is responsible for advertising and advertising only, although there are many, many duties of his that touch on advertising only peripherally. He is highly involved in every step of the genesis and production of the "Do You Know Me" commercials. Together with the people at Ogilvy & Mather and his management, he determines what commercials should be added to the pool of existing commercials for the coming year and which personalities should appear in these commercials.

"Once a person has been signed," Gilbert explains, "I'm still involved in every step of the commercial—choosing the director, the shoot, editing, etc. The agency presents me with three directors, and if I don't know their work I ask for reels and look at them. I use outside cost consultants and my own knowledge to go over the bids and decide if there is any fat. I also get very involved in choosing locations. When we shot Lord

Wedgewood in China, we looked at hundreds of polaroids of locations in Beijing before we decided where to shoot. At the preproduction meeting we talk about every conceivable issue that could come up on the day of the shoot so we won't have to address it then, when the meter is ticking. I'm present at the shoot and I deal with issues that always come up."

Gilbert's job sounds in some ways like the best of account management and creative, and in some ways it is. But, he points out, "Though working with the agency is the part I enjoy most, there is also a lot of administrative work that comes with the territory. The budgeting process is very comprehensive—how you spend these millions of dollars has to be very closely tracked, and you're either asking for more money and justifying this or you're being asked to cut money. I do a lot of work with the research department on questionnaire development, which, while it might culminate in guiding copy development, is really consumer marketing and consumer research. I do a lot with competitive analyses, which services the other credit card companies offer, what prices they have. There are weekly status reports, monthly presentations updating senior management. In fact, the administrative component can be a substantial portion of the job." Those whose true love is advertising might find the administrative aspect and the hierarchical structure of client organizations a real downside of the job. Typically, there might be a vice president of marketing, who reports to the senior vice president of marketing, who reports to the executive vice president of marketing and on and on, seemingly forever.

Gilbert himself has a fairly compact staff: there is an advertising manager and an assistant advertising manager, and that's it. The advertising manager runs the Gold Card print program and handles a lot of the key research projects. The assistant manager works a lot with the budget, keeping close tabs on how the money is spent, and also does a lot of work in competitive analyses. Salary levels are comparable to those at companies using the product management system, that is, higher than advertising agencies.

Though Glen Gilbert himself does not have an MBA, he concedes that he is a bit unusual for someone working on the client side. If you want to break into advertising at American Express or a similar company, your best bet would be to get an MBA, interview well with a recruiter on campus, and try to get a day at the company and wow people. There are, however, other routes. Gilbert's last two assistant managers have been bright secretaries who showed promise, took on nonsecretarial responsibilities, and jumped at the chance to work harder. American Express is now paying for them to get MBAs at night. And, of course, there's Gilbert himself, who came over from the agency side, another fairly common route into companies of all sorts. As for American Express, Gilbert says "the company is very good about hiring people—each year we hire dozens and dozens of graduating MBAs. There is never any lack of people coming in."

In general, though it may not be quite as hard to break into advertising on the client side, you still have to be good to get hired.

Retail

Yet another source of advertising jobs on the other side are national retailers such as Sears, K Mart, J. C. Penney and large department stores such as Macy's, Bloomingdale's, and I. Magnin. For the most part, large retail outlets do their advertising work themselves and may retain the services of an advertising agency only for corporate advertising or national campaigns. The nuts-and-bolts advertising is done in-house. This means that people must be hired to perform all the client-side and agency-side jobs. A department store of the magnitude of Macy's or Bloomingdale's will employ a large advertising staff including copywriters, art directors, production managers, traffic managers, TV producers, and media people as well as promotion and marketing people who spend a lot of time organizing special store "events." The advertising staff works closely with the merchandising managers and with department store buyers, who usually will submit requests for specific advertising and then check over the ads in an early stage to make sure they describe the merchandise accurately. The pace of retail work is fast. There may be a need for fifty or more ads a week as well as a new catalogue every month. The ads appear soon after they're written and the impact on sales is tracked immediately to judge the effectiveness of the ad. Frequently, the departments are divided into a group responsible for newspaper ads, a group turning out catalogues, and another group on special in-store promotions.

While retail does offer a full range of advertising jobs, it is considered somewhat of a breed apart in the advertising world. Because of the pace of the work and the relatively small scope of most of the ads, which will usually appear for one day only in newspapers, retail advertising, particularly on the creative side, can be a bit of a grind. "Retail advertising departments tend to be factories," says Charles Rabkin, veteran advertising executive who has worked for agencies, on the client side, and in retail. "There is no time to do copy research or to worry about the finer points. You're turning out ten to twenty ads a day on all different types of merchandise, so they need people who can work quickly. They don't have to be prize winners, they just have to be ready."

Retail advertising is ultimately more closely allied to merchandising than to the image-making and persuading that ad agencies specialize in. For this reason there is not a lot of crossover between retail advertising departments and ad agencies. There are, however, some rather stunning exceptions. Mary Wells Lawrence, chairman and founder of Wells, Rich, Greene and the "first woman of advertising," got her start writing copy for McKelvey's department store in Youngstown, Ohio, put in some time as advertising manager for Macy's, and then moved over to the agency side. McCann-Erickson snapped up her copy skills and made her a copy group head, and she did some brilliant work at Doyle Dane Bernbach during its creative heyday before opening her own agency. If you've got the talent and the drive, retail can be your steppingstone to a brilliant advertising career.

INSIDE THE MEDIA:
SELLING TIME AND SPACE

From an advertiser's point of view, an ad in a magazine or newspaper or a commercial on TV is a vehicle for bringing in business. From the point of view of advertising agency people, ads and commercials are products that they create and place for maximum effectiveness; but from the point of view of the people who run the media, advertising is a matter of space and time for sale. It's a commodity and, in the case of television, it's a commodity that is bartered on an extremely volatile market. The major concern of the people inside the media sales departments is getting the best possible price for those thirty- (or sixty- or fifteen-) second spots or getting the most possible pages of advertising to float the articles, news columns, and features. The media are the third major link in the great advertising chain of being and the third major source of advertising jobs. These jobs may be removed from creating advertising, but they're closest to the people the ads are made for. The primary consideration here is with the size, makeup, and cost of readers and viewers. "What we do is sell people," one network salesman told me, "people who are willing to watch a commercial."

TELEVISION: SELLING TIME ON THE AIR

Let's start with television because it's the most pervasive, the most complex, generally the highest paying, and, for the choice jobs, the most difficult to break into. American television has grown up in two separate but overlapping spheres: the networks and the local individual stations, known in the business as spot TV. The networks consist of three giant entities—CBS, NBC, and ABC—that broadcast television shows (and commercials) nationally and usually at the same time within a time zone. Though national in scope, the three networks are based in New York and that is where about seventy-five percent of the network buying and selling is done.

While there are only three networks, there are more than 500 local stations all over the U.S., each with its own airtime to sell. Programming on local stations is a mixed bag: since each station is affiliated with a network, there will be some network shows, some locally produced shows (for example, local news), and some syndicated shows (non-network programs distributed by independent outfits). The strictly local advertising is usually handled by the individual station's sales force. For example, a hardware store in downtown Des Moines may want to run a commercial advertising a big sale. The station salesman will negotiate the sale and decide which programs to run it in, and the station may even produce the commercial as part of a package deal. This commercial might run not only on locally produced shows but in the breaks (times left for commercials and announcements) in the network shows or syndicated shows. So getting a job on the sales force of a local station is one way of getting into TV sales.

When it comes to selling time to national advertisers, the local stations generally use national rep firms to handle the sales. The rep firms cover the major advertising centers and deal with the spot buyers at the advertising agencies. One rep may handle as many as eighteen small local stations. The reps know the availabilities of times on a station's shows (known as "avails") and they match up the avails with the advertiser's needs. Being a rep involves a double dose of salesmanship: you not only are trying to convince the agency spot buyers to place their clients' commercials on the local station you represent, you're also trying to convince the local stations themselves to retain your services. Media salesmen, like all salesmen, have to be outgoing, persistent, positive-thinking, and able to spring back fast from a setback or rejection. It's obviously not everyone's cup of tea.

The largest sphere of all is covered by the networks. One person I spoke to who moved from a national rep firm to one of the networks explained the similarities and differences between the two: "The job description is basically the same, but the audience that your advertisers have the potential to reach is a lot greater. You're dealing with the entire country as opposed to New York only, or Chicago, or San Francisco, or whatever the marketplace happens to be. For example, a network rating point would be worth 859,000 homes, whereas a rating point for a city like Des Moines might be worth only 2,000 homes. There's a lot more money involved and a lot more people, but the job is no different. You're still selling airtime."

THE NETWORKS: HOW THEY WORK

What exactly does the job of selling airtime for one of the networks involve? George

Cain, vice president and manager of eastern sales at ABC, opened it up for me. The networks divide the television schedule into dayparts—there's prime time (from 8 to 11 in the evening, Monday to Friday), daytime, Saturday and Sunday children's programs, early morning, late night, news, sports, and specials. Each daypart has its own sales force. George Cain works in prime time, and there are eleven people in the Eastern Sales Division who report to him. Cain explains:

"These eleven people have the title of Account Executive and they are responsible in the territory we cover for representing the ABC television network. Their jobs are probably eighty percent direct sales to ad agencies and twenty percent public relations to clients. An individual account executive will be assigned to specific agencies and specific clients. Now, let's say an advertiser who is using BBDO has a budget of $2 million. When that budget occurs, the network buyer at BBDO will call the account executive at each of the three networks and say, 'I have a budget in the area of $2 million for the fourth quarter and I want a half plan.' That means he'd like each of the three networks to submit on $1 million. So two networks are going to get $1 million and one network is going to get zero.

"The buyer tells us the target audience he is interested in pursuing and, since this business has such extensive research, we have track records of how different programs do against different demographic profiles. Through our Sales Proposal Division (see below) we'll pull together what we call a network plan or proposal. That plan will have a mix of programs that should have strength against the particular demographic that the advertiser is pursuing. In addition, if there are certain shows in which he expresses special interest, then we try to make sure those shows are part of the program mix. What we present is a package of a group of programs.

"Then we get into the negotiation process. Since one network is going to end up with zero, there's a little bit of stress that comes into the process at this point. The buyers will evaluate each of the three packages against their specific requirements—such things as income levels, family size, perhaps educational level, and also the primary demographic. Ultimately, the lowest common denominator is a cost per thousand (CPM) against the demographic profile. The buyers compare the CPMs offered by the three networks and size up the mix that we've given, and then we'll go back and refine the plan to bring it a little closer to the advertiser's needs. This is the second round and by this point we should have a package that the buyer is happy with in terms of mix, and now we're ready to talk price. The buyer may come to us and say, I have three packages I love, so now it's just a question of price: what is your best offer? The account executive has to make the determination of what level of discount we have to go to in order to get that piece of business. It gets to be a situation of being able to read the marketplace so that you know how you have to price your inventory, because when you come right down to it, we're probably in the finest supply-and-demand business that exists. In some ways, it's like the airlines business: once an airplane takes off, if those seats are empty, they generate zero dollars. Once that program plays, if all the units aren't sold, they generate zero dollars—and, of course, we try to avoid the empty-seat syndrome."

Network selling is also a *huge* business: in 1985, some $2.4 billion was spent in the "upfront marketplace" (upfront buys are the major commitments advertisers make for airtime for an entire year, on a firm basis or on a six-month basis. The upfront buying season usually occurs in late May through July, shortly after the networks announce their schedules for the season). During this frenzied selling period, anywhere from $700 million to $1 billion comes into each network, all during a sixty- to seventy-five-day period. The pressure is intense, the pace often frantic, and network salespeople, like their counterparts in buying at the advertising agencies, put in long, grueling days while a lot of other people are on vacation.

Though the audience numbers involved in the sale of a unit of network time are far greater than those involved in spot television sales, the number of people who have responsibility for selling these network units is far, far smaller. In fact, the network buying *and* selling community consists of perhaps 1,200 people, with the majority of them in New York. Smaller groups of network salespeople work in Chicago, Detroit, and Los Angeles. Yet even in New York, employment opportunities are very limited. One network executive estimated that a total of seventy-five salespeople handle the network sales in New York. Obviously, these high-powered jobs involve a lot of responsibility and prestige, but they're also extremely difficult to land.

The account executives, the people who actually make the sales, make up only one segment of the network sales departments. Working closely with them is a group of people known as the Proposal or Planning Division. These people develop a package of programs to suit the specifications provided by the agency. Like the account executives, they are broken down by dayparts: at ABC, for example, three people prepare the plans for prime time and they report to a manager and a director, while another three people and a director handle daytime; the proposal group for news consists of two people. Working in the Proposal Division is an excellent way to put yourself in line for a job as account executive. Though you're not actually selling, you are immersed in the commodity that the account execs sell and you gain intimate knowledge of all the aspects of the daypart in which you're working. To land one of these jobs, you must have three to five years of related experience, which means working in the media department of an agency or working within the network in some position that gives you exposure to the sales group. Pay range for these jobs is estimated to be $30,000 to $50,000.

Account execs in each daypart report to a vice president/sales manager who is responsible for inventory control and for providing guidance on pricing. George Cain, who holds this position in the prime time area at ABC, says he "takes an overview position with respect to the negotiating process. My function is to be aware of what's happening in the marketplace as a whole." He'll work closely with the account execs to keep abreast of marketplace conditions and he will also maintain contact with client and agency personnel. Cain reports to a vice president of eastern sales, and above him there is a vice president/general sales manager, whose jurisdiction is national: the Chicago, Detroit, and Los Angeles offices as well as the New York office report to him.

All networks have Sales Service Departments whose basic function is to schedule the commercials within the programs. A group of commercials that run together during a break in a show is known as a "pod." The people in sales service make sure the pods don't contain conflicting commercials, for example, you wouldn't want a dog food commercial to run in the same pod with a McDonald's or a Chevy commercial to run on an action show in which a Chevy is blown to smithereens.

Pay for network account executives consists of a base salary, bonuses based on review, and commissions. The more you sell, the more you make—it all adds up generally to between $70,000 and $125,000 a year, another reason why so many people want these jobs. Prime time, which many consider to be the top of the network ladder, will usually have account executives with five to ten years of experience working in it. In terms of overall status and responsibility, the progression goes from morning shows to news to daytime and sports and then to prime. Though network sales managers don't get commissions, they are very well compensated for their work. Salaries range from $85,000 to $200,000 for those at the higher levels.

Sales jobs frequently lead to the corporate management of the network. A number of people who now run the nation's most visible medium have come up through selling time to advertisers. This makes a lot of sense, since advertising is what the whole television industry rests on.

In addition to the advertising sales groups, each network staffs an advertising department that handles the network's efforts to advertise itself. An advertising agency might be brought in to help devise an image-building campaign, but much of the work is done in-house, for example, coming attractions of the new season's shows. Publicity and special promotions will also be handled by this department; in addition, each subdivision within a network—entertainment, news, radio—may have its own promotion group that produces or commissions an ad agency to produce promotional campaigns. While these jobs are quite separate from the area of selling airtime, they offer a good way to get into advertising at one of the networks.

BREAKING IN

Selling time for one of the networks sounds like a pretty terrific career: the pay is excellent, you're working with top agency media people; you're in the volatile, "glamour business" of television, and you could conceivably rise to the top of it. So, how do you get one of these jobs? There are several paths. First, I should point out that you can't get a selling job or a job in the proposals division without previous work experience. Even a communications degree from a top school and excellent references and contacts won't open the door to these positions. It might, however, open the door to a job as a sales assistant, a position that is staffed by people coming right out of college. Basically, you'd be doing administrative work, keeping files on program content and pricing, answering phones, working on the computer, keeping the account executive organized. It's a great foot in the door, but, naturally, competition is fierce—and jobs are scarce. A sales assistant could move into sales planning (proposal division) after a year or two, and from planning could jump into selling as an account executive. Or a sales assistant might go into media buying at an agency and then return to the network side. Unlike the agency world, where hopping from one shop to another is the rule, the networks generally operate more like families: once you're associated with a network, you're likely to remain with it throughout your career in television.

Another route into network sales is through spot sales or national rep firms. There used to be a wall separating the networks and the world of local stations, but this is no longer so true. You can now gain experience in spot sales and use this to boost yourself into one of the networks. Again, it's not easy because the jobs are limited, but it's a way in. Another common route, as mentioned earlier, is via an advertising agency media department. George Cain believes this is a good way to "gain a broad perspective. Agency work gives you exposure to print, local TV and radio, and all dayparts of network TV. A couple of years in media planning would give you a basis of what advertising is all about. Another course of entering is through media research. This gives you an appreciation for the elements of the business—ratings, shares, household-using television rates, etc. Many go from planning or research into buying and from buying into selling." Cain cautions, however, that it's always difficult to break into this business because of the limited number of positions. "In this business, your reputation precedes you, and when a network looks for a salesperson, they're looking for a person about whom an agency would say, 'Gee, I've heard you've hired so-and-so—I'd love to have that person call on me.' In a way, you have to be somewhat of a known quantity before you get in." Cain got to be a known quantity by working first in finance and then in advertising at Colgate-Palmolive, doing a two-and-a-half-year stint managing all network TV and radio buying for Colgate in cooperation with its agencies. Though Cain went on to work in product management, he kept in touch with his agency and network contacts, one of whom approached him about working at ABC. "I wasn't sure about making this move," recalls Cain, "because I'd already made three career changes and this would be the fourth; but after a couple of conversations with the people at ABC, I saw that this was really a unique opportunity, a real challenge for which I was ready. I came here and loved it."

Another executive I interviewed got into network sales from working at a rep firm. He emphasized the importance of that old faithful quality—persistence: "When I got into this business, I knew no one. I just made the rounds and I was persistent. I started off in research and I used to go in almost every day and tell someone I wanted to be a salesman. I got passed over three or four times, but finally my day came. There is no easy way to break in. You must present yourself properly; it's a good idea to research the company you're interviewing at; and, of course, it helps to be in the right place at the right time."

SELLING MAGAZINE SPACE

Things work slightly differently inside the magazines. First of all, you're selling space and not time, and one crucial distinction is that the rates are not negotiable (or shouldn't be, though some shady operations have been known to break the rules, offering what's known as a "rubber rate card"). Magazines determine the price of advertising space by a base rate, a guaranteed minimum number of readers that they will deliver. Prices do vary depending on whether the advertiser wants to run a four-color, two-color, or black-and-white ad; there are incentives in the form of discounts for advertising more frequently; and certain especially prominent pages (for example, inside cover, back cover, sometimes opposite table of contents) will be sold for a premium; but all of these variations derive from the set base rate. There is no supply-and-demand market situation of bids and counterbids as there is in the networks. Another key difference is that there is no fixed limit on inventory as there is in TV: a magazine will usually run as many ads as the sales force brings in, increasing its editorial content accordingly to keep the set ratio of advertising to editorial pages that the magazine's management has determined.

Given this, it may sound like the space salesperson's job is a piece of cake: just get out there and sell, sell, sell without worrying about the crazy-making, up-and-down marketplace of avails that besets the television salesperson. Happily or unhappily, it's not quite that simple. Cheryl MacLachlan works as an associate advertising manager at *Esquire* magazine in New York. Young, enthusiastic, and extremely personable, MacLachlan can clearly get out there and sell, sell, sell with the best of them. But, as she explained to me in a recent interview, she also does a good deal more than that. Her area is men's fashion and fragrances, a $3 million piece of business that she manages while at the same time overseeing the *Esquire* Collection, a twice-annual fashion magazine that is bound into an issue. Managing a running account (an advertiser that has already run ads in the magazine) means keeping her contacts up to date on where the magazine is going, how the magazine sees its audience responding to them, and what steps they're taking editorially to make sure that magazine-reader bond remains intact. "We also reinforce our position in the marketplace," says MacLachlan, "and by that I mean demonstrating why we still make sense for them from a marketing point of view, how we will bring their customers to them, how *Esquire* will enhance the image of their product—in short, how their visibility in our pages will translate into sales for them."

The first job with running business is to try to get back the business that ran the previous year, and if possible to increase it. This means not only selling the advertiser on the magazine, but knowing the advertiser's company, market, special needs, and problems inside and out. As MacLachlan puts it: "A good salesperson would be there, would tell the client what the magazine is up to, would reinforce our position, but a *great* salesperson would go in and say, 'You're having distribution problems in California. Let's talk about that. Why is there resistance to your product? How can we work on that? Maybe what we need to do is to create a live seminar for you in some of your

California department stores—it will be a joint endeavor between you and *Esquire*.' A great salesperson really becomes that company's marketing partner. Beyond what we can offer them through advertising in the magazine, we might have specific merchandising programs for them; for example, we might supply point-of-purchase counter cards of their ad 'As seen in *Esquire* . . . ,' or we might develop a direct mail brochure for them to go to their trade contacts or to consumers. It all serves to reinforce the message that they're making through *Esquire* magazine."

Of course, people contact is a huge part of the job, but it's no longer the buddy-buddy, slap-on-the-back, how're-the-wife-and-kids style of salesmanship that prevails. More important, according to MacLachlan, is knowing how a company's stock is performing, how well a product sells in urban versus rural stores, what market conditions the advertiser is competing in, and figuring out how to position your product, which is the magazine, to make it most attractive to the contacts. She travels a fair amount because many of her accounts are in other cities. When traveling on business, she prefers to conduct business, not wasting her time or that of the people she's selling to.

Bringing in nonrunning business (i.e., new accounts) really demands great salesmanship ability, because here you're convincing people to take a chance on something untried. They may actually be negatively predisposed toward the magazine for some reason, or it may be a new company or new line of products within an existing company. In either case, you've got to do your homework and figure out to whom they're trying to sell, and then base the sales pitch for your product on that information. MacLachlan estimates that 70% of her business is running to 30% nonrunning.

Advertising agencies play varying roles in this process, depending on the companies and the type of business. In MacLachlan's case, agencies are not involved in most of her accounts because fashion and fragrance companies tend to handle their advertising in-house. But when she does work with an agency, MacLachlan feels that "a good relationship with the agency people is a tremendous benefit: they can steer you in the right direction, and if they like you and like your product, they're going to do everything they can to help that sale happen. They might even point out things that should be brought into focus for the client, and facilitate getting meetings with the client. Of course, deference should be paid and you should approach the agency on any particular matter before approaching the client. But in my judgment, a good agency encourages contact with their client."

Though in magazines there is no programming issue, as in TV, there is the whole question of the placement of the ad in the magazine. This, says MacLachlan, "can be a huge problem in the fashion and fragrance industry. We will literally have people saying, 'If I can't be the first fragrance in the book, you don't get my business.' Fragrances are without a doubt the most difficult category to handle positionwise. The decisions are made usually by the advertising director, though every salesperson tries to protect the interests of their own accounts."

THE MAGAZINE ADVERTISING DEPARTMENT: POSITIONS AND PAY

Generally, the titles within a magazine advertising department are account manager, group manager, and advertising director at the top. This person reports to the publisher, who is usually an important figure in the advertising end of things and the one who makes the final decisions, sets the strategy, and outlines objectives.

An account manager is on the line every day, handling an account list, presenting the magazine to running and nonrunning business, keeping abreast of all aspects of the accounts' businesses. At *Esquire*, to continue with this example, the New York-based accounts are divided up by category—MacLachlan handles fashion and fragrance, someone else will sell space to liquor companies, someone else to electronics makers, and so on. At the regional sales offices (located in the major advertising centers and consisting of one to three people), the account managers will handle any business that happens to be in their territory. The San Francisco people may manage everything from Apple Computers to Esprit clothing.

A group manager has two or three (or sometimes more) account managers reporting to him or her and is responsible for setting guidelines in these categories, for assisting account managers in particularly difficult sales situations, for generating promotional ideas, and often for making the decisions about placement of the ads. This person acts as a kind of filter of information and ideas to the advertising director. The job description of the advertising director is essentially the same, only he or she handles all categories, looks after the entire department, has pretty much final say on ad placement, and spends a good deal of time troubleshooting.

At *Esquire*, there are about twenty-one advertising salespeople, which includes group managers.

Salespeople starting out in New York could expect to earn about $25,000 a year, and if they were really good at it, might get $2000 more in commissions. The commission system differs from magazine to magazine, but two common methods are a percentage (often 2%) of net sales and the quota system, in which the cutoff might be one hundred ad pages and you get no pay-out until you bring in eighty and then full pay-out only when you reach one hundred. Once a salesperson is well established, he or she can start earning about $40,000 a year. After five or six years, a good salesperson will get between $70,000 and $100,000 a year. An advertising director at a good magazine earns anywhere from $85,000 to $120,000.

In reaching for the higher salaries and better positions, hours tend to be rather long. MacLachlan says she puts in an average of ten to twelve hours each weekday, and then maybe two to three hours on Saturday and Sunday. There are, however, crunch periods when she finds herself working seventy-five hours a week for several weeks in a row. The day I interviewed her, she'd arrived at her desk at 5:30 A.M. and expected to stay there until 6:00 P.M.

BREAKING IN

This may sound a bit circular, but probably the best way to break into selling space is to be a good salesperson. If you can sell yourself, you've gone a long way toward demonstrating your ability to sell something as complex and multifaceted as a magazine. There is definitely a salesperson personality type, perhaps best described as outgoing, self-confident, good with people, thick-skinned, and persevering. You've got to be able to bounce back quickly because you're going to hear the word "no" a lot more often than "yes."

Cheryl MacLachlan feels that "It may be helpful, but it's not absolutely necessary, to have a degree in marketing or advertising. With a liberal arts background, an awareness of the world you live in, and strong communicative skills, you can be quite successful. Selling is the ability to convey passion for a product. Education and previous work experience aren't the final determinants."

MacLachlan herself came into this area with a good deal of interesting but unrelated experience (teaching physical education, running a gymnastics program, modeling, and then applying her education in exercise physiology as an assistant researcher at Yale Medical School's Department of Physiology). How did she go from this to selling space to the fashion and fragrance industries in *Esquire*? She explains:

"When I was at Yale I reached that critical juncture when we all wonder, Do I want to be an academic, remain in this intellectually stimulating environment, and be a pauper for the rest of my life? Or do I want to go to New York, find an equally challenging job, but this time make some money? I had a friend who was a publisher who felt I would make a great space salesperson, and he became my mentor. My first job was at a network of in-flight magazines, and here's how I got it: I did the usual mechanics—called up, sent in my resume. They showed a reasonable amount of interest and invited me back for a second interview. Between the first interview and the second, I created my own presentation to them as if I were them, and they were a client. I went to La-Guardia airport and interviewed people coming off of the planes with their in-flight magazines. I asked them if they had read the magazine; if they enjoyed it; if they remembered any of the editorial content, any of the ads; the kinds of products they had at home; the kinds of careers they had—just a basic demographic study. I compiled that information. It clearly demonstrated the high quality level of the audience. Then I did two other things. I have a friend who's a creative director at Doyle Dane Bernbach. I asked him if I could talk to some of the management supervisors on accounts that this magazine network was not getting business from. With that connection, they all agreed to talk to me. I asked them why they weren't buying space in these magazines and what they would like changed. I synthesized all of that. Then I went to talk to a couple of publisher friends and asked them what they thought were the strengths of selling a network of magazines versus selling a single magazine. I then took the strengths of the network system and incorporated them into the presentation.

"I came back to the second interview with this presentation and essentially it was 'WOW! You're hired!' I stayed there for a year and a half and received many inquiry calls during that time from other magazines. None of these positions was exactly what I wanted. It got to the point where I said, 'I'm not going on any more interviews unless *Esquire* calls,' and, unbelievably, *Esquire* called the next day. The reason I wanted *Esquire* is that I loved the magazine. Beyond that, I'd heard about the management team here—it's led by two extraordinary young men, Phillip Moffitt and Christopher Whittle. My mentor said to me that these are the two brightest guys in the industry, if you ever get the opportunity to work there, if you have to, you pay *them* to get in. It has absolutely lived up to my expectations."

MacLachlan may have been a little more fortunate than most because she had a few key contacts in the business, but there was no element of luck in her idea of putting a presentation together that demonstrated her research abilities and business acumen. That was a stroke of job-hunting genius, and just the kind of push that makes all the difference in getting hired. Notice also that MacLachlan didn't start at the magazine of her first choice. This is something else to bear in mind about breaking in: you might have a better crack at a small, regional magazine, a trade magazine, or a rep firm. Magazine rep firms represent a number of small magazines or out-of-town magazines to national advertisers, the same way that national rep firms in television represent a number of small, local stations. A Denver-based magazine, for example, may use a rep firm to go after advertising in New York rather than maintain a New York office. All of these routes are possibilities.

MacLachlan sums up: "My advice is to be well prepared for any magazine that you're going to interview at, and as soon as you see a slight gleam of interest, go all out. Take a real interest in their sales approach and special problems. No advertising director would mind if an interviewee called up and said, 'What categories are you having difficulty with? I'd like to bring back something for your consideration.' In fact, I would shout to the heavens, 'Thank God for someone who really wants to work here!'"

As with selling TV time, the world of space selling is centered in New York, but there are some opportunities in all the major advertising centers—Chicago, Detroit, San Francisco, Los Angeles, Boston, Dallas, Atlanta—and most major magazines maintain regional offices there. There may not be as many jobs, but then again there's not as much competition to get those jobs.

PART FOUR

THE JOB SEARCH

GETTING HIRED

"The easiest way to get an advertising job," Charles Rabkin, a long-time adman who has held a slew of them, confided, "is to have your father buy the advertising agency." Barring that, however, you're going to have to do a little hustling. Or maybe a lot of hustling. For a lucky few, getting a job, and particularly a first job, is a breeze: their college roommate's father is a management supervisor at McCann-Erickson; their favorite professor's best friend is head of personnel at Doyle Dane Bernbach; their portfolio hits the desk of the creative director of BBDO the same day a $50 million account moves its business to the agency. These are wonderful ways to get into advertising, but unfortunately, most of us can't really count on them. Here are some hard facts, specific information, and good advice that you *can* count on in landing that first job, or switching from a job you already have.

EDUCATION AND BACKGROUND

When asked for the one trait that distinguished a successful job applicant at Young & Rubicam from a reject, Alex Kroll, its president and chief executive officer, replied: "Almost none of them ever study advertising." This may be stating the case a bit baldly, but Kroll is not alone in emphasizing the importance of the broadest range of interests and experiences as being far more valuable credentials than marketing courses, copywriting courses, or what have you. What this translates into in terms of education is liberal arts. A bachelor's degree in just about anything from history to art history, psychology to political science is probably the best background for getting yourself into position for an advertising job hunt. (The exception here is the aspiring art director, for whom training in commercial art at one of the better schools—Pratt, School of Visual Arts, Syracuse, the Art Center in Los Angeles—is a real benefit.) Of course, if you do have some marketing courses, that's not going to hurt you; and, despite what Kroll said, advertising majors do get hired at major agencies all the time. But the point is you shouldn't rule yourself out if you haven't devoted your college years to studying advertising or marketing; and, furthermore, if the only thing you studied was advertising, you may come off as a bit limited, especially for jobs in research and creative. In general, advertising attracts (and favors) people with a broad range of interests and experiences, and the creative and research areas in particular seem to have the most heterogeneous staffs. These days, Renaissance men and women are doing better with the advertising hiring honchos than are specialists or technicians.

The rather vexing question of whether you need an MBA to get into account management is considered in detail in Chapter Five *[see the "Breaking In" section]*. I'll just add here that an MBA is pretty much required for most marketing jobs on the client side, for instance, the highly sought-after product management positions. An MBA, however, may actually hurt your chances of getting a media, production, or traffic job at an agency because it will make you look either overqualified or bound for account management. A number of people I interviewed were actually encouraged to leave this credential off their resumes when applying for these jobs. So, don't go rushing off to business school just because you've heard it's the thing to do in advertising. An MBA offers you a very limited advantage in getting hired on the agency side.

If you're still determined to major in advertising, you can obtain a list of colleges that offer advertising majors by sending $1 for the booklet "Where Shall I Go to College to Study Advertising," put out by Advertising Education Publications, 3429 55th St., Lubbock, Texas 79413.

Probably more important than your education credentials is your ability to demonstrate a real interest and commitment to advertising. This means entering any advertising contests that your school or the various associations *[see Chapter Fifteen]* may run. In the case of media, it means working on school newspapers or magazines or perhaps getting a summer internship (helpful for any advertising discipline, in fact) with a local TV station. Any kind of survey work or analysis sets you up for research jobs. For creatives, it's not only important, it's *necessary* that you demonstrate interest in the form of a portfolio of sample ads (see below). Sales jobs of any sort are also excellent related experience because they show your interest in selling (which, after all, is the essence of advertising) and also acquaint you with the tastes and habits of consumers, something advertising people go to great lengths and spend much money trying to figure out. In fact, almost any sales or business-related job can be valuable if you position yourself right. You may have considered your part-time job behind the counter at

Burger King a rather grueling way to earn spending money in college, but you can score a lot of points at an interview by bringing up your observation that teens unaccompanied by adults spent more money and time at the outlet than teens with adults or parents. When you start thinking like an ad person, you'll see the value and benefit in your jobs and hobbies. Remember, a job hunt is really an advertising campaign for *you*. You're the product and what attributes of yours might appeal to the "consumers" (those who are going to hire you) should be brought to the fore and stated in the most positive way possible.

GETTING ORGANIZED

Focus. This is one of the great buzzwords of the job-hunting process. Focus is what separates an organized job search from a vague and painfully prolonged one. Focus is a great way of relieving the anxiety and panic that many people experience when confronted by the immense number of possible jobs, people to call, leads to follow up, companies to consider.

First, focus on yourself and try to figure out why you want advertising, what you hope to get out of it, what your preconceptions are and how they measure up with the realities out there. Lots of books can help you at this stage; perhaps the best known is *What Color Is Your Parachute?* by Richard Bolles *[see Chapter Fifteen]*. A lot of people come out of school convinced that they must be a copywriter or account executive or product manager without really understanding what these jobs are all about or realizing that maybe being a media planner or producer is more up their alley. It makes sense to think about why you've become so set on one area—in some cases, it's because that's the fashionable job you've heard other people talking about; in others, it's because you know in your heart that it's you; in still others, you may have simply lit on it and never let go. Then there are people who know they want advertising but have no idea which branch, which department, or which area. Reading through the job descriptions and interviews in this book can help you focus on a single advertising discipline or perhaps a few related disciplines, which is absolutely essential before undertaking a job hunt.

A word of advice: Talk to people. The more people the better. Obviously people working in advertising can give you the best insights into the various advertising careers, but almost anyone you like and can open up with can help you sort out your thoughts. Friends or mentors may be more aware of your strengths than you are; relatives may have contacts in the advertising world that you never suspected; roommates can give you pep talks when all else fails. Thousands of advertising careers have been launched by a friend or teacher telling someone, "You know, I always thought you'd be terrific at selling space or account management or working in a production company . . ." Usually the people who think these things have a way of helping you realize them. *[For more on talking to people, see "Contacts," page 241.]*

Geography. The action in advertising today is happening in seven key cities—New York, Chicago, Detroit, Los Angeles, San Francisco, Dallas, Boston. Minneapolis, Miami, and Atlanta also have thriving advertising scenes. But the country (some would say the world) really has only one advertising center and that's New York. So if you happen to live in or near New York or one of these cities, it makes sense to focus your search there. It's not quite as simple if you don't live near an advertising community, because then you're probably going to have to think about moving. The best advice here is to do some preliminary research, put out a few feelers, talk to people, and then make a decision about which city you'll concentrate on before you launch a major search. Conducting a heavy-duty job hunt in two or more cities at the same time is all but impossible. *[For more on where the action in advertising is today, see Chapter Three.]*

For a lot of people, picking a city on which to focus will come down to tackling New York. Keep an open mind. A number of people I interviewed said they'd been knocking their heads against the wall in Boston, Philadelphia, or L.A. when someone advised them to try looking in New York. It was, in many cases, the best advice they ever got.

Of course, choosing where you want to be will depend to some extent on what agency or company you want to work for, which brings us to another area of focus.

Narrowing Down the Possibilities. The Agency Red Book *[see Chapter Fifteen]* lists over 4,000 advertising agencies. The Advertisers Red Book has over four times this many companies that advertise. Then there are the hundreds of media companies all over the country. How do you decide where to apply? There's no easy answer to this question, but here are some good pointers to get you started.

Most advice givers agree that it's better to concentrate your job hunt on a few companies and really go after them in a personal, thorough way than to spread yourself all over the place with form letters, mass mailings, and perfunctory follow-ups. So, narrow down the number of agencies, corporations, or media companies you're going to pursue to some workable initial figure, say, ten to twenty (you can always add more later). One way to do this narrowing-down process is to get your hands on the special edition of *Advertising Age [again, see Chapter Fifteen]* that is relevant to your area. This vital organ of the ad business publishes a special edition each spring profiling America's leading ad agencies; there's a summer issue devoted to the leading media companies; and a fall issue on the nation's leading advertisers. You can get hold of these issues at your local library, or call *Advertising Age* and arrange to have one sent to your home. As you thumb through these magazines, you'll get a sense of how the various companies are organized, how big they are; in the case of agencies, what new clients they've landed and what old ones they've lost; in the case of advertisers, what new product lines they've launched and what agencies they're using to handle which products. Certain company names will stand out and attract your attention for one reason or another. There might be an agency whose work you've always admired that just opened a branch office in your city. Or a company with a product you feel you could market in some new way. Or a media company expanding into pay cable, an area you happen to know a lot about. These special *Ad Age* issues will contain this sort of information. So check it out.

Here, too, talking to people can be invaluable. People in the business have a way of knowing who's hot and who's hiring, both of which change constantly in advertising. They'll give you the inside scoop on company reputations and relay rumors about areas of growth, new accounts, etc.

Then there's the trade press. In addition to *Ad Age*, there are a number of other magazines and newspapers devoted to advertising and marketing *[see Chapter Fifteen for listings]*. An immersion in these journals will introduce you to agencies, key advertising people, marketing directors, creative directors, new companies, new products, and best of all, new opportunities.

Awards annuals and the numerous (and well-reported) awards ceremonies are other sources of information that can help you decide where to apply. The advertising industry pats itself on the back all the time with such awards as the Clio (the Award for Advertising Excellence), the ANDY (awards given by the New York Advertising Club for outstanding creative work), and the One Club Show awards given by the One Club, an organization for copywriters and art directors *[again, see Chapter Fifteen]*. Find out who won the major awards in any given year and go after them. It never hurts to try and hitch your wagon to a star. One art director I spoke to said she organized her job search by poring through the awards annuals; not only would she find the agency names, but also the names of creative directors and writers and art directors who worked on the winning campaigns. She had an instant entree simply by calling up and saying, "I loved your award-winning work on such-and-such, loved it so much I want to work with you on that account. Will you take a look at my book?" Stroking egos never hurts.

In pulling together all of this information, you'll probably find that there are a few places where you're dying to work, a few that you have good reason to suspect are hiring (because they've landed major new business or opened a new office), a few where you have contacts, and a few that you've been reading a lot about and so they're on your mind. That's your list. That's where you begin your job hunt.

Even after you've determined which agencies to focus on, keep your ears and your options open. New possibilities and new situations arise all the time in the advertising world. If you hear about a good lead, follow it, even if it means dropping everything else for the moment. Revise your list whenever it's in your interest to do so. In job-hunting, it pays to be quick and stay on your toes.

CONTACTS: HOW TO MAKE AND USE THEM

The first rule of contacts is that *almost anyone* can become one. The word itself carries a certain aura of mystery and exclusiveness. When you hear other people talking about their contacts, you imagine old family friends, close relatives who have been in the business for years, members of Grandpapa's club. Maybe some people have these sorts of contacts (doubtless very few), but your contacts can be people you've met on the bus, in a course, or even over the phone—and they can be just as helpful as the other guy's cherished cousin. A contact is really any insider who will talk to you and let you use his/her name in making other contacts. You notice someone on the bus who happens to be reading *Adweek* and you strike up a conversation, explaining that you're new in town, just out of school, eagerly job-hunting. This person just happens to be a creative director at a small agency. His place is not looking for anyone in media (your chosen area) right now, but he happens to know a media director at a mega-agency and he recalls hearing that they are looking for a few good assistants. You ask if he'd mind if you jotted down that person's name and, without being too pushy, you obtain permission from your bus contact to use *his* name when you call the media director. Of course he agrees because you're so charming and obviously capable. You leap off the bus and find the nearest phone, calling that media director and introducing yourself as a recent acquaintance (or friend or contact or neighbor) of this fellow on the bus. You explain that he told you to call and ask if you might send your resume and come in for an interview. You do not mention anything about the bus.

You've just made two contacts.

That's the way it works and, advertising being a fairly small and talkative industry, you can contact your way around to a good number of the major agencies in any city in no time.

The second rule of contacts is that, without resorting to accosting people on buses, you probably have a lot more potential contacts than you think. Start talking—to *every-one*—friends of your parents, parents of your friends, friends of your friends, relatives of your relatives, teachers, alumni/ae of your school. Mention to all of these people that you're looking for an advertising job (be as specific as possible as to area) and ask if they can help or know anyone who could. Talk to anyone who will talk to you. If possible, go in and meet them in their offices and treat these meetings like interviews. Make sure you ask each new contact for names of *other* contacts. Keep meeting people, even if they say they're not hiring. One copywriter I talked to said she "networked" her way to a job by talking to anyone she came across who might be helpful. She met a woman at a party whose father was an account supervisor and he put her in touch with the copy director, who in turn helped her put a book together and hooked her up with a number of creative directors. "After that," she recalls, "it was a matter of knocking on doors until somebody had an empty desk." It took her several months and she got thoroughly sick of calling people she didn't know and being charming—but it worked.

The third rule of contacts is never be afraid of calling on someone "high up." Executive creative directors, agency presidents, research and media directors are always looking for new talent. That's you. Yes, directors are busy and important and maybe even famous. But part of their importance depends on getting people like you to add your fresh ideas to the company. It's strange but true that top management is sometimes more accessible and willing to talk and help than people in the middle or on their way up. Go after them. Impress them with your abilities and your knowledge of their backgrounds. And then diplomatically ask them for names of other contacts or people in the company who might be interested. There is no better entree than being able to say, "I was talking with the president of your agency yesterday and he mentioned that you were looking for someone to do . . ."

A resourceful art director told me how she would make contacts with top agency people during her job hunt: "I had no connections but I wasn't scared to call and I would call anyone. All the big creative directors talked to me. I would look in *Advertising Age* and if I saw that an agency had won a new account, I'd go and ask to speak to the creative director on the account. Sometimes I'd just call the agency and ask the receptionist who the creative director on the new so-and-so account was. The receptionist would give me the name and then I'd call back and ask to speak to him."

A few tips about contacting contacts: If you're calling someone cold (without a previous introduction), it's always better to speak directly to that person than to go through a secretary. Lots and lots of people don't return phone calls and there's nothing you can do about that. So try to call before 9 or after 5, when the secretary is not around. Or write and specify a time when you'll be calling (this sometimes works). Or leave a message that you'll be calling back later. If nothing works, forget it. Cut your losses and move on.

Tips on keeping contacts: it's usually a good idea to drop a contact a thank-you note after he or she has met with you. It also helps to stay in touch. Your contacts will keep you up-to-date on any changes in the job situation and perhaps think of other people for you to get in touch with. Remember, these are your future colleagues. Before you know it, they'll be calling on you for the inside word.

Applying

Research. Even before you contact a company or agency with your cover letter and resume (see below), go to the library and absorb as much information as you can. Nothing makes a better impression than demonstrating a real familiarity with the place where you're hoping to be hired. This means knowing something about its staff, its executive officers, as well as its major accounts, creative successes, and recent newsworthy accomplishments. Research is an essential first step in the application process. Read through the listing in the Red Book. Examine the company's annual report. Check the periodical index and the business index for any recent articles or news stories. Familiarize yourself with the major accounts or products, the recent advertising campaigns, awards, corporate acquisitions, new offices, personnel changes, etc. Not all of this information will be immediately relevant in an interview, but knowing it will make you feel that much more comfortable in answering questions and aware of the key issues facing the company. And some of it will be crucial. For example, if you've just read that the agency has reorganized its research department to take advantage of new findings on consumer attitudes and psychology, you might mention this fact in your cover letter as something that has drawn you to the company. Perhaps you wrote a term paper on the emerging importance of psychographics in advertising. You'd be a perfect fit in the new department and, because of your own research, you can let the company know this as soon as you make contact. Any interview involves a certain amount of surprise. You never know quite what you're going to be asked or quite how you're going to respond. The more prepared you are through research, the more you'll be able to make the surprise factor work for you.

The Resume and Cover Letter. No matter how many contacts you've succeeded in making and how many insiders you've befriended, at some point you're going to have to sit down and compose a formal cover letter, attach your resume to it, and send these to someone inside the agency or company *[for creatives you also have to have a portfolio; see below]*.

No one likes to put a resume together, but some people get so traumatized by the process that it becomes a major stumbling block in the job hunt. A resume may not be fun, but it needn't be as much of a deal as some make of it. It does require some fussing, but only over certain details. Fuss with getting every word spelled correctly, fuss over the format and organization so that the resume highlights your major achievements, fuss over the precision and clarity of the language so that your objectives match up with the job you're applying for and your experience makes you look qualified and competent. Do *not* fuss over fancy and expensive typesetting, elegant or strangely shaped paper, zany gimmicks (see below).

If you're applying for your first "real" job, make sure your resume fits on one page. At the top you'll center your name, address, and phone number. You'll include a line or two on your *objective* in which you state as precisely as possible what job you're seeking (assistant account executive, junior copywriter, etc.— *not* "creative trainee," "key position in the media department"). If you're hunting simultaneously for jobs in different areas (e.g., media and account management), make up two different resumes. Next, organize a section on *experience*, in which you include any interesting or related work experience (summer jobs, internships, part-time work) and a section on *education*, in which you relate the basic facts of your schooling, including any awards or publications and relevant extracurricular activities. Make sure that someone can gather all the major information about you by glancing at your resume. That means make it simple, clear, and organized with headings that stand out from brief, descriptive text.

A resume is just the bare bones of your credentials. You fill in all the fascinating details at the interview.

Your cover letter also requires careful attention to key details. Always address a cover letter to a person, never to a company, department, institution, or title (e.g., "Dear Mr. Account Supervisor"). Find out the name of the department head (from the Red Book) and address the letter to him/her. To be sure, it's a good idea to double-check by phoning this person's secretary and checking the spelling of the person's name and his/her correct title. It never hurts to write both a department head and a personnel director. It shows you're really interested. By all means, take the time to proofread every cover letter carefully. Make sure your grammar, spelling, and punctuation are flawless.

The best cover letters are the most personal, displaying some familiarity with the person you're contacting, or with the company. Explain why you've selected that person to write to, and try to tie it in with some aspect of your talent, ability, or career goal. For example, *Time* cited this creative director for his stunning MTV-style commercials, and you happen to have worked with some college friends on a music video. Mention both items in your letter, along with the fact that you would be a natural as a production assistant. The management supervisor you're writing to has just been assigned the new cosmetics account that the agency landed, and you spent last summer selling door-to-door for Avon. Again, draw the connection in your cover letter.

Try to think of your cover letter as a conversation rather than as a stiff presentation. Be warm, brief, eager, and direct—don't brag, but don't be shy or coy about pushing yourself as a first-rate individual. The good cover letter serves two main purposes: it displays your interest and knowledge of the company (and person, if possible) that you're applying to, and it arouses the interest of that company in you. Always keep these purposes in mind when you sit down to write. Copywriters need to pay special attention to the cover letter since it's the first writing sample they're showing (see below, "Attention Creatives").

Basics: Always state the purpose of your letter right up front—don't make the person wait to find out you're writing for a job. Keep it short, but don't be so blunt and businesslike that you fail to establish your own tone. It's a good idea to end your letter with something like: "I'll phone you on the morning of November 4 to see if we can set up a time to meet. Even if you have no openings at the present time, I'd love to sit down with you and talk about the X Agency and what I might bring to it in the future." If you wait for them to contact you, you'll wait forever. Always try to set up an interview; no interview is a waste of your time.

For in-depth treatment of the subjects of resumes and cover letters, see *Getting Hired* by Edward Rogers *[listed in Chapter Fifteen]*.

T HE INTERVIEW

Interviewing for jobs is kind of like riding a bike: at first, you'll be awkward and land on your face a lot, but with practice you'll find yourself cruising along with ease and confidence; soon you won't even have to think about things like changing gears, maneuvering around bumpy sections, starting from a dead stop. Also, as with riding a bike, once you learn how to interview, you never forget.

The moral of the analogy is: practice. Madeline Lewis, a management director at Foote, Cone & Belding in New York, advises job seekers to save the interviews at the places they really want to work for last: "Before you go to these chosen agencies, talk to a million people and get good interviewing experience. There's a real art to interviewing and you really need to get the experience under your belt of fielding questions and thinking things through. So when you finally do see those six key agencies, you'll come across as knowing what you want and knowing what you're getting into."

The next piece of interview advice is: be prepared. This means not only researching the company, but researching the area in which you're applying. Know what the job is all about and what the entry-level position will entail (you can find this out by reading the relevant section of this book!). Nothing makes a worse impression than saying something like, "I want to get into traffic and production, but I don't really know what it's all about." A lot of people I interviewed singled this out as the greatest failing in a job seeker. As soon as they sense that the person they're interviewing has no idea about the basic functions of the department, they strike that person from the list. Why hire someone who is going to start at square zero, when you can get someone for the same price who's starting out two jumps ahead?

At the end of most interviews, you'll be asked if you have any questions, so again, be prepared. The more you know about the job and the company, the more intelligent your questions will be. Jot down questions as you're doing your preliminary research If necessary, practice them. Make sure the questions are not obvious and that they reflect a real interest in getting down to work. "How soon can I expect a raise or promotion?" is a real turnoff. More impressive would be something like: "I understand you're trying to land some travel-related accounts. I worked in a travel agency last summer, so this is a real area of interest for me. As an entry-level person, would I have the chance to rotate from a packaged goods account to a travel account?"

Even more than ignorance about the job functions, advertising people complained about arrogance in job hunters. It's reaching epidemic proportions. People come in boasting about how they were at the top of the class and wondering why they have to start at the bottom of the agency. The attitude is, I'm too good for this lowly job, but if that's the only way to get to the top, I guess I can bear it for a while. The response, increasingly, is—drop dead. No matter how great you think you are, to any company you're only as great as your ability to contribute, and that's pretty small until you learn the ropes. Desire and eagerness score you major points. These qualities are the best antidotes to arrogance. Yes, you might become a little bored numbers-crunching on the computer for the first year, but you don't have to let that show at the interview. The attitude you project should be: I can handle whatever you throw my way; I know I'll be starting at the bottom, but I want to prove to you how quickly I can make myself indispensable to your business. All I want is the opportunity to work hard.

Maybe the best suggestion is to put yourself in the shoes of the interviewer. What kind of person would you want to encounter at an interview? What would make you choose one person over possibly hundreds of others? You know you've got those qualities—now you have to work on letting them shine. Be yourself—but be your best self in any interview.

Beyond that, there are a few matters of interview etiquette, decorum, and custom. Always arrive for an interview on time. Be nice to the secretary and receptionist: they have a way of passing information on to the boss. Always thank the interviewer before and after. Don't smoke unless the interviewer does and you ask permission. Dress up and look neat, businesslike, and comfortable in your clothes; look and feel both at ease and ready to work. Bring an extra copy of your resume to the interview. Don't do all the talking—interview back, asking questions about the company, the staff, the philosophy. Even if you're desperate for a job, don't appear to be. Always stress the positive: I'm really eager to get down to work soon at such-and-such; not: I'm totally broke and if I don't get a job this week I'm going to have to eat my plants. At the end of an interview, always ask how you should proceed: call again in a week? wait for their reply? further interviews with others in the department? Try to get names of other contacts from your interviewer, but if he or she resists, drop it. Don't get depressed about a lousy interview, cut your losses and move on. Always write a thank-you note after an interview, especially to someone you'd like to stay in touch with.

AFTER THE INTERVIEW

Staying in Touch. Most interviews end inconclusively. Either there are a number of other people interviewing for the job, or there is no job open and the interview was merely an exploratory let's-get-acquainted session, or there hadn't been a job open until they met you, or you're a very strong candidate but they want you to meet some other people in the company. Whatever the case, it's in your interest to stay in touch. That doesn't mean calling every day, but more like twice a month. If you have doubts about the appropriate frequency, ask the interviewer, "Do you mind if I call you in a couple of weeks to check in?" Many people talk about "being in the right place at the right time" as the real secret of job-hunting success, and they attribute this to luck. Yes, there is a strong element of luck in this process, but you can bolster your luck by pushing a bit. Keep your name in circulation by picking up the phone and reminding your contacts and interviewers that you're still out there. You'd be amazed at how eager people will be to help you if you've made a good impression and you stay in touch. There is definitely an advertising community in every city, and even in the advertising capitals it's not overwhelmingly large. Word has a way of traveling about a good, qualified job candidate. But it's up to you to get the word out in the first place.

Going that Extra Bit. "As soon as you see a slight gleam of interest, go all out," is the advice that Cheryl MacLachlan, associate advertising manager at *Esquire* magazine, has for job seekers. MacLachlan followed this advice when she was hunting for her first job, and it paid off immediately. *[For the details on what she did, see Chapter Thirteen.]*

Going that extra bit might mean digging deeper in your research into a company, offering to work for free on a trial basis (if you can afford it), or working up a presentation similar to the one MacLachlan devised. The great thing about her idea was that she demonstrated her ability to do the job she was applying for. Focus on this when you're trying to come up with ideas.

ATTENTION CREATIVES

Your Book. You can't talk your way into a creative job at an ad agency—you must show samples of your work. This means putting together a spec book or portfolio with sample campaigns. Catch-22, you may be thinking: how can I show samples of my work if I've never worked? The answer is: you make them up. You choose products you're familiar with and devise advertising campaigns for them. You choose ad campaigns you're familiar with and improve on them. Luckily, there is an excellent book written about this very subject by a woman who recruits and screens creatives at Dancer Fitzgerald. The book is called *How to Put Your Book Together and Get a Job in Advertising*, and the author's name is Maxine Paetro. It's published in paperback by Hawthorn Books. So if you don't have a book and don't know how to make one, check this title out.

The One Club offers portfolio review sessions to its members and many art schools give seminars or workshops on how to assemble a spec book, so take advantage of these if you can.

Some good advice on this subject appeared in *Advertising Age* (May 2, 1985) in an article by John Sweeney, former associate creative director at Foote, Cone & Belding/Chicago, and now a teacher of advertising at the University of North Carolina at Chapel Hill. Among other suggestions, Sweeney recommends the following: if you're looking in New York, do packaged goods and play up print. Agencies in smaller markets will be more impressed by regional accounts such as hotels and banks. Keep your book small: It's better to have a small, first-rate book than a mix of mediocre work. The worst that could happen is the creative director will ask to see more work. Choose a range of products and come up with a range of approaches, and make sure at least one campaign includes all the major media—TV, print, radio, and outdoor. It's OK for writers to include primitively drawn art. Avoid products which have already been advertised with celebrated, award-winning, world-famous campaigns: you're only inviting comparison with an impossible standard. It would be better to choose products you like that don't have super campaigns. Make sure your TV scripts time to thirty seconds.

Copywriters' Cover Letters. A copywriter's cover letter should be something special. Treat it like a piece of copy—captivate your audience (the creative director or copy chief), arouse interest in your product (yourself), be as charming as the constraints of clarity and persuasiveness allow. Don't get so carried away with some literary conceit that you forget to identify yourself and the reason for writing the letter. Make yourself distinctive in a good way—you want to stand out as exceptionally talented, not exceptionally crazed. If you write a long letter, you better make it a masterpiece. And, as with all cover letters, the more you show an interest in and knowledge of the person to whom you're writing, the better received your letter will be. Tell the creative director why you want to work for him or her. Rare is the person who doesn't warm up to a little admiration.

On Gimmicks. There are a few creative job-hunting gimmicks that have entered the annals of advertising history. The T-shirt with the resume printed on it that arrived in a Brooks Brothers box. The resume that unfurled on a giant banner on the building across the street from the agency's office. The guy with a sandwich board announcing that he was an unemployed copywriter who paraded around Grand Central Station handing out copies of his resume. The pizza box containing a resume and a genuine (greasy) pizza. There are some less famous ones that also worked. And then there are slews of totally obscure gimmicks that not only didn't work, they backfired. The person would have been better off with a normal resume and cover letter. Be aware that in using a gimmick, you're taking a gamble. If you come up with something that you're convinced is fabulous, try it out on a few people, preferably ad people, before you hitch your career fate to it. Remember, creative directors and recruiters have seen just about everything before. Be very sure your gimmick is clever, original, and not stomach-turning; otherwise, the people who count are simply not going to be impressed. And anyway, the best even a classy gimmick can do is get you noticed—it's not going to get you a job. Only you can do that.

TRAINING PROGRAMS

Training programs at advertising agencies have a way of coming and going. Some years they're out recruiting, other years they're not taking on juniors. The rules change too: enrollment procedures vary, formats shift, even location of which branch office offers the program moves around. One thing, however, does not change: training programs are very difficult to get into. The simple reason is that positions are scarce and applications plentiful. One personnel staffer at a large New York agency estimated that 12,000 people apply each year for the eight to ten openings in the account management program; others have given much lower figures—1,200 applicants for ten spots—but it's still not too encouraging. Even so, it's worth a shot, because if you do get in, you're going to receive lots of special attention, attend seminars and presentations, be fussed over by concerned senior people, and really learn the business well and quickly.

Here is a rundown on which agencies offer training programs in which areas as reported in *Advertising Age*. Be sure to check with an agency before applying to make sure that the program is still running and how to go about getting in.

Account management programs: N W Ayer, Ted Bates, BBDO, Benton & Bowles, Leo Burnett, Campbell-Ewald (Detroit), Doyle Dane Bernbach, Foote, Cone & Belding, McCann-Erickson, Needham Harper, SSC&B:Lintas, J. Walter Thompson, Young & Rubicam.

Media programs: N W Ayer, Ted Bates, BBDO, Benton & Bowles, Leo Burnett, Campbell-Ewald (Detroit), D'Arcy MacManus Masius (St. Louis), Foote, Cone & Belding, McCann-Erickson, Needham Harper, SSC&B:Lintas, J. Walter Thompson, Wells, Rich, Greene, Young & Rubicam.

Creative programs: Dancer Fitzgerald Sample, Ogilvy & Mather, SSC&B:Lintas, J. Walter Thompson, Young & Rubicam.

(Creative training programs, by the way, seem to be enjoying something of a resurgence. Both Dancer Fitzgerald and SSC&B have started up programs recently and both went to colleges to get recruits. Thompson scouted out copywriters for its training program through a full-page newspaper ad headlined "Write If You Want Work." More than 1,400 people replied, nine have been hired to date.)

Research programs: Ted Bates, BBDO, Campbell-Ewald (Detroit), D'Arcy Mac-Manus Masius (St. Louis), Foote, Cone & Belding (Chicago), J. Walter Thompson and Young & Rubicam are willing to consider student applicants.

Training programs tend to be considered something of a luxury, and usually only large agencies can afford them. Keep your eye on the trade press and college and university bulletin boards for announcements, or contact the agencies themselves to get up-to-date details.

EXECUTIVE RECRUITERS

Executive recruiters, also known as headhunters, help companies find the right people to fill available jobs. Generally they restrict their services to executive positions to which fairly healthy salaries are attached. The agencies simply don't want to pay a headhunter's fee for a low-level, low-paying job, especially when so many people are knocking down their doors to get these jobs. Still, it's good to know their names for future reference (or present reference, if you have experience and want to change jobs), and, of course, there are exceptions. Some headhunters do routinely help entry-level people (these are indicated below), and others are willing to take on a really talented person, a lucky person, or a stray whom they happen to like. Even if they won't find you a job, they may give you good advice.

Here are the major operations:

Berger Jacobs Kozuck
104 E. 40th Street
New York, N.Y. 10016
212-682-9610
Only handles creatives.

Roberta Brenner Associates Inc.
104 E. 40th Street
New York, N.Y. 10016
212-682-0700
Specializes in account management.

Fabian & Altschuler
215 Park Avenue South
New York, N.Y. 10003
212-477-3373
Creatives only. Does handle some entry-level people.

Jerry Field Associates, Inc.
515 Madison Avenue, Suite 1120
New York, N.Y. 10022
212-319-7600

Judd-Falk
124 E. 37th Street
New York, N.Y. 10016
212-686-1500

Placement Associates, Inc.
80 Fifth Avenue

New York, N.Y. 10011
212-620-7620
Leading public relations placement firm, also does creative and account management placement for advertising agencies.

Sussman and Morris Associates, Inc.
509 Madison Avenue
New York, N.Y. 10022
212-758-3411
Known for media placement, also handles account management and creative.

Judy Wald Agency Inc.
110 E. 59th Street
New York, N.Y. 10022
212-421-6750
Also has offices in Los Angeles, Chicago, and London. All areas; sometimes handles entry-level people.

F YOU DON'T GET THE JOB YOUR HEART IS SET ON

Don't give up! And don't conclude that advertising is not for you. William Phillips, chairman of the Ogilvy Group and of Ogilvy & Mather Worldwide, says his "first advice" for people who want to go to work in an ad agency is to get a job, any job: "Get a job as a secretary or in the mailroom or in *some* department, and you can usually wiggle your way on up if you are good. One of the big mistakes is that ninety percent of the people going into the agency business want to be in an account management training program. But remember, agencies hire a wide spectrum of people."

Almost any job inside an agency is better than pounding the pavements or waiting on tables. Copywriter jobs are notoriously scarce, but there are frequently openings for copy typists. *What?* you might be thinking, with my terrific book and my BA in English—*typing?* Remember—it's just a steppingstone, not a career. When the junior copywriter gets married and moves to Arizona, the creative director is a lot more likely to fill the spot with you—the cheerful, witty, tireless typist with the terrific book—than with some stranger from the outside.

Some positions can become a trap or a deadend, but for the most part almost any starting job depends on what you make of it. A network salesman I spoke to started in research at a rep firm; if he hadn't pushed, he'd still be there today. Everyone knows it's tough to make the move from spot TV to network sales, but he succeeded in getting out of the "spot slot" because he wanted to badly enough. Tom Clark, president and chief operating officer of BBDO, started in the mailroom. Glen Gilbert, director of advertising at American Express, started in the messenger room at Young & Rubicam. If you know you're good, don't be scared of getting your feet wet in this way. You won't be a messenger for long, and besides, it makes a great story in later years.

If you're really serious about wanting advertising, it makes sense to look on job hunting as a job. You may be at it for a while. Six months is by no means unusual. For some people it took an entire year. You may have to take on temporary work to support your job hunt; sometimes the temp work itself can turn into a real job. Keep your job hunt organized and update your research, files, contacts. It may encourage you to know that you'll never have to go through this again: landing that first job is probably the toughest job you'll ever have. Keep hunting. It will happen to you.

Resources

Professional Associations

Professional associations can help in your job hunt in a number of ways. Many publish brochures, some offer career counseling or portfolio review for creatives, others conduct seminars at which you can learn about advertising and meet top ad people. It won't hurt to get your name on the mailing lists of the relevant association and attend what functions are open to you. Here are some of the major organizations and what they make available to job seekers:

The Advertising Club of New York
155 E. 55th Street
New York, N.Y. 10022
212-935-8080
Devoted to bringing together people from all segments of advertising, marketing, and public relations, the club sponsors the ANDY awards for creative/communication excellence. It offers members such services as "special event" luncheons, during which industry luminaries speak, social gatherings, a newsletter, and advanced advertising continuing education. Those starting out may be interested in the twenty-lecture advertising and marketing course.

Membership available to students as well as young professionals under thirty or who have worked less than two years.

Advertising Women of New York, Inc.
153 E. 57th Street
New York, N.Y. 10022
212-593-1950
Has a Career Council for people who want to get into the advertising business.

Group meetings of five to six are held and additional counseling on a one-to-one basis is also available. This is a free service open to both men and women. There is also a yearly College Career Conference held for people who are studying advertising in college and scholarships for women studying advertising. Contact the association for further details.

American Advertising Federation
1400 K Street NW
Washington, D.C. 20005
202-898-0089
  A grassroots organization with members from the ranks of advertisers, agencies, the major media, printers, production companies, etc. Contact them for available literature and for information on their educational programs.

American Association of Advertising Agencies (the 4A's)
666 Third Avenue
New York, N.Y. 10017
212-682-2500
  Most American ad agencies of any note belong to this prestigious association, whose purpose is to furnish agencies with information that will increase their usefulness and to make legal, historical, media, and government-related information available to member agencies. The organization also acts as the industry's spokesman to government and the news media. The 4A's does, however, have several brochures directed at job seekers, among them "Advertising Agencies: What They Are, What They Do, and How They Do It," "Advertising: A Guide to Careers in Advertising," a listing (as of 1983) of agencies with training programs, and a list of publications about the advertising business. There is also a minorities advertising internship program for minority college students who have completed their junior year. Internships are with an agency in New York, Chicago, or on the West Coast.

Direct Mail/Marketing Association, Inc.
6 E. 43rd Street
New York, N.Y. 10017
212-689-4977
  If you have any interest in this aspect of advertising, contact this organization, which

offers a wealth of pamphlets on pursuing careers in direct marketing as well as lists of books on the subject and information about seminars and conferences. Through their Direct Mail/Marketing Educational Foundation (same address and phone) they offer seminars on the subject. Ask for their catalog on Books for Direct Marketers.

Magazine Publishers Association
575 Lexington Avenue
New York, N.Y. 10022
212-752-0055

Most of the services of this trade association for the magazine industry are restricted to members (consisting of many of the nation's trade and consumer magazines), but they do publish a useful booklet called "Guide to Business Careers in Magazine Publishing." Write or call for a copy if you're interested in selling space.

The One Club
3 W. 18th Street
New York, N.Y. 10011
212-255-7070

An organization devoted exclusively to copywriters and art directors and a great source of information and contacts for those who want to break in. Its many services include career counseling; portfolio review (an opportunity to meet some agency big shots); an extensive library; portfolio crash course; seminars and workshops (usually about one a month) on such subjects as presentation skills, computer graphics, and copywriters' future in the industry. The One Club keeps contact with agencies about job openings and passes on this information to its members, and members receive a copy of the One Show Annual (a compilation of the winners of this yearly awards ceremony). Currently, yearly membership costs $60 for people already working, $45 for students.

MAGAZINES AND NEWSPAPERS

If you read all of these every day (or week) cover to cover, you probably won't have much time left over to look for a job. However, familiarizing yourself with the trade press is crucial to keeping abreast: it will introduce you to current ad people and issues, tell you which agencies are winning new accounts and awards, give you pointers on how to focus your job search, and offer tidbits of information to include in your cover letters and drop at your interviews. There's no better opening line than, "Hey, I saw that terrific profile of you in *The New York Times . . .* "

Here are the trade journals that advertising people tend to read, quote, and refer to most:

Advertising Age
Crain Communications
740 Rush Street
Chicago, Ill. 60611
312-649-5200

If you're only going to look at one trade journal, make it this one—it's to advertising what *Variety* is to the entertainment industry. Published twice a week. Essential for job hunters are the "special issues" on America's leading agencies (spring), the top 100 national advertisers (fall), and leading media companies (summer). If you can't get your hands on these at your local library, contact the magazine and order them.

Adweek
A/S/M Communications, Inc.
820 Second Avenue
New York, N.Y. 10017
212-661-8080

Adweek is really seven different magazines—*Adweek/East, Adweek/Southeast, Adweek/Southwest, Adweek/Midwest, Adweek/West, Adweek/Northeast,* and the *National Marketing* edition. Articles of national interest and columns run in all the editions, while news pertaining to the geographical area will fill out the pages of the regional editions. Tends to be a bit more gossipy and irreverent than *Ad Age*. Those hunting jobs will want to make use of their posting of "positions wanted" ads free of charge for three weeks. Also of use to job seekers are various special reports published throughout the year, including annual agency report cards in March, annual salary reports in June, and reports on the magazine world in January, on TV in March, and on direct marketing in June.

Madison Avenue
Madison Avenue Publishing Corporation
369 Lexington Avenue
New York, N.Y. 10017
212-972-0600
Follows advertising trends and the people who make them. Slick graphics, good coverage of magazine publishing.

Marketing and Media Decisions
Decisions Publications, Inc.
1140 Avenue of the Americas
New York, N.Y. 10036
212-391-2155
Read by media people and account people and worth looking at if you're eager to get into either area.

Media People
P.O. Box 3905
Grand Central Station
New York, N.Y. 10163
212-573-8582
This focuses on the media, the people who run, buy, and sell them, and media-related topics.

The New York Times
229 West 43rd Street
New York, N.Y. 10036
212-556-1234
Read Philip H. Dougherty's "Advertising Column" in the business section, Monday through Friday. Comb through the want ads for possible openings.

Television and Radio Age
Television Editorial Corporation
1270 Avenue of the Americas
New York, N.Y. 10020
212-757-8400

Interesting issues relating to the broadcast industry are covered here. Spot and network buyers and sellers should check this out.

The Wall Street Journal
22 Courtlandt Street
New York, N.Y. 10007
212-285-5000
Covers events in the business world. Like the *Times*, it has excellent classified ads which job hunters should make a habit of looking through.

DIRECTORIES

Your two best reference tools for job hunting are the *Standard Directory of Advertising Agencies* (which everyone calls the Agency Red Book) and the *Standard Directory of Advertisers* (the Advertiser Red Book). The Agency Red Book lists some 4,400 ad agencies and includes such information as address and phone number, branch offices, billings and breakdowns by media, number of employees, and names and titles of agency executives in all major departments. What more could you ask? It's published in February, June, and October and updated monthly. Look for this volume and the Advertiser Red Book at your local library. The Advertiser Red Book lists some 17,000 advertisers and, like its companion volume, gives names of company executives, addresses, budget information, and the names of the advertising agencies the company uses. The *Ad Change Weekly* updates changes each week.

Other useful directories include:

The Creative Black Book lists ad agencies, photographers, unions, schools, production houses, and suppliers of creative services of every stripe. Has samples of the work of major commercial photographers, designers, etc.

O'Dwyer's Directory of Public Relations Firms/O'Dwyer's Profiles: 25 Largest PR Operations—those who want to get into public relations will find these useful.

Standard Rates and Data Services—individual volumes broken down by category (for example, newspaper circulation, spot radio, consumer magazine) provide information on the rates for advertising and list media personnel. A good source of information on just about any fact related to the nation's truly astounding array of media.

The Direct Marketing Market Place covers the direct marketing field with names and addresses of companies that do direct marketing, suppliers in the field, and creative services, including listings of advertising agencies and freelancers specializing in direct marketing. If you're a freelancer in this area, you may want to think about getting your name in the directory. Published annually. Available at libraries.

Books

Reading is never a substitute for doing, but until someone gives you a chance to *do* by hiring you, you may find it useful, or at least entertaining, to read up on the subject of advertising. The most inspiring books are those written by advertising greats who impart secrets of success. The most fun are the books that show the brilliant campaigns of yesteryear or the comic reminiscences of "those zany days back when . . . " There are also a slew of textbooks and how-to books that will actually take you through the mechanics of each job description. In this category, try to get hold of the most recent— even books from the seventies are already outdated in many respects. If nothing else, reading books on advertising will give you something to talk about in your interview, aside from your education and your determination to work hard. Dropping a famous name, book title, and amusing anecdote makes you look informed and truly committed.

These books should get you started:

Arlen, Michael. *Thirty Seconds*. New York: Farrar, Straus and Giroux, 1981. The making of one thirty-second television spot for AT&T's "Reach Out and Touch Someone" campaign. Takes you through every step of the commercial process and introduces you to all the people involved.

Bovee, Courtland L., and Arens, William F. *Contemporary Advertising*. Homewood, Ill.: Richard D. Irwin, 1982. A recommended textbook that takes you through all the advertising basics. Illustrations are clear and relevant.

Bolles, Richard Nelson. *What Color Is Your Parachute?* Berkeley, Calif.: Ten Speed

Press, 1983. The now classic work for those embarking on a job hunt or career switch. Gets you started and helps you answer those tough "philosophical" and practical questions.

Buxton, Edward. *Creative People at Work*. New York: Executive Communications, Inc., 1976. Good advice and information for getting in and getting ahead in advertising.

Caples, John. *How to Make Your Advertising Make Money*. Englewood Cliffs, N.J.: Prentice-Hall, Inc., 1983. Lots of excellent advice for copywriters and would-be copywriters. Also see his *Tested Advertising Methods*. Englewood Cliffs, N.J.: Prentice-Hall, Inc., 1984

Cone, Fairfax M. *With All Its Faults* . . . . New York: Little, Brown, 1969. The Cone of Foote, Cone & Belding offers his thoughts and reflections on the business of advertising.

Della Femina, Jerry. *From Those Wonderful Folks Who Gave You Pearl Harbor*. New York: Simon & Schuster, 1970. The creative revolution of the 1960s really *was* a time of insanity, vitality, and excess, if Della Femina is to be believed. A goldmine of advertising anecdotes, told with raunchy humor.

Dobrow, Larry. *When Advertising Tried Harder: The Sixties*. New York: Friendly Press, 1984. Great illustrations of those golden ad campaigns from the golden years of the creative revolution.

Ellenthal, Ira. *Selling Smart, How Magazine Pros Sell Advertising*. New Canaan, Connecticut: Folio Publishing Corp., 1982. A good grounding in magazine space selling for anyone interested in getting into this area.

Fox, Stephen. *The Mirror Makers*. New York: Random House, 1985. A fine history of the advertising industry in America.

Glatzer, Robert. *New Advertising: Twenty-One Successful Campaigns from Avis to Volkswagen*. New York: Citadel Press, 1970. The ads may not be new anymore, but they're still great.

Hopkins, Claude. *Scientific Advertising*. Chicago: Advertising Publications, Inc., 1966. Originally published in the 1920s and still a great introduction to the principles of advertising. A classic.

Meyers, William. *The Image-Makers*. New York: Times Books, 1984. A look at how "psychographics" is transforming today's advertising and what it is doing to today's consumer. Brings up some interesting issues, although the tone is a bit ominous.

Nelson, Roy Paul. *The Design of Advertising*. Dubuque, Iowa: William C. Brown, 1981. Aspiring art directors might want to look at this clearly written discussion of the elements of design.

Ogilvy, David. *Ogilvy on Advertising*. New York: Crown, 1983. Legendary advertising creative leader David Ogilvy (founder of Ogilvy & Mather) shares his views on how to run an agency, how to write great selling copy, how to make commercials, advertise for travel, use direct marketing effectively, and much more. Slickly illustrated, entertaining, and informative. Also see his *Confessions of an Advertising Man* (1963) for more secrets and anecdotes and his amusing autobiography, *Blood, Brains and Beer* (1978).

Paetro, Maxine. *How to Put Your Book Together and Get a Job in Advertising*. New York: Hawthorn Books, 1979. Everything a creative needs (except talent) in order to assemble a portfolio that will land him or her an advertising job. Highly recommended.

Pocket Pal. New York: International Paper Company, updated annually. Covers the graphic arts field with lots of useful information; especially handy for people in print production.

Reeves, Rosser. *Reality in Advertising*. New York: Alfred A. Knopf, 1968. Reflections and ideas from a tough, reality-minded ad man.

Rogers, Edward J. *Getting Hired*. Englewood Cliffs, N.J.: Prentice-Hall, 1982. The director of personnel at N W Ayer tells you how to put together your resume, write a cover letter, and interview effectively. Very useful.

Roman, Kenneth, and Mass, Jane. *How to Advertise*. New York: St. Martin's Press, 1976. Covers the basics of advertising briefly but intelligently. Copywriters might also be interested in looking at *How to Write Better* by Roman and Joel Raphaelson. New York: Ogilvy & Mather, 1978.

INDEX

INDEX

ABOUT THE AUTHOR

David Laskin worked in book publishing as an editor and an advertising/promotion copywriter before starting a freelance writing career. The author of *The Esquire Wine and Liquor Handbook* (Avon Books, 1984), he has also written articles on travel, home entertainment, and manners. His work has appeared in *Esquire* magazine and *Travel & Leisure*, among other publications. He lives outside New York City with his wife, their daughter, and two large dogs.